THE COMMUNAL FUTURE:
THE KIBBUTZ AND THE UTOPIAN DILEMMA.

by
JOSEPH RAPHAEL BLASI

THE COMMUNAL FUTURE:

THE KIBBUTZ AND THE UTOPIAN DILEMMA

by

JOSEPH RAPHAEL BLASI

Director, The Project For Kibbutz Studies
Center For Jewish Studies, Harvard University
Lecturer, Social Studies

Volume I

KIBBUTZ, COMMUNAL SOCIETY, AND ALTERNATIVE SOCIAL POLICY SERIES

NORWOOD EDITIONS, Norwood, Pa. 19074
1980

Library of Congress Cataloging in Publication Data

Blasi, Joseph Raphael.
  The Communal Future. The Kibbutz and the Utopian Dilemma.

 (Kibbutz, Communal Society, and alternative social policy series;v.1)
    Bibliography: p.
  1. Collective settlement – Israel. I. Title II. Series
HX76.P3B53   334'.683'095684   78-7876
ISBN 0-8482-3425-1 lib. bdg.

Manufactured
by
Norwood Editions
Norwood, Pa. 19074

To

Susan Lyn Sklar

who poetically fueled
my interest in community
and turned me to the kibbutz
without realizing it.

ACKNOWLEDGMENTS

Many persons have lent crucial assistance to this work. I am most grateful to my advisor, Professor Donald Oliver of Harvard University, whose thinking, influence, encouragement and criticism have been central in the success of this project. Dr. Menachem Rosner, Director of The Institute for Kibbutz Studies, and Professor Joseph Shepher, Chairman, Department of Sociology, both at the University of Haifa, have assisted unselfishly in all stages of this study for several years, and its completion is as much a result of their constant effort as my own.

The members of Kibbutz Vatik of the HaShomer HaTzair Federation and Kibbutz Tzair of the Kibbutz Ha Meuchad Federation contributed endless hours out of a dedication to sharing their social and educational experience. Dr. Avraham Yassour of the University of Haifa has in the last year been a helpful colleague and friend, especially with his lessons on kibbutz social history and assistance in many areas. Professor Yechil Abramson dedicated many afternoons to teaching me the Hebrew language. Ruth Shapiro and Schmuel Chermoni, Ruthie HaCohen and Sara Tal helped coordinate the research at Kibbutz Vatik.

Susan Liberman, the main translator, worked without end on the translation of documents and interviews. Terry Tivnan's careful and continuous help with the long and complicated job of computer programming and print-out enabled me to get the most out of the research. Mordechi Bentov of the International Communities Desk, HaShomer HaTzair Federation and Aharon Yadlin, Israeli Minister of Education, provided significant encouragement and support.

James Keen and Cheryl Hollmann Keen, my roomates, helped me to appreciate deeply the value of fellowship and always aided me. My parents, Angelo and Jean, and my sister Tina were always willing to support and encourage a study that took them some time to appreciate. They and my Italian peasant family taught me the meaning of community. Susan Lyn Sklar has been a constant companion and has helped to refine ideas and plan the research in all its stages. She helped to edit many original documents connected with the research and took full responsibility for directing a group of persons who coded all the data. Her influence in this work has been global.

Over the last few years Vicki Steinitz and Joseph Feather-
stone have counseled and guided my study and shaped my development with their brief but significant criticisms.

The following persons provided important assistance:
Rachel Aharoni, Eli Asher, Robert Boozer, Professor S. N. Eisen-
stadt, Angela Erisson and Billy, Yehuda Elkana, Avraham Fein,
John R. P. French, Paul Freundlich, Brian Herrnstein, Gideon and
Golda Jacobi, Yosef Yerushalmi, Professor Rosabeth Kanter, Susan
Katchko, Marcus Liberman, Dov Liberman, Dianna Murrell, Geula
Pariser, Yehuda Paz, Phillip Perlmutter, Robert Rosenberg,
Eliza Samuel, Avishi Shafrir, Moshe Shavit, Sherman Starr, Laurel
Steinberg, Roberta Steinberg, Tami (of Kittutz Tzair), Amnon and
Amalia Tamari, Tsvi (of Kibbutz Tzair), A. Tigue, R. Pollack,
Mr. and Mrs. William Weiner, Charles Wilber, Yura Wi, Dalit
Yassour and Ori Zmur (in memoriam), G. Posnik and D. Varisco.
I especially wish to thank my new family Bernice, Donald, and
Richard Sklar for their continuing encouragement, Benjamin Beit-
Hallahmi for his recommendations on publishing the manuscript
and my publisher Jerome Weiman for his patience and interest in
this project and the complete series. I also thank Shelly Wood.

This book is based in part on a research project funded by
the United States Department of Health, Education, and Welfare,
National Institute For Mental Health, Center For The Study of
Metropolitan Problems. I am grateful to the staff of the "Metro
Center," especially Richard Wakefield, for their assistance.

This work would have been impossible without the continued
support of the Bydale Foundation and Phillip Warburg who has given
me advice and confidence, and I especially note their ongoing support of this and other projects connected to the Project On the
Kibbutz and Collective Education at Harvard University.

The final manuscript's form was much aided by my editor
Cecily Bradshaw, the typist Norma Panico, Ann Guletsky, Rona
Kurtz, Janice Falzano and Mary Beth Leu who did the final edi-
torial review, and has been a faithful assistant. These persons
worked with or helped the research significantly at one time or
another. Many others in Israel and the United States aided me,
and I am also indebted to them.

TABLE OF CONTENTS

These thinkers were urging a science that
would be about values, but would stop short
of actively promoting new values.

Ernest Becker

The Confusion of Utopian Thinking

Utopias make us uncomfortable because we are suspicious of
societies and human groupings that have the audacity to claim
perfection. The discussion and study of utopian societies is
often viewed as a leisure-time activity that is divorced from
normal life. Normal life is concerned with the compromises of
progress, the exigencies of making a living and withstanding the
ever-threatening crises.

Still we are plagued by dilemmas in normal life. Is it
really possible for people to feel comfortable with each other
and experience themselves as a social body when, for normal life,
the family is breaking apart, neighborhoods and towns are losing
cohesion, and each person looks out for his or her own private
welfare? The debate continues whether citizens can have a strong
sense of political power when people with whom they have little
or no contact represent their interests, when decisions are made
on such a high and remote level, and when there is no commonly
accepted set of values upon which decisions are based. Can rationalized bureaucracies not submerged in a common, visible,
small community or not connected with the citizens whose lives
are affected continue to make decisions that affect the quality
of peoples' lives?

Mutual obligations, or what the economist Kenneth Boulding
calls 'unrequited transfers,' are being more widely replaced by
a utilitarian ethic in personal relations as the 'contract' replaces the 'relationship' in all spheres of life, replacing the
communitarian spirit. An exemplification of this is the mounting
significance of differential economic rewards, and the pricing of
all forms of human behavior, from leisure counseling to spiritual
growth. Economic resources and a good standard of living cannot

be justly and equally available to all when full employment
costs too much, when most of the wealth is concentrated in the
hands of a few, when every speck of life must be paid for, when
family background, education, personal connections, attractiveness, ability to manipulate others, luck, profession and class,
rather than the human right of economic sustenance through work,
determine a person's wage.

In an earlier time extended families, ethnic communities,
and a greater capability in the population for self-sufficiency
moderated the stress of competition. Once society loses its community character the individual personality is alienated in the
social environment. Mass society devoid of fellowship leaves the
person with the rules of individualism, competition and prestige
maximization, and rationality - the mediator of success - forces
the person to adopt the schematized behaviors that work in a complex society. Greater centralization of governmental functions
which intrude into more areas of life, and the increased importance of money as the mode of connection between persons, drain
economic, social, political and educational transactions of their
local, interpersonal, and moral, significance. Speaking of the
resultant schematization, the sociologist Ferdinand Tonnies says,
"One's own activities take the form of commodities."

The key point is whether people can be happy when modern
life is so fast, so stressful, so complicated and so threatening,
when the drugs of body (nicotine, alcohol, narcotics) and of mind
(television) are the dominant modes of adjustment, and when they
are involved with ever-shrinking circles of individuals from whom
they can expect an unconditional form of association.

Control over our world and history is not possible when
technocrats surround us with ever more machinery and technology
that creates our world and transacts our business, when we neither know, can find or can understand those who determine the
values and criteria of such technology and its consequences.

Schooling becomes oriented to the preparation of individuals
who can function in this mass society. In good part, school requires intensive competitive training, socialization in preparation for living in corporate hierarchical nonpersonal settings,
and the acquisition of skills necessary to fulfill roles in a
complex technological society. The training ground of the school
can never strongly encourage children to challenge the moral imperatives of the overarching technological society. This not-
withstanding, parents still emphasize the importance of values
such as neighborliness, cooperation, participation and democracy,

ii

ethical discrimination, closeness to nature, and control over technology. But these are abstract ideas of another era in a foreign structure. We are finding it harder and harder to pass on any kind of values to children because a more person-centered humanistic education is too expensive and the school is divorced from the community and agreed-upon values are hard to come by.

This is the modern scene. Human fellowship without community. Political participation without social contact or consensus. Economic justice without the rights of economic equality. Mental health without simplicity of life. Control over our world without knowing where the levers are. Education without locally generated and agreed-upon values.

Indeed, if Utopia is a society whose claim to "the good life" must merit suspicion because of its lack of reality, then we live at present in this type of Utopia. The fact that this mode of social organization represents our best hope for the future is certainly a leap of faith. Once we strain to step outside of what the sociologist Peter Berger calls our "social construction of reality," it is then much easier to realize that it is nothing more than a form to which we have become accustomed and socialized. The form must stand the test of human moral interrogation. For, is it out of some mysterious mystical notion of 'modern society' that we defend this as the road to human perfection? Have we not lost the capacity to think about how the 'good life' is created? Indeed, we do not know how to analyze the quality of our lives. This is the confusion of utopian thinking. We regard utopian visions as unviable, yet we avoid examining the moral assumptions upon which our own world is based.

We are wont in our infinite chauvinism to make fun of other 'so-called' Utopias. Is the funny dress of the Hutterite cooperative communities of the Midwest any more bizarre than our current belief that the small, local visible community of friends and acquaintances is no longer a garment of a fitting social life for humans? Is the inefficient direct democracy of many communitarian societies (and the use of consensus by others) more inefficient than the huge national bureaucracies that now decide almost every aspect of our lives? Are the much touted crazy dances of the Shaker communities dizzier than the dance and twirls by which our economy provides and rewards dignified work? Is the fact that a kibbutz community will pay for all the medical expenses of members without any relation to how fast or how much they work a maladjusted way of dealing with the problem of human satisfaction? Is the sacrifice, in some cooperative communities, of innovative machinery and new technology in order to safeguard

iii

satisfying jobs more alien than the assembly line at Ford Motor
Company? Can the communal practice of children sleeping in peer
groups in children's houses not far from their parents' dwellings
compare unfavorably with such distortions in our own society as
often-absent suburban fathers, child abuse, and doggedly competitive systems of grading?

Yes, Utopia is a scary phenomenon. But the fact is that
modern society is itself a frightening utopia. It involves
mystically weird belief systems. It shuns a normal way of life.
It claims perfection without any knowledge of what people really
want. It prescribes inappropriate methods to reach 'the good
life' that do not work. It leads people on by promising happiness and joy when complexity and slavery are the true consequences.

The unfortunate event of our time is that demonstrated creativity in making our society what it could be is a vanishing
skill. If the general population did not share this malady, if
it were the unique crippledness of the sociologists and educators
among us, that would be bearable. But the debate about the
'quality of life' is increasingly an argument about the status
quo, not about alternatives.

We abundantly verify paltry facts to argue about the causes
of our predicament; we continue to document the spreading disintegration of norms and values to claim that a 'new era' will be
upon us when certain unspecified developments take place; we complain about the rigors of modern life with its crime, violence,
and anonymity and wonder what we can do, since we work hard, love
our mates, provide for our children and cannot possibly recognize
our own responsibility in the morass of dilemmas; we discuss
which government program and what federal expenditures are necessary to reconstruct society; we worry about 'interior spiritual
growth' and plan our conversions, and those of our fellows, hoping that holiness will make us forget and will 'trickle down' to
the rest of the world, thereby solving all problems; we pray for
the day of 'final revolution and liberation' when the oppressing
classes will be overthrown and some benevolent power, committee,
leader or world government will deliver us. Those high priests,
the sociologists among us, continue to assure us that modern society is 'evolving' and 'developing,' that if the neighborhood
and community fall apart, new forms and structures of social life
will emerge to take up their functions. Equal promises are made
for the passing family and couple. Soon similar promises will be
made for nations.

This 'sociology of the present' is shared by both the sociologists and the citizens. Sociologists analyze and explain the

functioning of each new mutant social mass; they offer no alternatives, just analyses. Society is not an intentional fellowship providing a good quality of life. The essential modern definition is that, in America, society is what accidentally develops next, receives the approval of the citizens, and comes to be identified by sociologists as the thing worth studying, and by educators as the thing worth teaching. The federal government then must fashion policies and worry about how people's needs will be met in each evolving situation. This is not exciting dialogue about social reconstruction.

Society is not created by the scientist, the philosopher, the responsible man or woman in the street, the religious person, or the revolutionary. Society is not the province of the lone moral individual, nor does it come into being as a result of the moral public policy dispensed by the federal cash register. Neither does it come into being as a chance development of modern times. Society is a web of mutual obligation to which the individual feels a sense of belonging, for which he or she works and gives commitment, and from which he or she derives benefit.

We need to examine models of responsible societies that place real social alternatives within our reach. We need to recover the moral strength upon which to base our relearning and education in social organization. This book is the first in the Kibbutz, Communal Societies and Alternative Social Policy Studies series about alternative 'social constructions of reality' that are still within the reach of modern humankind. As one of the most visible and recognized utopias of the modern age, the kibbutz provides for us a different calculus by which to begin measuring the yearnings for a 'good life.' Further works in this series will complete a library of modern alternatives.

The purpose of the present study is to examine one such model, the kibbutz of Israel. We have purposefully chosen a vibrant, existing system of cooperative communities oriented toward the amelioration of human life in order that we may clear up some confusion concerning utopian values. This study describes minutely and documents the workings of an existing kibbutz society so that its details and mechanisms are more obvious to those among us who are trying to participate in constructing social alternatives. The make-up and attitudes of its population are dissected so that the diversity of membership allowed by a small communal society will dispel the fears of those who do not themselves countenance social reformers, special individuals, ideologues, or possessors of the oft-touted 'herd' personality of communal citizens.

The Status of Kibbutz and Communal Studies

Two decades have passed since Melford Spiro first described kibbutz life in his classic ethnography, The Kibbutz: Venture in Utopia. Since the publication of that work there have been numerous general descriptions of kibbutz life and myriad studies of specific aspects of the kibbutz, but there has never been a study which is both general and specific; that is, one which assesses the community's advantages and disadvantages in the context of an ethnography while at the same time addressing itself to the interlocking dilemmas that cut across social, political, economic and educational concerns in the commune. This study updates our knowledge of kibbutz life in the light of more recent research and methodology. It attempts to provide a substantially more detailed account of the utopian community in the kibbutz and the activities that take place in that community.

A common feature of general descriptions of kibbutz life is that the bases for the author's conclusions are seldom identifiable. In contrast, we have relied heavily upon systematic methods of observation which, it is hoped, will be as open to criticism by the reader as are the conclusions drawn from those observations.

Specific studies, of which there are many, of various aspects of kibbutz life (e.g., bedwetting in children, or work branches in the commune) do not portray sufficiently the total and organic nature of community life. Because of such studies, a reader may see the commune as an arbitrary mixture of sociological mechanisms while missing the originality and the exact natural order in this social construction. In addition, the uniqueness of individual cooperative communities is lost when a particular slice of life - for instance, the economy - in one kibbutz is then put into the context of a more general ethnography of another. Also, despite the ready availability of kibbutz literature, no one item presents sufficient detail to allow for richer secondary analysis by researchers or readers. Our hope is that this project's data will lead to a variety of secondary analyses since a greater factual knowledge of communal societies will encourage more creative thought about social alternatives.

For reason of limitations of space two crucial secondary analyses of material on Kibbutz Vatik have not been included in this volume; however, they bear extensive comment because of their relevance in assessing a communal future. They are:

<u>Kibbutz Vatik in the Light of a Value Geography of Individualis-</u>
<u>tic and Communitarian Community Options</u> and <u>The Quality of Life</u>
<u>According to the Diversity of Membership</u>.*

The first analyzes the specific mechanisms of social life of
Kibbutz Vatik in the light of a philosophically developed theory
of the quality of life which uses insights from Ferdinand Tonnies'
theory of Gemeinschaft and Gesellschaft. The costs and benefits
of kibbutz life are assessed vis a vis those of modern society
and other communitarian forms in greater depth than in this volume. The second summarizes a complete expanded computer analysis
of the data presented in this study by cross-tabulating all the
questions by diverse paired membership groups. (See the Appendix
for Outline of Quality of Life Data for the Kibbutz Research Project.) Thus, men and women are compared minutely along all the
measures of attitudes and satisfactions, as are old and young,
first and second generations, service and production workers, and
twenty other demographic groups in the kibbutz.

Our goal was to assess the attitudes and satisfactions in
kibbutz life, to determine whether or not there were strong and
significant differences distributed along crucial lines of human
diversity such as sex, age, and place of work. If this were true,
the picture of Kibbutz Vatik that emerges in this work would be
opened to doubt. The distinctiveness of kibbutz organization
would have to be tempered by the fact that there existed within
it a predictable amount of stratification, organized along clear
demographic lines. In fact, however, the research showed impres-
sively that such correlations were few and were very weak. Advantages and disadvantages - when the issue was satisfactions -
and attitudinal clusters - when the issue was perception of kibbutz life - were neither predictable nor significant according to
a wide variety of diverse membership groups. The kibbutz, overwhelmingly, does not divide its population into exploiters and
the exploited.

Both secondary analyses illustrate the importance of contemporary dissection of communal societies. By pursuing the problems of modern life in the halls of a few social alternatives, we
may be able to make some clear statements about social reconstruction. Thus, the approach undertaken by this volume in

---

* The full text of both analyses is available as a research report of the Project for Kibbutz Studies Center for Jewish
Studies, Harvard University.

particular, and by the Harvard Project in general, differs distinctly from that of many communal studies long considered germane to thinking about social amelioration, many of which derive from historical works on communes. Kanter's analysis (1971) of the problem of commitment and the mechanisms for its attainment in her discussion of the success or failure of communal experiments, and her book of readings on communes (1973), present in tandem one of the best bibliographies of historical sources on communal life. Kincade (1974) and Communities Magazine (1975) provide general descriptive accounts of current secular communal attempts, including a variety of strikingly stable communities, with some ongoing analysis of the nascent movement in the United States and around the world. Hostetler (1968) and Zablocki (1971) exemplify ethnographies of contemporary religious cooperative communities in their respective studies of the Hutterite communities of the upper western United States and Canada and the Bruderhof of New York, Pennsylvania and Connecticut. Zablocki's more recent work (1974) actually analyzes a variety of sociological and psychological processes in contemporary communes. Most of these genres of communal studies present the novice social reconstructionist with distance: the historical communities are far away in time; the secular communities are often far away in lifestyle, being populated mostly by the post-sixties young; the religious communities are frequently distant in their beliefs.

The special quality of the kibbutz lies not particularly in its proven success vis a vis these other communal societies. It has yet to outlast some of the societies studied by Kanter; it has yet to fascinate the young of Israel as does the Walden Two Twin Oaks Community described by Kincade; it has yet to prove definitively that it, with its openness to many changes in modern society, will have a greater effect on the quality of life than will the more closed and traditional contemporary communities which are based on religion. Further, attempts to define the kibbutz as distinctively Jewish or Israeli are open to question once the considerable similarities between it and other communal alternatives are observed.

The kibbutz is special because it is a communal alternative that much of the American population could visualize, were they to opt for cooperation as a way of life and develop an intention for fellowship. The kibbutz provides a level of cooperation that critically alters social life and markedly eliminates gross social, economic and political problems, yet it does this in the context of a normal secular society of grandmothers, grandfathers, aunts, uncles, sons and daughters, with a strong respect for individual human rights and an attempt, albeit a complicated one, to relate responsibly to national obligations. Its members are diverse; their religious beliefs are mixed and are, in fact, distinctly secular; the lifestyle is comfortable yet radical, participatory but not intrusive, industrialized but not technocratic. These elements exist in part in historical and contemporary secular and religious communities, but no other community actualizes them all.

The kibbutz movement does so with one hundred thousand people in two hundred and fifty communities. Despite this tremendous advantage as a model for utopian thinking, the kibbutz, as the reader will see, is not a perfect society. Having eliminated the most serious forms of social, economic, political and educational fragmentation and violence, the communal group is left with the complicated and mounting problems of keeping a fellowship alive and well. Many choices remain, many mistakes are made and, oftentimes, the stark dilemmas of existence remain fully untouched. Probably this fact will limit the discussion far short of the consideration of nirvana and well within the reaches of some reasonable and moderate proposals for developing more responsible, self-reliant communities.

Any implications of this work, and of future books in this series, will come from the attempt to further our dialogue about our education toward a communal future. Before turning to the kibbutz, let us sketch in general terms the possible communal future and the fragmentation that demands this dialogue and this action.

A Possible Communal Future

The goal of this work is to encourage a fuller understanding of the concrete realities involved in bettering society on a local level. The goal is not to persuade quick adherence to a carbon-copy 'kibbutz ideology' for improving social life. The intention for fellowship and the energy to visualize and create social alternatives must be deeply felt and must have a persistent significance for the individuals who try to create a local community within a larger society. The substance of this intention and the plan for an alternative cannot be copied. The central point is that such a plan must direct the citizen-pioneer's energy effectively and must take into account wisely the possibilities existing in the present environment. Thus, in the face of these realities, many social alternatives are theoretically possible.

Existing neighborhoods could be identified and webs of mutual cooperation and obligation developed within their perimeters. Developing such a 'cooperative infrastructure' might become a very creative task for a social science and citizenry more oriented toward self-reliance. Decaying small towns and villages could be saved if inhabitants were to realize that the pattern of their social relations and the degree of mutual labor they would commit themselves to might insure the community's continued growth just as much as would welcoming the new factory of a large corporation.

In more hostile urban environments, whole cooperative communities could be developed in the ashes of a declining city with community-owned businesses and services, such as daycare and medical care, provided by an association of citizens. Larger towns would decide that the weight of federal dependence and insoluble social problems should be thrown off for a reorganized municipality based on an association of smaller governmental units and worker-managed industries.

The government might develop a program of federally subsidized community homesteading projects whereby rural settlements with insured full employment would receive federal land, technical assistance and long-term, low-interest loans to develop 'communal' settlements. The urban communal household could become increasingly acceptable as a response to the alienation and economic press of modern life. Still, some groups might decide to buy land themselves and actually build cooperative communities (kibbutzim), hoping to develop a movement which would grow steadily and act as a catalyst to continued expansion of a self-reliant and locally controlled string of communities. The government could at one time decide to give special tax incentives to such groups if they could demonstrate that they would create fewer gross social problems and thereby put less strain on federal financial and bureaucratic resources.* In a less extensive way, some elements of the communal endeavor, such as cooperative daycare centers, communal homes for senior citizens, or worker-owned firms, might be more universally adopted.

---

* This is already a reality in parts of the United States. The Hutterite Federation of Communities practices mutual aid among almost 200 communities with a population of over 25,000. In 1976, the first contemporary Federation of Egalitarian Communities was founded, tying together five secular cooperative communities in the United States.

Worker-managed and employee-owned firms show promise of becoming a popular method of encouraging economic independence and enrichment of the workplace. Nevertheless, the less a preferred social alternative coherently touches all the elements of a citizen's life (i.e. producing, consuming, deciding, educating, celebrating, associating, maintaining psychological self-balance) the greater the risk that it will be wiped out by the forces of modernization. The kibbutz, for example, provides a stunning laboratory study, for those interested in employee ownership, of what can be done when the concepts upon which self-management of firms is based are applied to the life of the smaller surrounding community.

Marxists will oppose a communal future because communitarian self-reliance might satisfy the 'quality life' urges of the radical elements of the population and thus undercut the possibility of a complete revolution in which hierarchical power and privilege society-wide would be eliminated. However, the track record of Marxist revolutions and of even the tamer democratic socialist states is not persuasive proof to feed a very long wait. This approach does not even take issue with the assumption that justice and dignity and equality can be attained by violent revolution or bureaucratic fiat; these two uniquely hierarchical methods we reject categorically. On the other hand, the same criticism that Marxists apply to cooperative communities - that they coopt social radicalism - may soon be leveled against such alternatives as employee-owned firms or cooperative daycare associations by opponents of a communal future. Can you satisfy people with a little fellowship, a little participation, a little cooperation, a little locally controlled education, a little power over technology, a little more mental health so that they will feel so much better - relatively speaking - that they will seek no more, when such changes themselves are so superficial and non-pervasive that they never touch the grossest social ills? The day must come when the majority of the population enters into healthy argument over this point.

The study of the kibbutz, communal societies, and alternative social policies can at least provide us with the grammar of a communal future. We lack at present even a novice's knowledge of the means of constructing the intention for a better life. Attention to the experiences of those who have tried and are currently succeeding in social reconstruction can be inspiring. However, it would be hard to develop sound generalizations on inspiration alone! By pursuing detailed studies of social alternatives such as the kibbutz, possibly more people will become aware that the options for the following statement are real: "I intend to join with others in creating a better local fellowship."

For sociologists this means confronting again what Ernest Becker calls the fact that the science of humankind is fundamentally a moral problem, opposed to the notion that ". . . there is nothing left but to work within the ongoing social ideology, gathering data and hoping to patch things here and there." The communal future means a systematic, exploratory, and careful scientific evaluation of communities, experiments, visions and practical proposals which really can restitch the nets of human fellowship.

Fragmentation and Its Consequences

The possibility of return to some romantic, just community is not within our reach. Those who do remember such things disagree on their value. Most of us simply do not remember. Besides that, the fact that humankind is not necessarily getting better and better along a straight raising line of progress does not suggest that return along the decreasing line of regress to the past is the prescribed solution. The kibbutz sheds much light on the critical function of the elimination of privilege and hierarchy in arriving at social betterment. Yet privilege and hierarchy were crucial features of past communities, from small town America to the Middle Ages. Many who reflect on society would agree, therefore, that it is not the development of privilege and hierarchy which constitutes the modern age so much as it is the invisibility, the concealed power, of these things which, in short, can be traced to the phenomenon of fragmentation in our society.

The seeds of a communal future may reside in the obverse of the modern scene.

Most citizens never examine the assumptions of modern life. One cardinal assumption is that human activities can be divided among different reference groups quite without limit. In most traditional and primitive societies, and certainly in many villages and towns of the nineteenth century, humans worked, played, worshiped, affiliated, consumed, produced, decided, learned and suffered together. Modern life takes each human activity and creates a corporation to 'run' it. The corporation has hierarchical authority to which we generally do not belong, an admission fee, a set of specific rules, and a specific reference group. The corporations are usually not closely situated. Their administrators do not know each other, and the lone individual is left to pilot his or her course among them. We work, play, worship, affiliate, consume, produce, decide, learn and suffer in different corporations. Increasingly, there is further specialization. Consumption, for example, is spread among a large number of ever expanding corporations. Affiliation for the purposes of help is also highly specialized, with a panoply of counselors, caseworkers, weight-loss and ego-massaging organizations. The more no one human setting includes the essentials of a whole life, the more new corporations must be developed to provide the service required. Modern society is built for the individual who has enough money and time and 'cool' to pass to and fro among these exponential transactions and 'get what he or she wants' without hurting anybody. Society is a switchboard.

The quintessential corporation is the government. The federal government must step in to incorporate and organize the activities of human groups that no rational being would choose to make a business of: the hungry, the poor, the single parents with dependent children, the disabled, the aged, the retarded, the 'maladjusted.' These people used to have a network of mutual aid and acceptance in primitive communities; now they are at the mercy of a vast bureaucracy. The government grows with the destruction of community, for it was community that provided many of the free human services we now associate with bureaucracies. Older parents lived in with kin and took care of children. Now we need agencies for the children and the parents, staff to staff them, inspectors to monitor the staff, and social scientists to figure out why the system does not work.

The corporate social model tears each activity from an individual's life and requires that that individual learn different rules and different sets of behavior for the varying reference groups and develop an ability to function in a variety of hierarchies where he or she has very little power, very little friendship and very few mutual obligations with the reigning staff. The state, through a system of taxation - which replaces social fellowship and mutual aid as the new 'neutral' obligation - maintains the system.

A brief overview of modern fragmented society and its recent history has led to several 'safe' generalizations:

1. The fragmentation is continuing. The distance from old-age homes to weight-loss corporations to massage parlors to assertiveness training corporations gets smaller and smaller.

2. The tendency is to replace free mutual aid as a solution to social needs with paid-for services and therefore with

commercially organized corporations that must turn a profit to
exist. The disenfranchisement of the aged, the daycare crisis of
children, and the problems of nursing home corporations are cases
in point.

3.   The mounting evidence of large-scale social illness, gained
from statistics on crime, suicide, drug and alcohol addiction,
mental illness, corruption, administrative inefficiency and lack
of compassion, may indicate that humans do not function well
under the conditions of fragmentation and lack of fellowship.
Possibly, we do not appreciate that as a human group increases
exponentially (10, 100, 1,000, 10,000, etc.) the social dynamics
alter drastically in a way that efficient bureaucracies may never
be able to humanize!

4.   The government becomes the screen upon which the ineffectu-
alities of modern society are projected. We are seduced by one
quick solution after another, but it must be realized that:
a) tax dollars and bureaucratic planning cannot replace fragmentation with integrated social settings; b) even if this were
possible, the taxes could not go high enough, nor could the
bureaucracies, in reality, grow big enough, to solve our deepest
social problems, since this would not be practical, this would
not pass the Congress, and the redistribution of wealth required
would be politically unfeasible in the near future; c) questions
remain as to whether welfare payments improve the quality of life
of recipients and unemployment compensation does not create jobs.
In short, fiscal solutions do not give poeple whole lives; they
only maintain their existence.

5.   There is no evidence that our social problems will lessen; in
fact, each day, new studies and new analyses reveal ever greater
and unimagined problems in areas we never considered.

6.   These events are occurring not only in the United States.
Communist and capitalist societies alike continue to buckle under
the weight of modern problems. At the same time, the 'developing'
countries hasten to become modern. The dilemmas are global and,
indeed, the perception of global crises related to the quality of
life must be tied closely to the worldwide lack of self-sustaining
social fellowships that fulfill the needs that people have.

7.   As the crisis warms up, national and international politicians, 'scholars' and information media are hard pressed to give
people at least a sense of potency, a notion that the solution
has been found and the experts are setting it in place. The sub-
standard lives of millions in the United States who are living in

economic and social deprivation can be improved by a 'Welfare
Reform Package' that, miraculously, will not cost the taxpayers
much more money! Unemployment can be solved by bringing the unemployment rate down to the 'acceptable' level of 4 or 5 percent!
Sociologists redefine community as the 'community of interest,'
the healthy network tying together all the isolated individuals.
To 'give' people a 'sense of community,' the thing that they do
and the place where they do it is so called. So is born the
Harvard Community, along with the Intelligence Community. The
tough questions about social fellowship, economic justice, political participation, control of technology, coherent values for
responsible local education and childrearing and positive mental
health supported by a trustworthy commonwealth are never asked.
While the shadows of such questions remain, corporate bureaucracies, believing they are answering them, consistently cook up
unsatisfactory solutions which miss the point.

8. On a global level, the many believers in the modern corporate
state act as if they are threatened by one another. They arm
themselves against multiplied nuclear destruction, wastefully
using resources and labor that might be directed toward social
betterment, and missing the creeping internal enemy of fragmentation. Liberation movements and revolutionary parties, hoping to
gain control, fight to wrest the power to determine national
options. Throughout the world, the notion of responsible local
life is puny, hidden and unrecognized. Political, and social,
policy egos, revolutionary and non-revolutionary, fight it out to
determine the shape of the future. Since bureaucracy is an inefficient substitute for the benefits of a deeply committed, organically acting group, hysteria, empty promises, media blitz, or
violence and suspension of human rights are more and more necessary in those countries where more bureaucracy is not a feasible
solution.

     Sadly, many who offer alternatives to this disheartening
situation claim simple solutions. Fragmentation is caused by the
capitalist system of ownership. Fragmentation is caused by lack
of belief in God. Fragmentation is caused by body tension, lack
of self-awareness. The track record of surefire sociologies and
psychologies is not encouraging. Criticism of capitalism becomes
Centralized Marx, Inc. Belief in God is Multinational Spiritual
Enterprises, Inc., promising eternal deliverance that is often
blind to the mounting social crisis. Self-awareness is marketed
by Growth, Inc., whose Seminar and Super-seminar can make you
more responsible.

     Where are the whole alternatives that address directly the
important political, spiritual, and personal issues and provide

another setting apart from the modern corporate existence? They are generally forgotten.

Cooperative communities and communal societies provide one substantial set of examples from which to choose creative ideas for social amelioration. The kibbutz, as one example, is real and is open to examination, and provides specific starting points for the social reconstructionist. It solves social problems by changing social relations. It is built on mutual commitment and obligation among a group of people, a commodity within reach of all. It calls for grouping human activities under 'one roof,' encouraging people to conduct most of their affairs within a fellowship based upon consistent rules, similar reference groups, and little hierarchy, and thus opposes the fragmenting tendency of modern society. It prescribes mutual aid that is free once the intention for fellowship is present; this costs little, requires minimum administrative supervision, promises a sure profit, and is something to which most people believing in its virtues can adapt themselves. The kibbutz could lead to a reversal of widening social problems and a possibility of responsible and responsive control over local life. It promises less government, more local self-reliance, and thus increases the possibility that government might again be respected for performing the constitutional and protective functions it is best fitted for.

To some extent, the kibbutz crosses ideological lines. Is a progressive, non-violent, voluntary, self-reliant, democratic, cooperative social fellowship Republican or Democratic? Is it Communist, Socialist, Fascist, Capitalist? It speaks to the regeneration of human culture around the globe and sublimely addresses the possibility of the fellowship of humankind and the reversal of the rape of developing countries.

The main disadvantage of the communal future is that this will not be an easy or a mass phenomenon. The development of a wide variety of communal and cooperative associations and communities of citizens will be a slow process. Learning and education will be central, and the person who is most in pain from modern fragmentation may least understand or be able to visualize such an alternative. For this reason it is no panacea. It requires no endorsement by the Secretary of Health, Education and Welfare, no mention in the State of the Union address. Should this ever happen the government would only remove the stigma which Americans put on the right to independent voluntary changes in patterns of human fellowship.

And that indeed is a value choice, for it is easy phenomena like fragmentation, and mass movements like modernization, that got us where we are. Finally, the logic of the technological fix asks the final question: If we cannot administer and mass produce it for everyone, can this be worth anything? This is probably the central decision. The communal future takes a stand on the moral issues of our time, but it is not in the last analysis the winning combination according to the criteria for social development our society accepts at present.

J.R.B.

INTRODUCTION

This study will examine the quality of life in an Israeli kibbutz through a detailed description of six major areas of community life: the historical development of the community, social arrangements, economic cooperation (and work), participation in politics and culture, education and childrearing, and personality. Our methodology will rely on a combination of two approaches: anthropological, and social psychological. From an anthropological point of view, we will utilize the notes and observations resulting from extended residence and participation in Kibbutz Vatik. Central issues of life in the kibbutz relate to many areas of community activity. For example, the quality of work has (much) to do with social arrangements through the provision of close-knit fellowship in which work takes place. Too much of a dependence upon statistical data generated from questionnaires might shadow these issues rather than reveal them. Thus, excerpts from intensive interviews conducted with community members will be used along with field notes to focus on issues for which other methods were inadequate.

From a social psychological point of view, we will report on the results of questionnaires. The goal of the questionnaires was to provide a common medium to describe differing amounts of agreement and disagreement about areas that proved to be a major concern for many members. Nevertheless, there are times when we are suspicious of the questionnaire data, and both the ethnographic and social-psychological data shed little light upon the subject. At these times the author's personal judgment is relied upon, and the premises upon which an argument is made are clearly put forth. (See Appendix I for detailed information on Research Background, Materials, and Methodology.)

The normative perspective we have is simple: the time has come for the field of education to give proper attention to more than the search for statistical truths about the methods of education, or better ways of administering school programs and creating curricula. The critical resource of the future is the quality of life of our people, the ultimate shape it will take, and the advantages it will deliver. We must examine whole societies as learned human settlements.

How can many diverse individuals be orchestrated into reasonably constructed roles in a common social setting? (Oliver, 1976, p. 148) We shall explore this perspective, which has been

1

persuasively explicated by Oliver in <u>Education And Community</u>, by examining one kibbutz community. Throughout the examination we do not seek to romanticize "small communities" or the experience of community life in the past or present. For example, there have been other conditions of humankind - like the feudal period - which contained more community, but were not necessarily free of crime, class struggle, starvation.

Rather we are concerned by the lack of integrative neighborhoods and supportive communities in our society and the ever-increasing trend towards alienation, mental illness, crime, economic dislocation, and the lack of self-sufficiency. There is a uncertainty about the use of technological options, and concern over the ever-widening influence of centralized government and its continually expanding programs of human welfare, directly related to the absence of integrated community life, and human support systems. (Taylor, 1972) A former HEW cabinet chief predicted that the immediate future of the welfare state would be that one half of the population would be supporting the other half with as much as half of its income. (Hickel, 1975) There are many groups in our society who oppose welfare programs and simply want to balance budgets, but they have no alternative.

We want to increase the quality of life, to maintain valuable services, to prevent suffering (all without making other groups passive recipients), but we recognize that the present way of massive bureaucratic expenditure is not a reasonable option at this time. Thus, the aim of this work is a critical examination of one kibbutz as a model of integrative community on a small scale, where changes in the quality of life can be brought about without continuing the process of atomization in our society or the dangerous road of government centralization and programs.

The Kibbutz will not be compared with other kibbutz communities or other community systems. No attempt is made to judge whether the kibbutz has a better or worse quality of life than any other social arrangement. Rather, in the ensuing chapters, a community is described which is at least acclaimed as an attempt at creating a better life. (Cantril, 1965) This description takes place in the context of a review of the literature on the kibbutz movement as a whole. Where the articulation of the specific case study and the literature conflict, that will be pointed out.

CHAPTER I

HISTORICAL BACKGROUND AND THE DEVELOPMENT OF KIBBUTZ VATIK

Introduction

Misconceptions about the nature of the kibbutz are corrected and the size, origin and present state of this community system outlined. The special influence of persecution and the lives of East European Jewry on the formation of the movement is explored in terms of an alienation from the narrowness of life and power-lessness and a struggle with the definition of progress. This and Zionist socialism led to the movement to establish the kib-butzim that evolved in an unorganized manner from intimate com-munes to the cooperative village/towns of today, of which Kibbutz Vatik is an example.

The Kibbutz Movement

One problem of considering community as both a more desir-able learning environment and a social policy alternative is that few concrete examples exist which have been tested over time on a large scale. Because of the possibility that the traditional forms of small community life will encounter stress under the press of modern change, their importance in our quest is mini-mized. On the other hand, while many communes exist and some ex-periments are quite impressive (Kincade, 1974), they still remain only shadows of the stable community life that can endure.

We need then a modern community that has a fairly long his-tory and on which a substantial amount of research has been done. Most importantly, it must exemplify a voluntarily and purpose-fully applied communitarian ideology whose goal is to achieve a better life. We must be able to scan whole areas of its life to view the reality of learning, and yet in the end focus on those institutions (schools and child care) which are concerned more with learning and development.

The kibbutz is probably one of the most studied societies of the world. (Shepher, 1974) Its unique system of collective local child-rearing and education is well known. Most significant, however, is that kibbutz life has been a purposeful attempt to learn and develop more just ways of achieving the quality of life. This effort imbues the whole life of the community, not just the schools and nurseries. Therefore, it is crucial that we put aside our inclination to go to the kibbutz schools first, and consider the interconnected nature of its life.

This work will serve as a review of the main trends and findings which are available in English regarding the kibbutz movement and in a specific description of the community under study.

The kibbutz movement of Israel (Shulman, 1973) offers a unique and invaluable example of a large number of people living in cooperative small communities in an industrial society. Because the kibbutz exists in a foreign country, because a great deal of research and writing material about this society is shrouded in Hebrew, and because so little comprehensive and up-to-date English literature on the kibbutz exists, the movement has still to be recognized with the global importance it deserves. In fact, a number of myths hide the logic behind its historical development.

The word kibbutz comes from the Hebrew word kvutzah which means group. The first kibbutz was really a rural commune founded in 1909. (Baratz, 1949) As the movement expanded and the communes became communities, the word kibbutz was invented to denote a larger community group. Today, there are some 240 kibbutzim with a total population of about 94,000 people (about 30,000 each of men, women, and children), or approximately 3.3% of the total Israeli population. The population of an individual kibbutz may be anything from 50 to 2,000, though most are between 250 and 500. The size of most settled communities is between 500-700. (Criden and Gelb, 1973)

Our community, called by the pseudonym Kibbutz Vatik, was founded in 1936, almost 30 years after the beginning of the movement in Israel. Its historical development can be viewed as a result of the previous three decades of "perfection" of the kibbutz structure. That is, Kibbutz Vatik did not develop by chance. Its members were trying to build a social form which for thirty years had been replicated consistently and regularly throughout Israel. Jeshua, the counselor at the kibbutz high school, in his sixties, discussed some of the preparations he and other Polish Jews were making years before they founded Vatik in Eastern Europe.

The youth movement from which this community
sprung was founded in Poland in 1928. Many
of our members even before then were reading
a lot of philosophy, examining their con-
sciences, and pursuing the issue of social
life on a very high level. Ours, unlike
other Zionist movements, put a great emphasis
on kibbutz. Our newspapers stressed this
theme. Some of our preparation came from the
Pfadfinder, an apolitical countercultural
youth movement which developed in Germany in
the twenties. It emphasized a return to
nature through scouting groups, freer relations between people, and not simply following in the footsteps of our parents. The
youth often asked themselves if this style
was a game. How long could we play it without changing our lives?
(Conversation reconstructed from notes.)

Background For A Counterculture: Persecution And Its Special
                                   Influence On Vatik

   Despite its stability as a well-defined settlement today, to
understand the historical development of the Kibbutz Vatik one
cannot ignore the influence of the conditions affecting European
Jewry at the turn of the century. Jeshua, a member, addressed
this issue in our conversation:

   The Liberalism of Europe at that time gave
   much power to a move to secularize the Jews.
   Many felt that they could be intellectuals
   and begin to branch out into many professions
   in the universities. Many a person went to
   Berlin or Budapest to study and never returned. They changed their names and put off
   other forms of Jewish identification. But
   anti-semitism continued to rear its head.
   Jews helped in the Russian revolution and
   afterwards they were liberally killed. We
   felt like the oil on the wheel of history.
   Our group wanted to build an independent and
   just future and strive for what we called the
   independent realization of our ideals.

At the same time, however, the Jewish youth were questioning the nature of their lives for reasons not connected to persecution. A prominent defender of this kind of questioning of the day put it this way:

> We are an ancient people, submerged by too much inheritance, by a deluge of thoughts, feelings, and values transmitted to us, so that we can no longer live our own lives, just be ourselves; our dreams and our thoughts are not our own, our will is not one implanted in us; everything has been taught to us long ago; everything has been handed down to us. Everything is confined and defined within set limits and boundaries, measured and weighed, ruled and legislated, so that those among us who crave to fill themselves are lost and can never discover themselves. Is it possible to begin again after fundamental changes in our lives and hearts....There is no construction without prior destruction, and there is no being without ceasing.
>
> from an early critic of established Jewish life, M. J. Berdechivsky

The founders of the kibbutzim were mostly of East European origin, especially from Russia and Poland. Vatik was founded mostly by Polish Jews from Galitzia.

Galitzia, an area of Poland on the Austrian side, was part of the Austro-Hungarian empire before World War I. When the members of Vatik grew up there it was under Polish national control. The Jews there spoke German; this factor contributed to the central influence of the German counterculture on the early Jewish youth groups.

Kibbutz Vatik differs from other kibbutzim founded in the twenties and thirties in two ways: first, while most of its population was from Galitzia, many of them never saw anti-semitism. For them, the question of achieving a new social identity as Jews was influenced by what they knew about persecution rather than how they experienced it. An older woman, now principal of the Ulpan (Hebrew school for foreign volunteers in the community) explains:

6

> We were Israelis when we founded this kibbutz
> (referring to the first group) and we formed
> our youth movement in Israel. We were the
> first ones and we really had many ideals. We
> came from well-to-do homes, we did not come
> from any holocaust, and we didn't come from
> starvation. On the other hand we were not
> rich, because there were not rich families in
> Israel, but we lived and studied because we
> really wanted to do something special. We
> had an ambition not to be like the other kib-
> butzim which were formed by Jews coming from
> Europe. We wanted to be better than them.

The fact that the first founders of Vatik were born of Eastern European families who had already emigrated to Israel had a
strong effect on the founding of the kibbutz. The initial founders were not running from anything. They were already in
Israel, and they sought to build a cooperative rather than a
private life there.

Later, the small group of 20 or so initial founders were
joined in the early thirties by about 50 youths from Galitzia.
This group had been in the leftist socialist - zionist youth
movement there, and like the Israeli founders, their experience
of anti-semitism was not strong. The Jews in Poland of the
thirties were prey to a more vicious kind of persecution:
economic anti-semitism, discrimination in social situations, and
a rightist Polish nationalism that was suspicious of minorities.
They had been members of the youth movement begun in 1913. Persecution as a factor had a more indirect effect on the founding
of Vatik.

Vatik also differed from its peer kibbutzim of the thirties
in the socio-economic background of its members. Unlike the
richer families of Germany and parts of Russia, these members'
families were lower middle or middle class, mostly craftspeople
and small business people. Thus the educational standard of
members of Vatik differs radically from that of kibbutzim where
the parents of members provided a more university and study-
oriented youth. Despite these differences, these Jews knew their
long history of persecution, which included not only social discrimination but also physical attacks and pogroms. From the time
of the Roman destruction of Jerusalem and dismemberment of the
Jewish state in 70 A.D. European Jewish life was a series of
grand attempts to build small communities, which were destroyed
when the local Christian ruler changed his attitude or wished to
appropriate their property or art. (Durant, 1957)

7

Several other aspects also define their experiences at the turn of the century: alienation and the narrowness of life, powerlessness, and a struggle with progress.

Alienation And The Narrowness Of Life

Alienation meant that although many Jews lived in stetls (ghettos) which were fairly closeknit communities, they were continually uprooted. The use of identifying badges, the fact that by law they could not own land, which prevented a normal involvement in land-based farming, labor and manufacture, forced the Jews into business requiring little use of land, emphasizing exchange of commodities (trade), work that could be done with little capital or need of space (crafts), and the more abstract services (law, education). A hundred years before a lifestyle detached from the land became popular in the West, the Jews found themselves forced prematurely into the modern lifestyle of root-lessness and exchange. (Spiro, 1956)

This situation resulted in a narrowness of existence. The early kibbutz members spoke in this way of the stetl:

> Why has the glory of the Torah declined? The
> Rabbis marry their sons to the daughters of
> the rich. The sons-in-law depend on the money
> of their fathers-in-law, which buys them the
> Rabbinate. Once in the Rabbinate they must
> satisfy the material appetites of their wives,
> who are unused to austerity. As a result they
> become servile flatterers. (Likert, 1973, p. 9)

Life in the stetl was radically hierarchical and unegali-tarian. The Rabbis and the pious Jews were at the top and were keenly aware of their station and power. A worker in the chicken branch of Vatik speaks about the near disdain with which the youth movement regarded traditional religious Judaism.

> In my house (the ghetto apartment house where
> his family lived) many of the young were in
> the movement, but our parents were very toler-
> ant. But in the same house, there was another
> family and the parents went to the police to

keep the child from going to the Shomer Ha
Tzair (Young Guard) movement.* Well, they
were very religious and they used to bother
us calling us "Goyim, Goyim"(non-Jews).

Powerlessness And The Definition Of Progress

Another formative experience for the early kibbutzniks of
Vatik was the powerlessness of their and their parents' lives.
From an exacerbated sense of the injustice of the religious
regime to disgust with the empty promises of liberty which the
French revolution promised to grant to all people and the Jews
in Europe, this group decided that power was not in filling
pleasant and excelling social roles. It was not having the right
to vote in a basically dominated situation, and it was not being
so divorced from the values of human cooperation and connection
with nature and the land. Even those born in Israel without as
many European influences sought to take greater control of their
present and future situation. They saw religion as being power-
ful because it resolved basic human dilemmas, as their early
Guru, A.D. Gordon believed:

> Authentic religion cannot live in such an
> atmosphere. If the person is to rediscover
> religion the proper balance between the two
> powers of the human soul--intellect and
> intuition--must be restored. The task of
> the intellect is to be the servant of intui-
> tion not to overpower and repress it. This
> balance can only be restored by our return
> to a direct and immediate relationship to
> nature...A genuine inner renewal of society
> can be achieved not by an accidentally and
> superficially related mass but only by an
> organically united community, the people.
> Nature has created the people as the connect-
> ing link between the individual and the
> cosmos. (Bergman, 1961)

---

* This was the youth movement from which arose the Federation
(Kibbutz Artzi) to which Vatik belongs.

9

Their experience of society and the radical kibbutz ideology that flowed from it was completed with a <u>struggle over the meaning of progress</u>. They asked: Why didn't the intense piety of the stetl life solve severe social and economic problems? For if anything, the bearers of piety intensified the inequality and were indeed the bearers of progress. (Lilker, 1973) This planted the seeds for a suspicious attitude toward individual wealth which become a central principle of the kibbutz.

Even during the infancy of the youth movement elements of communal sharing were practiced.

Yasha, a member who came to Vatik after living in a communal house in Poland, remembers those days:

> When there were poor kids among us, and we were going on a trip, the counselor would make us sell stamps in order to raise money for those who could not afford to go. There was a common treasury and every member gave a few cents, ten perhaps, a week. With that money we once bought a ping pong table.

Other members whose formative years were more ideologically informed (in the traditional Marxist sense) than Yasha's youth movement days, speak about hours of pouring over Marx and socialist writings.

These elements of persecution, alienation, narrowness of life, powerlessness, and suspicion of progress grew in the early 1900's in the minds of many Jewish youth, and became, together with influences of the German counter-culture and Marxism, the root of a critique of the establishment and a new personal philosophy that bore the kibbutz.

Emergence Of The Kibbutz Movement After Many Attempts

The kibbutz grew out of circumstances and conditions lacking a clear plan or direction. While discontent was seething in the communities of Russia and Poland (mainly Galitzia) and was generally directed towards leaving Europe and re-settling Israel, no clear social program had evolved other than a desire to transplant life to the other land. The strong zionist motivation in the early kibbutzniks was coupled with a desire to create a new society.

Groups had tried to establish cooperative communities earlier in Israel, in 1838, 1881, 1903, and 1905, but they all failed for one reason or another. Some of these groups bore close resemblance to the American utopian communities flourishing at that time. (Viteles, 1966)

The first kibbutz, Degania Aleph, grew out of an argument between a group of workers and their farm manager over visiting a sick fellow worker. The group left that man's farm and, with a small loan and a lot of encouragement from a settlement advisor, Dr. Ruppin, (1926) started a cooperative farm in 1909. An early visitor to the group before they got settled describes what resembles a commune in the country: primitive and innocent youngsters, wildly talking, singing and dancing as they gathered in a large room with a table in the center and long benches. The men and women did not have separate rooms.

After the first year they had a surplus and liked the efficiency and security of cooperation. The group grew in population and expanded with some long-term loans. The word spread and soon other groups began trying to settle the land in this way. By 1913 there were three communities. By 1917 joint childrearing developed. Around this time they began to receive youth groups from Europe.

After World War I, as after Vietnam, a counter-culture beginning in Germany swept parts of Europe. As Becker describes them:

> They loathed the world of their elders, and
> were ready to follow any Pied Piper whose
> mystery and power held promise of a new realm
> where longings found fruition. (1946)

This rebellion did not take the form of political revolution. It advocated escape from the present society into the world of nature and relationships "where the shams of the city were absent." Self-expansion, the simple life, sexual freedom, and equality became hallmarks of this movement. The Jewish youth quickly adapted this movement and the beginnings of their serious consideration of Marxist socialism to their desire to break with the old and found the new land. It was not until the tragic persecutions of the Polish Jews in the years following 1917 that these "countercultural scouting groups" added zionism to their original goal of changing Jewish life.

By 1921, the kibbutz structure began to take form at Degania and spread through trial and error. When finally 25 kibbutzim

11

met and formed a Federation in 1925 they defined a kibbutz: it was a small community based on economic cooperation and social understanding supported by frequent democratic assemblies, refusal to give leadership to any one person or group, collective rearing of children, emphasis on concern for all members in the community without the interference of exclusive couple ties, the importance of work, giving up individual property, and cooperating with neighboring communities.

The Small Intimate Kibbutzim

As the movement got older, the Europeans who came brought with them a more refined background in the Movement (the counterculture), including some experience of living on preparatory kibbutzim and urban communes, and greater socialist radicalism. The early kibbutz movement tended to be extremely communitarian. As one member remembers:

> We sang a lot and sat around a lot and you
> must understand that each song was a value in
> itself. The substance was that you were young
> and you were creating something, creating a
> new ideal, and that attracted us a lot. Also,
> to build the land, to change yourself, the
> meaning of the pioneering spirit is that we
> threw our lives away THERE (in Europe) and
> came to this land to work together in an
> orchard, and that was an honor. Many farms
> had a communal shower: men and women washed
> together. There was a liberal period in con-
> nection with sex. The clothing room distrib-
> uted not your clothes but the clothes of the
> whole commune. So if you got clothes, every-
> one got them too. The ideal grasped the per-
> son more and more and the reality of unity in
> work held one more...There was little room
> for problems between people. There were at
> times four people in a little room. But the
> rightness, the ideal was all.

Kibbutzim still go through an extremely communal stage, although it tends to be shorter and much less radical, now that family life and marriage have been for many years accepted tenets of the movement.

In 1922, <u>Kaheilatenu (Our Commune)</u> was printed, containing letters, notations, diaries, and confessions of 27 out of 100 members of Kibbutz Aleph (later to become Bet Alpha, the kibbutz on which Melford Spiro's book is based). What is pictured is a group striving to realize utopian and mystical brotherhood and sisterhood:

> A direct relationship between a person and
> his or her neighbor is the first condition
> for the creation of society. In order that
> one may understand one's friend and forgive
> the person, one must know him...On the altar
> of creativity a group soul was formed...Arms
> were joined and wild song burst forth. (1964)

Members in kibbutz after kibbutz tell of the sliding nature of this constant feeling of brotherhood. In one community, we are told that when the first child appeared, the couple became more of an institution, the long talks and encounter sessions on the lawn receded, family life and friendship and intimate and work circles replaced the "one big happy family," and the kibbutz passed from commune to being a collective village. (Parsons, 1961, pp. 331-347)

Kibbutz Vatik was founded many years after Kahilatenu, the prototype of the small communal grouping that typified many early kibbutzim. The goal of Vatik's members was certainly more set than that of pioneer groups who had little preconception of the kibbutz social form. They would build a cooperative village, and it would be large. The practical economic and social considerations in constructing a successful community made the thoughts of a small communal grouping obsolete. Still, Vatik passed through this intimate communal stage. Rena, a founding member of Vatik from the Israeli group, recalls:

> We had a communal shower and we thought the
> difference in showers was not important. When
> new people came they did not like it, but we
> wanted full communality. I once was on a com-
> mittee of communal beds. This is not what you
> think it was. There were only a certain num-
> ber of beds and at times extra people and
> visitors had to be assigned to the places in
> the beds. When I first came here my parents
> gave me a clock. Someone told me, "Give me
> your clock because the man who works in the
> field, or the mother who works in the baby

house needs the time and it is not so important to you." So I gave away my clock and so
did others. It is true it was a remembrance
of father and mother, but, on the other hand
we thought that we would be the finest and
the most just. I do not laugh about it now.
I think it was important and right then, and
this is what gave us the power to overcome,
to make it, and to be something special, because, at that time, there was not too much
faith in the other Israeli youth.

A more detailed view of the initial "intimate commune"
(Tzur, 1975) emerges from discussions with founding members of
Vatik. Before they set up the kibbutz they lived in an urban
commune around an abandoned graveyard near Tel Aviv. Decisions
were made by consensus; all money was shared; couple relationships were de-emphasized, and group singing, group dancing, and
group ideological and planning discussions were the order of the
day. Even after making the shift to the present home of Vatik,
several members report that the sense of being one family continued. One member reported, "We sat outside every night and
talked and talked." Singing, dancing, communal showers, a communal work schedule that knew no regular limits on hours, a
decision-making procedure that lent itself to long encounter-
group type discussions (despite the voting character of the assemblies of older kibbutzim at the time) - all of these typified
the radical phase of Vatik.

Yonina Talmon, the noted kibbutz sociologist, developed a
theoretical description for these "first times," which capsulizes
the early history of Vatik:

The process of change in kibbutzim may be described as a transition from "bund"* to "commune." The main characteristics of the kibbutzim during the bund stage are: (1) Dedication to an all-pervasive revolutionary mission. (2) Intense collective identification.
(3) Spontaneous and direct primary relations
among all members. (4) Informal social controls. (5) Homogeneity. Kibbutzim are

---

* This term was coined by the German sociologist Smallenbach.

14

established by young unattached individuals
who share a comparatively long period of
social, ideological, and vocational training.
The social and economic systems are in a rudi-
mentary, almost embryonic, stage, so that
there is also little functional differentiation.

(Talmon, 1972, p. 2)

We shall examine Vatik's movement from "bund" to "commune," in
Talmon's terms.*

We have already commented on first members', revolutionary
ideology, their extreme collective identification, and the youth
movement and cultural conditions that encouraged their homogeneity. However, early members of Vatik stress the direct primary
relationships they had among each other, probably because this is
one characteristic that has so radically shifted in intensity and
importance. A founding member, now a scientist in the community's fish lab, speaks,

In the beginning of the kibbutz movement the
ties of the family were not so strong, and
people were joking and asking, when they came
to visit, if the children knew who their
parents were because of the communal way of
life. Of course this was a joke, because it
was never so. But nevertheless, the way of
family life was not so tight. The family was
not based on a moral basis as it is now, but
the building of the family that has taken
place in the kibbutz now, especially if I compare it with families outside the community,
from a moral point of view, has become a
strong and stable endeavor. But in the beginning, what I wanted to say was that there

---

* A commune is not a historically viable social form, if by commune is meant a small radically cooperative and experimental
group which constantly strives for religious or social intimacy,
and a wholly separate identity in all parts from the surrounding
society. This form, vs the communal village form, which is willing to accommodate a more normal range of people in normal times,
depends on crisis to exist.

were more cases of extramarital sex than there
are now. (Author's note: the much touted
free love of the early kibbutz movement was
the freedom of each person to be in love with
the person of his or her choice most appropriate at the time. Group sex, orgies, and
multilateral relationships were not part of
this freedom.)

Also, members of Vatik stress the informal social controls.
There was a strong community feeling against higher education,
and many regret now that much of the "intellectual leadership"
of the community left at that time over personal conflicts over
pursuing higher studies. Drinking and smoking were taboo, and
the introduction of the slightest personal luxury, such as a
private teapot in the room, a new dress received as a gift, or
a radio, caused great interpersonal tension, and hours of arguments in the general assembly. Today, the community is more
prosperous and such individual diversity is not just tolerated
but openly encouraged. The popular Hebrew phrase frequently read
in interviews was, "Each to his own likes and dislikes." The
attitude is similar to the motto of the grange, "In essentials -
unity, in non-essentials - liberty, in all things charity."

Talmon, who spoke above, ascribes much of the structure of
the "intimate commune" to the need to achieve overwhelming fellowship and to deal with conditions for building a new state.

Fellowship is rooted in a common idea and a
common will....As long as commitment to the
cause was all-absorbing and defined every
aspect of life, one's duty toward the kibbutz took clear precedence over kinship
obligations....The kibbutz acted as a vanguard of the emergent society. It was a
unique combination of agricultural settlement, training center, and military outpost
....It fought its way against great odds-
eroded and barren soil, a severe scarcity
of water, inadequate training of the settlers,
and lack of capital resources for basic investment. On top of all this lay the heavy
burden of self-defense in a hostile environment.

(Talmon, 1972, p. 3)

Emergence Of The Cooperative Village

In Vatik today, as in all but some recently founded kibbutzim, many changes with regard to family life point to the transition from "intimate commune" to communal village. Talmon sketches the theoretical framework for these changes:

> The processes that bring about the emergence
> of the commune are: (1) Differentiation.
> The original homogeneity of the bund stage
> is disrupted by the differentiation of func-
> tions and of groups that perform them. Most
> important in this context is the division of
> labor in the occupational sphere and the estab-
> lishment and growth of families. Another major
> source of differentiation is the persistent
> internal solidarity of the various nuclei of
> settlers who join the core of founders at later
> periods. (2) Attenuation and accommodation of
> the revolutionary ideology. (3) Decline in
> the intensity of collective identification.
> (4) Standardization of norms of behavior and
> formalization of social controls.
>
> This process of institutionalization may be
> observed in the history of the collective
> movement as a whole as well as in the develop-
> ment of any single kibbutz, and it of course
> affects the position of the family and family
> relationships.
>
> (Talmon, 1972, p. 2)

The lessening of intimacy and the concomitant increase in material wealth has a central place in explaining these changes. One cause of greater differentiation in Vatik was the introduction of a new layer of members from a different background than the founders. They are referred to as the "hashlama" (completing group) and almost a hundred joined the kibbutz in the years following 1948. They, unlike the founders, experienced virulent anti-semitism: some were in concentration camps; most had to go underground; all suffered much. Although their numbers were needed, their socialism and their youth movement education were similar, and even though many of the hashlama were from urban communes in Galitzia, Poland, the founders felt they came less out of ideology and more out of survival. A hashlama member describes herself:

17

> After all our sufferings in Europe we came to
> the kibbutz and things were very hard. We all
> had to work hard physically, in terrible cold
> and blistering heat. And I for example could
> not work in the fields, so I went from the
> children's houses to the kitchen, and there
> were a lot of problems, because when we came
> they (the founders) were already the vatikim
> (old-timers) who had <u>founded</u> the kibbutz. They
> lived here because they found it as an ideal
> way of life, but we came out of survival. So
> it was very hard to get together.

While our data (see Chapter II) do not corroborate the founders'
supposition that the hashlama had a weaker socialist-Zionist
idealogy, this distinction is a main point of contention between
the two groups. Some of the hashlama identified with this distinction; many of the founders believed it to be so. The differences did not let up. In the late fifties and sixties groups
from Austria, Italy, Switzerland, along with a smaller number of
Oriental Jews, joined the Kibbutz. All had varying degrees of
movement experience and vastly different backgrounds. At that
time the sons and daughters of the founders moved into their
teens, and a new layer of kibbutz-born members (and then their
husbands and wives from the city or other kibbutzim) mixed in the
population. Older members also point to the birth of the first
child and the initial "pulling back" of various family units as
the signal for the end of the intimate commune. In the forties,
the community quickly became more interested in its economic
growth and dealing with complex decisions. New economic branches
were developed. Members began to train for specific roles, to
seek work stability, and to develop special skills. The days of
"everybody equally competent for every job" passed quickly. The
hours of ideological discussion on the lawn, the continuous group
dancing and singing and encounter-type exchanges evolved into a
more normal life of work, family activities, individual time-
alone, social life with special circles of friends, and more
organized communal cultural activities. Culture was for enjoyment not for gathering together. The diversification of members,
activities and tasks only fueled the development into a large
village.

The attenuation of revolutionary ideology occurred with
equal intensity. The truth about Stalin and the failure of the
democratic experiment and respect for human rights in Communist
Russia crept up slowly on Vatik. One member stated that he saw
the failure of the Russian experiment when he realized the

inequalities that existed between the managers of the factories (who had dachas and special privileges) and the impoverished workers. The other members of Vatik critized him in 1948 as he told these stories. Nevertheless, the community never recovered from its rejection of the world socialist ideology once the truth of Stalinist Russia became impossible to deny. There was no world movement to develop human respect and an egalitarian socialist movement world wide was a joke. There was just kibbutz Vatik and several others like it. Ideology began to be tailor-made to the community's needs and its development. This strength-ened the desire for a higher living standard that small examples of economic inequality symbolized:

> Well, in 1937 and 1938 it happened that one
> of our girls got married. Her parents were
> from Haifa and they brought her a present,
> a radio, the first radio in the kibbutz, and
> she returned the radio to her parents. It
> was a sin of the kibbutz because, "We will
> not take presents and we will not allow you
> to have a private radio in your room." It
> was the rule. It does not matter that just
> several years later radios started to come
> in and they started to become private. What
> was the cause of this change? First of all
> in my opinion the big cause was evolution,
> slowly and gradually. Someone got a present
> and we decided not to bother them about it,
> to leave it, and close our eyes. This is the
> beginning. It starts with something, a small
> thing, and then we start discussing, why this
> is allowed and this is not allowed, and then
> find the border - what yes and what no - but
> then we do not know when to stop it. (While
> there was a big confrontation and a general
> meeting to fight the first private radio) the
> second radio came without a general meeting.
> It came in and people became a little tired
> of discussion, or they became aware that we
> will not be able to fight against this, and
> then we had two choices, to decide to fight
> this again or to buy everybody radios.

> Member, Kibbutz Vatik

The community decided to buy everyone radios but the use of initial inequality and ideological "sin" to raise the living standard continued, and was partially responsible for many of the

19

small practical adjustments made in the personal budgets of the members. This is often referred to as the kibbutz's "teapot scandal." A myth exists that this process began in one kibbutz (supposedly Degania Aleph, the first kibbutz) with the introduction of a teapot and soon spread to other kibbutzim. It has become the archetypal symbol of attenuation and accommodation to a change in the character of those first times of radical privatistic and rabidly egalitarian kibbutz ideology. The tightly reined social evolution of the commune was dead. Many members in Vatik said they value both the fellowship those first times helped forge and the good sense and reasonably desirable developments their fragmentation insures -- a trade-off indeed!

These developments in differentiation and attenuation of revolutionary ideology led to a weaker collective identification of the individual. The decision to have private clothes was a turning point. Usually all took the clothes they needed each week, often different clothes each week, which sometimes fitted, and sometimes did not. What changed was that people began to ask, "How essential is this? Are we less socialist if our clothes fit us and they are private?" This question of clothes is an excellent symbol of individuals beginning to identify with the kibbutz as a social form, rather than trying to infuse every minor activity with the mechanical demands of socialism; the egalitarian format behind clothes distribution not uniformity in sharing them, was the principle. So, too, there was less patience for the long-winded discussions of principle and feelings necessary to reach decisions on all these matters by consensus. More important decisions beckoned, such as where to build the new chicken house, or how many cows to buy. In short, being an individual and being different, and having separate interests coexist alongside each other was becoming affirmed. The general assembly meeting minutes for the period of 1950-65 show an increasing concern for making norms clear, spelling them out, printing them up, and rationalizing their operations. Life was becoming too complex to have the whole community examine every activity. So norms governing the distribution of clothes, food, the use of transportation facilities, the general nature of acceptable gifts, the responsibilities of members who worked on the outside, the hours that a pregnant woman could subtract from her workday depending on her time, the proper criteria for determining who and in what order members would go for higher education, were established to encourage the development of a diversified society, cut down on possible conflicts, rationalize administration, and offer the use of hard-earned economic development as a resource for greater choice and freedom for individual members. In brief, Vatik, like many other kibbutzim, became an institution.

Our coverage of the kibbutz's historical development may
seem like a patchwork quilt, but it is frankly hard to say
whether the private teapot or the first member who fought to
study nursing had the greatest influence on the structural change
that occurred in all aspects of the community's arrangement of
life. We can say this: the reorganization of economic life with
a view to greater profit and productivity (the industrialization
of agriculture and the development of workship and factory-type
operations), the increasing bureaucratization to achieve equitable and efficient arrangements of communal life, and the attempt
to add more of an urban flavor (emphasizing human diversity and
choice in non-essentials) was reached with a distinct loss in
communal intimacy. But as the senior female member who <u>was</u> the
first person to fight the community and win on getting a professional education (in nursing) says, advantages did come in the
trade:

> Now I feel there are more possibilities. In
> other places you would have to work long hours
> just to support the family whereas here you
> are free to choose what you want to do. The
> kibbutz gives you the opportunity to do what
> you want; whether you have two or four chil-
> dren, you do not have to work any harder.
> But in the city of course, if someone has
> four children and he wants them to live on a
> certain standard, and get a good education,
> he has to work very very hard. So he can-
> not spend time on his own interests, he just
> cannot. But on the kibbutz he can have the
> time to pursue his own interests.

CHAPTER II

DAILY LIFE AND SOCIAL ARRANGEMENTS

Introduction

The physical layout of kibbutz Vatik is described along with patterns in daily life. Members describe the community in their own words and we see the community through its obligations to members and their obligations to it. After outlining the composition of the population and the research sample, information in the following spheres is reviewed: the social organization, maintaining social relationships, the integrity of roles, boundary mechanisms, social ideals and their degree of homogeneity, social control, and attitudes towards the basic individual-community dialectic of kibbutz life.

Daily Life In The Kibbutz

Before examining the present social arrangements of Vatik let us look at the layout of the community and day-to-day life. It will help to place our description of Vatik into perspective. Kibbutz Vatik today looks like a cooperative small town. As the map (Figure 1) illustrates, all the aspects of normal life are found within its confines. The community itself takes up about 30-70 acres and is surrounded by several thousand acres of fields. The center of the community, the communal dining hall where members meet for meals, general assembly meetings, concerts and festivities, is surrounded by spacious lawns and wooded parks where people gather frequently to talk or play ball or sit with their children. Vatik is especially beautiful. To the left of the dining hall are some of the work areas of the community, the chicken houses, the grain elevators, and different workshops, along with storage houses for food. To the right is a spacious park with an on-going exhibit of the community sculptor's work. Behind the dining hall is a lawn used for outdoor movies in the evening, and the various outdoor activities mentioned above. The screen is on the side of a large cultural center that houses an auditorium for movies, visiting concerts and dance, a library, a reading room and coffee house, a discotheque for the younger generation, a patio overlooking the stream that runs through the

22

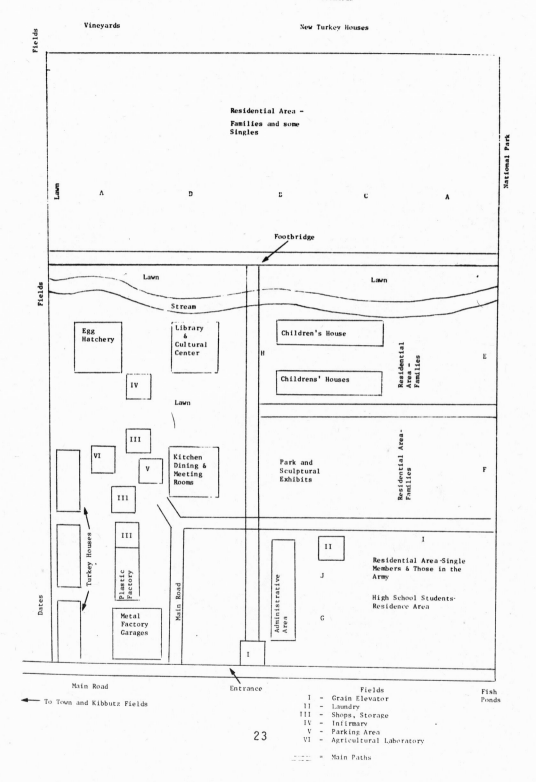

FIGURE 1
Map of Kibbutz Vatik

Olives

Orchards

Vineyards

New Turkey Houses

Fields

National Park

Residential Area –
Families and some
Singles

Lawn

A   D   E   C   A

Footbridge

Fields

Lawn   Lawn

Stream

Egg
Hatchery

Library
&
Cultural
Center

Children's House

H

Residential
Area –
Families

E

IV

Childrens' Houses

Lawn

III

VI

Kitchen
Dining &
Meeting
Rooms

Park and
Sculptural
Exhibits

Residential Area –
Families

F

V

III

III

II

I

J

Residential Area -Single
Members & Those in the
Army

High School Students-
Residence Area

G

Turkey Houses

Plastic
Factory

Main Road

Administrative
Area

Dates

Metal
Factory
Garages

I

Main Road   Entrance   Fish
Ponds

To Town and Kibbutz Fields

Fields
I   – Grain Elevator
II – Laundry
III – Shops, Storage
IV – Infirmary
V   – Parking Area
VI – Agricultural Laboratory

= Main Paths

23

FIGURE 2

Artists' Conception of a Kibbutz

Source: **The Family of Man: A Social Studies Program**
Kibbutz Family In Israel
Newton, Mass. : SEE, Inc., 1975.

middle of the community (used for wedding ceremonies), and a room
in honor of kibbutz sons who died in their country's defense.
On the other side of the park, not more than 100 feet from the
dining room, is the administrative area of the community. Located here are the offices of: the central coordinator of all
economic branches, the social secretary (similar to a mayor), the
technical secretaries who answer telephones, process a vast quan-
tity of mail and distribute morning newspapers, and help with
internal accounts and members' needs, the internal treasurer who
dispenses funds, the accounting office (with offices of the treasurer and economic planners), and the buyer of clothes. The
buyer of food has an office in the dining area. A member responsible for coordinating the work schedule has an office adjoining
the dining room, since most discussion of the work schedule takes
place before, during and after meals.

Harvest festivals, cultural events, occasional outdoor pic-
nics, and movies take place in the lawns, parks and fields. Most
apartments flank the stream; three to a house containing a kitch-
enette, bedroom and living room. The houses and apartments have
connecting lawns. Each couple or member (if single) may have a
flower garden, but fenced-in yards, private vegetable or fruit
gardens do not exist. The climate is usually hot and dry in the
summer, cold and rainy in the winter. To avoid working in the
heat members usually rise early -- 5:00-6:00 A.M. -- and work
until 2:00-3:00 P.M. taking a snack in the apartment or in the
kitchen, with a few coffee breaks at work, and more talkative
and extended breakfasts and lunches in the dining room.

Kibbutz life is fairly integrated. Most of the work branches
(the service branches, dairy, field, orchards, workshops, factories, fish ponds, poultry houses, and vegetable gardens) except
for the fields are within the village proper or close by. Because of the small population (about 600) members encounter each
other frequently, on the walks and bicycle paths that connect the
community. Cars are not allowed inside the community except to
approach the parking lot near the kitchen and the garage area
where a fuel pump is located. Even this track is limited to two
service roads through non-residential areas. People meet at
work, at the children's houses when parents go in the afternoon
to take their younger children from communal day care and when
in the evening, they take them to bed. Connections of mutual aid
and common life criss-cross the community endlessly. The woman
who is social manager (figurehead executive of the community for
all except economic management) may have a son in your nursery
group. Your husband may work with her husband in the orange
groves. Several times a year you may be on similar community

jobs, committees, or even taking the podium to defend a common
opinion.

On a daily basis each adult member works six to eight hours,
meets with various other members for community business (relating
to a work branch, a committee, personal arrangements such as a
new job, a wedding or a gripe), takes care of the necessities of
daily life (the house, the family, seeing the treasurer for
money, going to town for a certain book, making sure one's kitch-
en is well stocked with light food and snacks from the kitchen
and kibbutz "store").

In the afternoon most members take a nap and then prepare to
spend the early evening (from 4:00-8:00 P.M.) with their children, circle of friends or family, and at dinner. At 8:00 P.M.
the children are put to bed and usually people just spend time
together, go to cultural events (study circles, library). A
member lives with problems and joys but never needs to worry
about whether there will be work, whether there will be money,
whether the children will be able to go to school. Although each
branch and each branch manager tries to maximize productivity and
efficiency, and the community's economic planners for that year
must plan hard, individuals do not have to struggle and compete.
Money is distributed through individual "closed budgets," and a
community budget. Members' closed budgets, all equal (except
where objective events such as children's budgets or special
physical needs require), provide for clothing, transportation
(including use of community cars, public transportation, vacations yearly, and occasional trips abroad), spending money, for
personal matters and cultural events, and small luxuries which
can be purchased through an account at the kibbutz store. The
yearly personal budget (spending money outside of the "closed
budgets") is about $150-300.

The community budget provides: meals, services such as
laundering and household handywork, child care and education,
higher education, medical care, full old age social security,
housing, and cultural events and special community facilities
(pool, concert hall, darkroom) in unlimited fashion to all members without measuring who gets what or determining the amount
according to the status or work position of that member. The
general assembly and the committees determine the amount of funds
that can be spent each year in the community and personal "closed"
budgets. Daily economic life is relatively stable and imbued
with the cooperative principle. The community could not function
for one hour without thousands of mutual acts that usually take
place without much supervision, without immediate remuneration,

and without the presence of a police force or clear external punishments. One, for example, does not get a smaller cultural budget if one has been working poorly. Social control does exist, however. It depends on each member's awareness that the system works: if one does at least work and live peacefully in the community, many rewards are forthcoming.

Also, gossip plays a significant role, as described in Elsewhere Perhaps, a kibbutz novel. (Oz, 1973) The exchange of information about other people and the community is one of the main pastimes. In the intimate commune life was visible, needs were standardized, and options were limited; in the communal village, with greater privacy, people often limit the amount of information available about them by differentiating between their circle of friends and relatives and the rest of the community.

One of the founding members compares both times:

> Once people had very close friends, and had a
> very strong circle of friends. Some people
> still do. But now there are lots of children
> and there is not much time to meet and when
> we do meet after work sometimes it is only
> the family (referring to the extended family).
> We eat together in the dining hall, then come
> home and drink coffee. Before, when we were
> younger, and there were no children, then a
> few families would get together. Today,
> everyone has his own family except for
> special occasions, like when there is a
> birthday, when a lot of friends get together.

Another member, from the second generation, defined a more impersonal attitude:

> There are many people who, while they are
> fellow members, and I will say "Shalom" on
> the path, with whom I have no business. If
> I have to arrange a matter with them, I do
> it. Many people simply do not interest me
> personally.

In comparison to other kibbutzim Vatik has more age segregation. The map indicates age group areas consonant with each residential area. Apartment area A houses mostly second generation married couples and married couples from the city or overseas. Area B, closer to the community center houses the founding members. While the arrangements are not planned according to formally set out areas, there is some compromise. Area C has mostly hashlama, but D is more of a mixture between hashlama and founders. This is also true for area E, while F is mostly hash-lama. G is fully reserved for the high school age children, and H for the children's houses (babies to junior high). I is for volunteers and visitors, while J is for young single members who have just returned from their compulsory army duty or who are still in the army and use their rooms on vacations and weekends.

Except for general community celebrations, age patterns in the dining and meeting room are observable and the tendency to-ward age segregation holds up in the general assembly meetings, in the breakfast seating arrangement, and films. One exception is lunch, which is the hot meal of the day; people are seated as they enter the dining room so that the food can be brought out as tables are filled, so the age pattern breaks down. At the evening meal the seating is more familial (at both lunch and breakfast the main criteria for sitting is order of entry and work group - couples rarely eat together during these meals) with the age barrier breaking down in extended families. But these families do not always eat together; and one frequently sees senior members and their families eating separately.

The tendency to age segregation enforces the limitation of gossip in the community; in Vatik one knows more about one's peers.

Knowing the historical and physical arrangements* of Vatik and the pattern of daily life, we are now prepared to look at its social organization in detail.

---

* While a detailed and personal ethnography of the life of one kibbutz has yet to be done, several excellent studies of daily life exist, especially Spiro's classic description (1963), Criden/Gelb's running interview with members of their own village, (1974) and Oz's novel which more than all others gives one a sense of the interpersonal underbrush of the communal village.

Composition Of The Membership

Table 1 shows the composition of the community by age, and type of member. Also shown is the percentage of the actual population each group represents, the percent of that specific group that participated in our research, and what percent that group was of the whole research sample. Out of 380 members 158 participated in the research in proportions very close to their representation in Vatik's population. Because of the size and distribution of the sample, despite the fact it is not random, it makes a high degree of statistical reliability possible.

Of the 158 participants in the research 94 were men (59.5%), 61 were women (38.6%) and 1.9% or 3 people did not give their sex. Whether the participation of fewer women, given their relative equivalent as a component of the population, has any meaning remains to be seen. Yonina Talmon, in Family And Community In The Kibbutz, found that an astonishing and significant number of women favored private vs. communal attitudes and many would want to view their reduced participation as an expression of this hypothesis. This possible explanation will be taken up later. Table 2 shows the number of years different members have spent in the kibbutz. The average is 5.7 years.

While fully accurate census figures for Vatik are not available, our sample shows that 100 (78.7%) of the population of Vatik are married, 26 (20.8%) are single and 1 (.8%) divorced.

The approximately sixty couples in our sample have about 2 children per couple. About 50% of the population (according to our sample) have been to elementary school and high school, 20% to college, and 30% to vocational school. About 10% of those who went to both high school and college never finished. It seems probable that these terminations took place mostly in the generation of the founders and hashlama and were related to emigration, war, persecution, or the dislike of the youth movement for higher education, and not to the success rate of kibbutz-born students in the kibbutz high school. Of the 158 persons in the sample, 45 were interviewed from 2 to 6 hours in Hebrew by the author, in addition to completing written questionnaires. The purpose of these interviews was to interpret and provide a check on the questionnaires, attaining the same information in a more natural setting when members were allowed unlimited exposition of their answers.

TABLE 1

Population Composition Of The Community

	Male	Female	Total	A	B	C	D
Senior Members, Age 50 and over							
Founders	40	50	90	(29)	32%	23%	20%
Joined 10-20 yrs after*	50	50	100	(39)	39	25	35
Middle-aged members, Age approx. 26-49							
*Married	65	65	130	(52)	40	32	25.8
Unmarried, residing in community	20	20	40	(25)	62	10	7.5
In army**	10	10	20	(5)	25	5	3.8
Guest & Candidates (Non-members)	5	5	10	(5)	50	2	4.8
Younger Inhabitants, Age to 25 approx.							
High School	10	10	20	(3)	15	5	2.3
Lower grades	20	20	40	(0)			
Infants	10	10	20	(0)			

Total population   460 people

Total membership   380 members

Additional Residents

Temporary volunteers***   25
Ulpanim****   30

A. Number of persons participating in research

B. Percent of group participating in research

C. Percent of group of total membership

D. Percent of total research sample

*   This group includes several people who joined alone although we group them under the hashlama or group that came en masse in 1948-50.

**   Young Israelis give three years after high school to the army.

*** Usually young people who are interested in the kibbutz life or escaping into a different world, or Jews planning to settle in Israel who wish to give the kibbutz a chance.

**** Ulpan is an intensive Hebrew language program run by some kibbutzim, mostly for immigrants, involving part-time work and study, and hopefully settlement in the kibbutz or Israel.

TABLE 2

Years In Kibbutz Of Research Sample Participants

Category Label	Absolute Freq	Relative Freq (PCT)	Adjusted Freq (PCT)
1-5	7	4.4	4.6
6-10	4	2.5	2.6
11-15	11	7.0	7.2
16-20	14	8.9	9.2
21-25	19	12.0	12.5
26-30	46	29.1	30.3
31-35	18	11.4	11.8
36-40	23	14.6	15.1
41+	10	6.3	6.6
	6	3.8	Missing
TOTAL	158	100.0	100.0

Valid cases: 152
Missing cases: 6
Mean: 5.7

Social Organization

Each kibbutz is a self-governing entity, democratically organized and responsible for its own social, cultural, and economic development. The village is legally constituted as a municipality in the eyes of the Government for administrative purposes and as a cooperative society in the eyes of civil law. (Constitution of the Kibbutz, 1976.)

The social organization is not distinct from the decision-making structure or the cooperative economic structure. The structure, the norms, and the processes of change in the kibbutz all work to support its unique character: a mixture of organic community, fellowship and cooperation which welcomes individual diversity, a clear definition of human rights, and a measure of social change.

Members descriptions of Kibbutz Vatik's social structure are strikingly similar. The older woman who is presently social secretary speaks:

> People in the kibbutz try to live according
> to the will of the society, and it is "an
> alternative society." The important elements
> of this are that the member value the social
> group, be able to: talk about his life,
> make a ladder of values in terms of relative
> importance, sit together and talk, and live
> in a democratic way according to these values.
> And this is important; because it is an alter-
> native society, the kibbutz takes effort.

They emphasize a web of social agreement that is taken for granted. The netting of this web is not, however, seen as utopian. Zalman, a member of the hashlama, often a spokesman on ideological issues in meetings speaks:

> When someone asks why the kibbutz is the way
> it is, then my opinion is that there are
> things that happen during the life of a per-
> son which are brought out by life itself.
> It is the same in the kibbutz, in New York,
> in Tel Aviv. There are problems of young
> couples, problems of healthy children, prob-
> lems of sick children. Or another instance.
> Orphans. There are orphans everywhere. The
> father is dead. A couple divorces. There-
> fore when you speak about the kibbutz you
> have to make the distinction; what belongs
> to the kibbutz and what to life in general.
> Where is the singleness of the kibbutz? In
> the kibbutz people are able to feel the joy
> as well as the pain of other fellows. That
> is not the meaning of the kibbutz, only its
> expression, the expression of something
> deeper: the solidarity, the reciprocal
> responsibility. You see, for instance, at-
> tention is paid to the woman who has worked
> in the kitchen for a long time. She will be
> transferred somewhere else. She will get a
> job in the administration where the work is
> easier. Of course, if she needs psycho-
> logical care, she will get it.

Figure 3 shows the kibbutz structure. In the general assembly decisions are made on a one vote per member basis. Alternate labels for administrators and administrative parts of the kibbutz are used here and in the literature.

Secretariat - Executive Committee (in Hebrew, Mazkirut).
Secretary   - Social secretary, Mayor (in Hebrew, Mazkir).
Economic Coordinator - farm manager, farm coordinator
                       (in Hebrew, meracez merchek).

Decisions are executed by the secretariat (its members are the social secretary, and the economic farm manager, plus important branch and committee heads). Specific issues are dealt with, organized into program projects, and investigated through committees. The farm, educational and members' committees are the most important, initiating policy and making long range decisions on productivity and budgeting, learning goals, problems and resources, and the important social issues and rights and standard of living of members respectively.

Maintaining Social Relationships

How much is the image of the intimate commune realized? We examined the matrix of informal social supports in Vatik to check this, since there was little doubt and little success in finding members of the community with clear physical needs or critical psychological needs (such as depression about work), where one or several members were not helping that person, or the situation was not under active notice. The philosophical context of social help may indicate its extent and nature [Question 48].

Members of Vatik view human nature in strikingly similar ways. According to Table 3 more than two-thirds of the members view human nature as both good and bad, and place the emphasis · on the societal endeavor to make the difference. Few see egoism as a solution, and few view either human nature or society as impossible to deal with. The emphasis on the social agreement of mutual obligations now makes more sense.

But can the term "intimate community" be used of the kibbutz? Historically speaking, that period has passed. The intimate commune is gone. Also, members are clearly not interested in achieving or aiming for interpersonal honesty with everyone. To [Question 47]: "Despite what we would like, everyone has a practical approach to other people. Which agrees with your

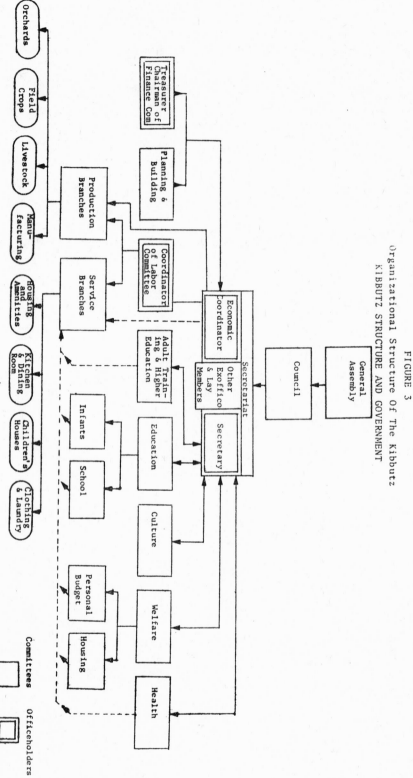

FIGURE 3

Organizational Structure Of The Kibbutz

KIBBUTZ STRUCTURE AND GOVERNMENT

(Howe, 1972, p. 72)

34

TABLE 3

Attitude To Human Nature

	Relative Freq (PCT)	Adjusted Freq (PCT)
1. Human nature is bad but a strong society can organize people and eliminate many bad things.	7.6	8.2
2. Human nature is bad and a person must be egoistic since the society cannot improve the situation.	3.8	4.1
3. Human nature is basically good and the society is not important.	2.5	2.7
4. People are both good and bad; the important thing is society.	78.5	84.4
	0.6	0.7
	7.0	Missing
TOTAL	100.0	100.0

Valid cases: 147
Missing cases: 11

---

approach?" Members answered in the following ways:* 5% said telling people what they wanted to hear was the best approach; 17.8% favored telling one's feelings no matter what the conse- quences (this brash trait is often identified with the Israeli sabra personality); 13.3% suggested that one should speak as

---

* Valid cases 116 - Missing cases 42.

little as possible to those not one's friends; a surprising 33.5% agreed that while honesty is better one simply cannot trust most people; 2.5% favored maintaining open relationships and 26.6% did not answer the question. This is no romantic Gemeinschaft. This describes a fairly normal distribution of attitudes in a village. The lack of interest in interpersonal honesty is startling when compared with the lofty descriptions of brotherhood and sister-hood in "the first times." While many members criticize the fact that Vatik has become a society of groups, there is clearly no desire to return to the level of interpersonal energy needed to create one group friendship.

A woman of 24 who works in the kindergarten describes her attitude:

> There are all kinds of relationships; there
> is one that I would not say hello to,
> another one I would say hello to, another one
> I would say more than just hello. It depends
> on how you relate to other people. There is
> no rule. Is there a rule for kibbutz members?
> There is no such thing. If you have a rela-
> tion with another person you talk to him or
> her; if you do not you do not talk and you
> only say hello or even you do not say hello.

Almost all members asked to describe the ideal relationship be-tween two members not friends agreed with this assessment: rela-tions would be friendly and cordial but one does not confide in this person or visit his house unless at a birth or death; if there is business to settle one should deal kindly with another member; extreme insults are out of the question. Even today, members will ask for and usually get a public apology before the committee on membership from another member who has called them names. Some members added that one should always be on the look-out for others who needed practical aid, and some felt one should say hello to everyone, but these opinions are not popularly shared. Most of the members do greet each other on the pathways, in the meeting rooms, offices and workplaces. When the time comes to work with or deal with them, a certain proper warmth has been built up.

With these philosophical and practical underpinnings of social relationships as background, the information on social supports will have more meaning.* Members were asked how willing others were to help them, to listen to them in times of diffi-culty, [Question 78 A-O]. The results are shown in Table 4.

TABLE 4

Pattern of Social Support**

	No One	Not At All	A Little	None or Little	Some- what	Very Much	No*** Answer
Fellow Workers	5%	6%	14%	24%	23%	35%	18%
Friends	3%	5%	9%	17%	32%	41%	7%
Branch Coordinator	14%	5%	14%	33%	14%	29%	24%
Partner	9%	2%	1%	12%	9%	68%	12%
Relatives	7%	8%	11%	26%	24%	34%	11%

---

* The social support indices were developed at the Institute For Social Research, University of Michigan. The assistance and advice of Dr. John R. P. French, a Research Director at the Institute, is gratefully acknowledged. The indices can be found in (Caplan, Cobb, French, Harrison, and Pinneau, 1975). The question was altered to refer to the community as a whole, not just to work.

** These figures represent averages of percentages in the four parts of Question 78. The number of valid answers fluctuated between 108 and 127, the missing answers between 50 and 31.

*** The question either did not apply to these people (high schoolers), or they were away (army), or studying, or they did not answer.

Members get the greatest amount of support from their partners, which is not unexpected. The large gap between the support people receive from partners and that from all others illustrates the attitudes they themselves described above. Members report that their friends support them almost as much as their partners. The perception of fellow workers and relatives as comparable offerers of support might indicate that the strength of the extended family has certainly not overtaken the "commune" in the kibbutz. 43% of the members see their branch coordinator at work providing support. Intuitively, this would seem to be far greater than one could expect in a mass society. However, in contrast to glowing descriptions of communitarian society, many members perceive no one, or just a little social support, available. The kibbutz gives certain supports to members but it is not a utopia. One trend in the data harkens back to the way many members defined the ideal relationship between two members not friends. It is a trend that the averages hide. For every reference group except their partners, members note that it is far easier to converse in general with people than to ask for personal help. For example, 22% feel that fellow workers will listen to their personal problems, 28% that they can turn to fellow workers in times of difficulty and 33% that their fellow workers are willing to help them generally, but 57% perceive it easier just to talk with their fellow workers.

Another matrix for viewing relationship is neighborliness. In Kibbutz Vatik, groups often move into three apartment houses near people they like or in their own age group. These groups often double as friendship groups. With 5.1% not responding, 41.1% of the members thought that their neighborly relations were very friendly, and 44.9% somewhat friendly. 8.9% agreed they were just neighbors and resided alongside each other. [Question 42].*

In short, while the community is organized as a society for mutual aid, a direct feeling of mutuality in most interpersonal relationships is neither the philosophical or interpersonal, nor the achieved, goal of the members.

---

* Valid cases 150 - Missing cases 8.

Integral Roles

Tonnies (1940), theoretician of Gemeinschaft speaks of consonant social roles. While differences in intensity of support exist - except for those who feel little support coming their way - the roles of family member, fellow worker, branch coordinator and relative are consonant, with the role of member. That is, there is no critical split between family and non-family in terms of social fellowship. Perhaps this has to do with the degree to which the kibbutz presents members with the possibility of organically related activity.

One aspect of this integration of roles is the broad range of voluntaristic participation in the society. In Kibbutz Vatik, there are about 32 committees that require members and coordinators.

Since 1950, out of our sample of 158 people, 42 members report having been coordinators of committees, 41 having been branch coordinators, 68 having been members of committees. In the last 25 years this same group remembered being on committees 194 times. For such a small society this is a remarkable amount of after-work volunteerism. These are not all the same members; first, there is a principle of rotation so that coordinators of committees, branches, and community administrators are changed every few years; secondly, few members report filling significant positions more than once.

Figure 4A lists the committees of Kibbutz Vatik and the work branches (Figure 4B). The committees touch all branches of life; such diffuse public participation contributes to the integration of roles in kibbutz life. By definition those filling administrative roles (also in Figure 4B) have intense and continuous contact with all these other associations.

Let us consider the example of one member, David, about 55 years of age, an accountant in the metal factory. David has not participated in important kibbutz roles very often. He has not been the social secretary, farm manager, or treasurer. His preference is more of a leavening role, behind the scenes, working at different issues from many directions. His involvement as accountant in the metal factory involves him with the administration and working staff of that branch (about 30 people). He also sits on the executive committee of the community and meets regularly with the main coordinators of the branches and administrative activities. Many of these poeple are his neighbors.

FIGURE 4A

Committees In Kibbutz Vatik

Education	Building
Further Education	Newspaper
Consumption	Nomination
Members	Security
Culture	Sport
Health	Farm Economy
Work	Industry
Youth Counsel	Youth Camps
Music	Political
Young People	Furniture
Absorption	Wedding
Outside Members	Army Returnees
Housing	Consumption Points
Vacation	Human Relations Personal Problems

Since 1950 the 158 members in the sample report the following committee participation:

    42 were coordinators of committees.
    41 were branch coordinators.
    62 were members of committees.

In the last 25 years this same group remembered serving on committees 194 times.

This group includes about 20 people. David encounters another group of five to ten people in his volunteer role as coordinator of the equality committee, members like himself who are trying to solve the problem of inequality in the community. He speaks to countless members about their ideas, and has toured all the houses of the community to gather information. Add to this the people he knows from many previous work branches, those kibbutz members he joined within the hashlama, the parents who were meeting him nightly to put their children to bed in the same children's house, his close friends and relatives, friends of friends he would encounter. In adding all this up the meaning of integral roles in the kibbutz comes into better focus. David is not an extremely heavy participant but he represents a cycle of activity of many members.

FIGURE 4B

Work Branches In Kibbutz Vatik

*Sewing (S)
+Carpentry Shop (S)
+Industry (P)
+Plastics Factory and Industry (P)
+Metal Factory and Industry (P)
*Education (S)
*Teacher (S)
*Special Education (S)
*Kindergarten (S)
*Metapelet (S)
*Baby House (S)
*Children House (S)
*Bookkeeping (S)
*Clothes Storage (S)
+Cows (P)
+Construction (P)
*Student (S)
+Dates (P)
+Non-citrus Orchard (P)
*Occupational Therapy (S)
+Fish Ponds (P)
+Landscape (S)
+Vegetable Garden (S)
+Garage (S)
+Chickens (P)
+Repair Shop (S)
+Agriculture (P)
+Shoemaker (S)

*Secretariat (S)
*Pricer (P)
*Nurse (S)
*Outside Work (P)
+Outside transporation
   (trucking) (P)
+Laundry (S)
*Export Company (P)
+Dining Room (S)
*Office Secretary (P)
+Upholsterer (S)
*Dental Assistant (S)
+Water Irrigation (P)
+Parts Storage (P)
+Citrus (P)
*Health Services (S)
+Grains (P)
*Lab Technician (P)
*Planning
*Full-time Kibbutz
   Administrator (S)
+Plumber (S)
*Research (P)
+Sanitation (S)
*Recreation (S)
*Library (S)
*Army none
+Engraver (P)

+ Indicates blue-collar branch.

* Indicates white-collar branch.

(S) Indicates service branch.

(P) Indicates production branch.

41

The social arrangement of a continuous communal village like the kibbutz contributes to a form of interpersonal alliance and administrative consanguinity that is hard for inhabitants of less interdependent communities to imagine. David, and other members, find an interpenetration of their roles, because their social life is lumped together and assembled collectively. When asked what type of participation best described their life in the kibbutz, members of Vatik showed an uncommon orientation towards community roles. [Question 54]* 13.9% said they were concerned with kibbutz problems and involved a lot in public affairs; 62% were also concerned but felt they were involved but not a lot, 13.9% were more involved in family life and their own comforts, and 10.1% did not answer. In short, the totality of social participation in Vatik is quite remarkable and shows a high degree of integrity between one activity and another. Individuals' evaluation of this social participation will be dealt with later.

Boundary Mechanisms

In order to maintain this amount of centripetal activity, Vatik needs a boundary, the place where the community ends and the outside begins. A few kibbutzim have tried to erase their boundary with little success. Joseph Shepher has pointed out that every urban kibbutz has failed and every kibbutz close to a city has run into serious problems because of the interference of city activities into the community's life. (1974) Personal communication. Vatik is not close to a city. It is three miles from a small development town to which most members seldom go. The town lacks cultural events and has no facilities which could attract the members. In a sense, the boundary is pathetic since many Oriental Jews live in this poor town and the contrast between the town and life in Vatik is stirring. People go hungry there. There are crowded conditions, unemployment, a growing crime rate.

Vatik's distance of almost 20 miles from the nearest medium size town reduces its boundary problems. The bus ride is time consuming and strenuous. Cultural life is sought within Vatik and at nearby kibbutz communities: we shall see later that many members are dissatisfied with the level of culture in the

---

* Valid answers 142 - Missing cases 16.

community. The difficulty in leaving (the limitations of community cars), the kibbutz six day workweek, and the limited outside possibilities all contribute to strengthening the boundary.
The resounding impression of living a year in Vatik is that members are not eager to leave the community frequently. Unless one
works outside or sees a special doctor, going out once every two
weeks would be frequent.

The considerations for going outside of the community are:
1) the desire to travel abroad; and 2) the attraction of working
outside. Vatik usually sends several members a year abroad for
vacations. This is not routine since most vacations of two-to-
four week duration are taken inside Israel and are paid for out
of a special vacation budget. The trips abroad are given out
according to seniority figured by number of years in the community. Since only a few members go each year, many younger members feel that their time is so far away that they will not even
have the opportunity, and wish to change this situation. About
50 members* work outside and sentiment on this issue is complex:
most members who do not work outside believe that outside member-
workers are the main cause of economic inequality, yet they favor
keeping the option available for members who have difficulty
suiting their special skills or particular life situation to
inside-community work roles. Many members have said that the
kibbutz uses outside work as an easy solution, too often and too
flexibly.

The heart of the boundary problem is illustrated here.
Small infractions arising from economic inequality rank as one
of the most serious problems of the community; most members reduce its initiating cause to a boundary problem. That means that
while inequality might occur without outside work roles, many
members perceive them as fanning the flame. Yasha, an older
member from the hashlama who has worked inside the community for
over twenty years, reflects on this:

> There are people who from a civilized point
> of view can acquire a position that is better
> outside the kibbutz. After a period of time,
> they get an important position outside the

* Only a small number of this group (less than 5) have worked
outside for years on end. Most return every three or four years
to work in the community as a show of humility and solidarity.

kibbutz and their lifestyle changes radically.
You work twenty or thirty years and you think
occasionally about this as members think and
you quickly swallow it. That all your time
you did the same work. Sometimes you are
satisfied, and sometimes you are not. It all
depends on the character of the person. The
first according to his ability got to a level
which is higher. So I've got to adapt to the
fact that he has a car to use all alone. He
gets up, gets in that private car and goes to
Tel Aviv. There he has a job. He didn't do
this against our will. We agreed, and got
used to the idea. So I accept that he has a
different ability and a different lifestyle.
Neither I nor he can ignore that his standard
of living is higher.

This kind of conversation arose an astonishing number of
times in interviews despite the fact that the questionnaires did
not touch outside work. After much probing it was found that it
is the private car that upsets most members and the occasional
trip abroad that a high government official or a kibbutz scientist gets that causes most bitterness. In Vatik, no more than
ten of the 50 outside workers have a "private car." This car is
usually supplied by the place of work, usually the kibbutz federation, a government agency, or a university (in this case the
community may supply the car).

These members must post when they are driving to work and
they must offer places in the car to others going in that direction. But some of them have apartments in the city (again not
more than six members in Vatik) because of the distance. After
all probing is completed, one finds that many members have worked
on the outside and they do introduce inequality. But members
think the kibbutz profits culturally and economically from its
contact with the outside. So, while the kibbutz has a strong
boundary with the outside, Vatik, especially has problems with
its management. Possibly, the reader is beginning to understand
a basic truth about the kibbutz that no amount of tables or statistics can communicate. If one describes the community in
sociological terms (like Gemeinschaft or Gesellschaft) and looks
for material to fortify these terms, one comes up with a neat way
to categorize what is going on. More often than not, however,
sustained and muti-directional observation shows that elements
of both categories exist simultaneously. Statistical and mathe-
matical techniques are to some extent unsuited to our exploration,

because they cannot accommodate these features of discontinuity, complexity and non-linearity that are the distinguishing marks of social and political life. (Berlinski, 1976) We try to keep these limitations in mind.

The matter is one of tendency and balance of forces over the long run. There is tension between forces moving towards uniformity in the social arrangement and the diversity of people and the variation of options (for the community recognizes it needs to change). Any examination of the social arrangement has to take original sources of this diversity into account. We will now search through the original motivation of members.

Ideals And Homogeneity

Despite the intensity of the "first times" and the overpowering implications of founding a society, no amount of ideological seduction can erase the fact that people came to Vatik for vastly different reasons. Even the members who say, "We came for zionism," or "We came to build a just society," must not be believed. They often really mean "I" not "We."

Many of the members of the founding and hashlama group came out of a ideological education nurtured in the youth movement. Zalman touched on this:

> Look you ask me why I came to the kibbutz
> when I arrived in Israel and why I did not go
> to the city. That is not a relevant question
> you know. We got a special education since
> we were children. In the youth movement.
> When we grew up we formulated some thesis.
> The thesis was right in its time and it is as
> well right nowadays, in spite of the fact
> that now one does not speak so much about it.
> Anyway the first thing in this thesis is the
> duty to immigrate to Israel. The principle
> was organically related to the idea of kib-
> butz, because we were a product of the youth
> movement. We were very much convinced that
> the Jewish people in the diaspora was leading
> an abnormal life and that it needs a state of
> its own. From an economic point of view the
> Jewish people fill up the holes in the capi-
> talistic regime. They are the merchants,

artisans, and shopkeepers in the thousands
and tens of thousands. They are physicians
and professionals. But we said we do not
only need a working class; we need a peasantry.
We need villages and agriculturists. So I
said to myself: therefore I must be a peasant
and live in a village. And we wanted to set
up a socialist society.

A founding member describes a different story:

I came here on a visit. All my life I wanted
to live on a nice farm with a little house.
I liked this village a lot and the others
were so friendly to me. Then, I met Micha,
my present husband, and we decided to become
a couple. When I think back it seems that
maybe I really wanted to live on a moshav
shitufi,* not a kibbutz, but I have been here
so many years....What can I do now?

This woman made sacrifices similar to those of the other founders.
She held difficult and time-consuming positions in the turkey
house, in the dairy and in the area of children's education. She
sang and danced with the others in the "intimate commune." But
her reasons are not the same as Zalman's.

A married member of the second generation describes reasons
typical of this group. Eytan worked for some years in the plastics factory in Vatik and now has gone to study in the university:

You grow up, you're educated, you make
friends, it is your home, your family, your
parents, it is a base. This place has a significance, when you live here you have to accept some standard of living that is accepted
here. If you do not accept it you have nothing to do here. This standard is on a very
high moral level. Of course it depends on the
individual, since everyone lives according to
his or her view of life and his or her nature.
There is a great variety but the standard is
very high. What maintains this high standard
is the social pressure. People who live here

---

* This is a landowners cooperative.

share the same ideas even if they do not say
it, they live in a structured arrangement.
Their view about their way of life is not
without variance, but it is pretty standard.
You have to look at it according to age. A
person of my age (young married) is just beginning to build his life, and we look for-
ward with this perspective: what am I, and
what do I want for myself. Afterwards,
people who are ten years older than I, they
are in the middle of activity (middle-age),
so much so that they do not have the time to
think of ideas, but mainly of practical matters. I do not say that they do not think
about ideas but their thinking is clearer,
the standard in their case is more basic and
permanent. People of my age are looking for
the implementation of beautiful ideas. The
gap between the desire and the reality is
huge. We are sensitive to small violations
of justice. I think young people are sensitive
about the subject of equality. They are
sensitive about work ethics, all the little
kinds of evils that occur in every day living,
things that you have to think about from time
to time, things like favoritism or relating
to a fellow member. Older people out of habit
have stopped relating to others or stopped relating to these problems. I want to live according to the beautiful principles and also
implement them. And what are they? That the
kibbutz will be really good for me because it
is my home, and that others and myself will
really reach this standard that we want to
reach, that life will be good!

Eytan typifies the young and middle aged married members of
Vatik. He respects the kibbutz as a social arrangement, with
little questioning, but not in a socialist language, and certainly not with the mention of Zionism. After all, he is an
Israeli and a son of the kibbutz. Zionism was always a reality
for him, not a choice. He does not have to remind you or himself
of that. Instead he focuses on the practical problems of maintaining the community and achieving happiness for the greater
number of individuals in the community. Not one man or woman in
the middle and young married group spoke to us of Zionism or
socialism. They spoke a secular ideology of equality, a good

47

life, working to solve social problems in the kibbutz. Many older members have said that with the "death of ideology" after the truth of Stalin and Russia came to the surface, that ideology in their kibbutzim became a matter of practical community ideas. But maybe, what "died" was never so standard.

In order to gauge the homogeneity or lack thereof of ideological motivation in the kibbutz, we examined the motivation for members' coming to the kibbutz [Question 8] and the motivation for their decision to remain in the community [Question 9]. Members were asked to rank the four most significant reasons in their decision, and these reasons were rated according to their closeness to original pioneering ideology. Tables 5A and B show the index of Ideological Strength To Join and To Stay in the community for different groups of members. There is a lot of variation in each group. The younger and older members cannot be viewed as separate blocks. In addition there is an attenuation of ideological motivation for most groups when the decision to remain in the community is explained.

TABLE 5A

Ideological Strength And Age

Decision To Join

	Low	Middle	High
Young	50%	25%	25%
Middle	10%	68%	22%
Old Founders	43.6%	14.5%	41.8%
Hashlama	36.5%	30.1%	33.4%
Rounded Averages	35%	35%	30%

TABLE 5B

Decision To Stay

	Low	Middle	High
Young	41.6%	10%	53.4%
Middle	20.5%	66%	13.5%
Old Founders	27.2%	37.8%	35%
Hashlama	37.7%	33%	34.3%
Rounded Averages	30%	36%	34%

Valid cases: 86
Missing cases: 72

N.B. The reason for the number of missing cases is that the
      Index was not computed where there were missing answers.
      Table 43 (Chapter II) was computed using all answers (even
      if a member only listed 1, 2, or 3 instead of four reasons)
      and the agreement between both sets of data confirm our
      conclusions about the population.

Does a particular kind of motivation to join or motivation
to remain in the community predict significant communal attitudes
during one's term of membership? If a prediction does occur then
homogeneity in terms of the original pioneering ideology has continued to matter in kibbutz life; if not then, we must look beyond the issue of homogeneity to explain the diversity of attitudes and beliefs in modern-day Vatik. No significant relationships were found when we cross-tabulated levels of motivation
with any other attitudes reported in the study.

There is not as much homogeneity of motivation in Vatik as
generalistic notions about the "Gemeinschaft" kibbutz would lead
us to believe. There is a variety of individual viewpoints.
What is common is not so much ideology as an acceptance of the
kibbutz as the place to live. Even non-ideological reasons are
contingent on the particular social arrangement that the kibbutz
represents. Some insight into social control will determine
upper and lower limits to this diversity.

Social Control

Vatik has no serious crime. There has never been a murder, suicide, or significant physical injury incurred by violence in the community since it began. Regarding the kibbutz movement as a whole, this is not exceptional. Joseph Shepher pointed out that one murder was committed in the kibbutz movement by a visitor. (1975) (Personal communication.) Several suicides have occurred in the last 15 to 20 years but the number is small and the cause often clear (for example, a parent would commit suicide after the death of a son in a war). In Vatik, one member once threatened another member over 20 years ago. The community felt the person issuing the threat was both serious and unstable. He had built up a reputation for some time and he was asked to leave.

Some petty theft occurs from time to time but each captured thief has been a visitor or an outsider. Several fistfights have taken place over the years. Surely, the discussion of social control will not bloom on this level, since the control is very strong, even though a police force or court does not exist. (The kibbutz is legally a municipality but it maintains no police force. Serious crimes, by arrangement with the government, would be reported to the local authorities.) The lack of serious need and inequality, the availability of work to all members, the mutual caring for the disadvantaged, the smallness and personalized nature of the community, the voluntary choice of members to live in the community, the press of gossip and social pressure are surely the main reasons for this lack of serious crime.

The level of concern is the conduct of one's life and its effect on the collective. The attempt to insult or malign another member or sustained sexual contact with another's mate has led to a Berur (Clearing Up) which takes place at the general assembly meeting, before the executive committee, or before the committee on membership. In recent years, the general assembly is no longer used much for such functions. This can be understood in the light of the change from a commune to a village. Instead, the two members involved will explain their gripes to the committee or the social secretary and come to some "clearing-up" of the situation. Community punishment or withdrawal of community rights does not exist. No attempt is ever made to adjust your economic rewards or the education of your children based on your behavior.

Two specific sides of social control can be elucidated in Vatik: what members consider unacceptable behavior and how members treat each other on a social level when the lines are crossed.

Based on a list of behaviors that came up in the interviews with 45 members we asked the whole sample which behaviors they considered a violation of kibbutz values [Question 23]. Table 6 shows the results.

TABLE 6

Unacceptable Behaviors According To
Percent Of Members Identifying Them

Lack of mutual aid among members	27%
Persons who do not work well or skip hours	66%
People who refuse to do toranut or mishloach	40%
People who abuse outside sources of money	43%
Personal habits of members I find disagreeable	21%
Dishonesty	44%
Do not consider these things important	6%

Valid cases: 132
Missing answers: 26

Disapproval of persons who do not work well, or who skip hours, makes sense since members evaluated the lack of a strong work norm as one of the major problems of Kibbutz Vatik. Refusing to do "toranut" or "mishloach" is related. These are Hebrew terms for "your turn" and "a sending." Certain labors the community considers it unfair to trust to one person all the time (for example: serving dinner on Saturday evening, washing pots, watching the baby house, doing the midnight watch at the gate) are taken in turn. "The Sending" refers to the late night loading of turkeys for market. Although the staff of the turkey houses is small the turkeys provide the second largest profit of any branch in Vatik. All male members must take their turns to load turkeys into cages and onto trucks. This is done at night when the birds are more docile, and it is a messy, cackling, hilarious job except for the huge breakfast at three o'clock in the morning.

Members disapprove equally of persons who get money from the outside and of dishonesty. Getting money from the outside is, as one member put it, "an accepted social sin. We know about it and turn our heads." In the days of the intimate commune all money and gifts were handed in no matter what the source or what

51

the size (a dress or a book was fair game for the collective till). It is now acceptable to receive small gifts, worth less than twenty dollars, but some members abuse this situation. It was very difficult to collect accurate information in this area; the author gave it some of his best hours. Since most members do not even talk to each other about these "little sins," it seems that indeed the author is one of the best sources. This information is based on interviews, gossip, and fairly honest special interviews with several community administrators who know a good deal about the personal affairs of members. Most members have received a television set, radio, small baking stove, air conditioner, or tape recorder from relatives in Europe, America, or even Israel who seek to do a good turn for their kibbutz family. These items are not extravagant but can cause a desire for everybody to use their "sources" to get the same thing and a serious discussion of "where our living standard needs to go" in the general assembly. Some members, often those who have worked outside the community and have sizeable bank accounts accumulated by saving their expense money, bring back a tape recorder from a foreign trip and sell it at a profit. As another example, the daughter of a kibbutz family may go overseas as a representative of the Israeli kibbutz youth movement. Her rich uncle in Canada may send her money for a side trip to France. Sometimes relatives send kibbutz members money to visit them for a wedding or a reunion. It is now an acceptable practice to accept such money. The issue is only if you have vacation days coming to you. But this decision was taken some years ago by default, and most of the members do not profit by it. The problem here is that almost everybody violates these norms, which explains why so little is done even though so many disapprove.

Dishonesty is more difficult to track down. Much of the dishonesty members reported was related to outside sources of money. For example, a member may get five dollars a day for meals when he or she is out of the community working, or at a meeting. Sometimes that member will ask the kitchen to make a lunch and pocket the five. Nevertheless, many members consider any flagrant abuse of outside sources as dishonest.

Our interviews are peppered with judgments of Vatik's attitude towards social control. "It is a weak kibbutz that let a few exceptions pass once and now has no choice." "We are a middle-income kibbutz and have to tolerate this because we do not have enough money to take care of these special needs." Members point to other kibbutzim which have not had Vatik's problems with social control. A neighboring kibbutz bought cameras for all the members and have encouraged an attitude that says, "We do not need to be dependent on the people from the outside even for

little things." Another decided that it was against kibbutz ideology for one person to have a television before others and
waited until an orderly transition to television sets for all
was made. Evaluating social control in the movement, however is
not so simple. Whether a kibbutz introduces components of a higher living standard by the book or through tension and last minute
planning, is not the question. There is simply a new social
situation in the kibbutz movement. Yonina Talmon pinpointed a
central cause of the standard of living controversy in the
kibbutz:

> A nonascetic trend is discernible in another
> element of the original ideology. We have
> already hinted at the ambiguity of the rela-
> tionship between socialism and asceticism.
> Raising the standard of living of the working
> man is one of the primary goals of the social-
> ist movement. Opposed to the existing world
> order on grounds of both justice and effi-
> ciency, it holds out a promise of material
> prosperity if all of its principles are put
> into practice and society is reorganized ac-
> cordingly. The kibbutz is supposed to be a
> model socialist microcosm. Since it has to
> compete with the surrounding nonsocialist
> economy, it must prove itself capable of pro-
> viding superior conditions for its workers.
> It is therefore hardly surprising that its
> members should also judge it by its capacity
> to fulfill their consumer demands. (1972, p. 210)

The problems of social control in Vatik are symptoms of
larger trends in the kibbutz movement as a whole and changes in
the community economy regarding consumption and the organization
of material life. They are based on a superordinate adjustment
that has been going on ever since the communal village was born,
an alteration in the norm that governs the relationship of the
individual to the community.

The Individual-Community Dialectic

The kibbutz defines a structure of mutual obligations between co-members where action on behalf of the community is rewarded in a more organized way than action solely on the behalf
of the individual. While preserving the notion of kibbutz the

social arrangements of the community have changed to accommodate a more normal society, a more diverse population, and a greater variety of options and challenges. Menachem Rosner, (1970) noted kibbutz sociologist and Director of the Institute For Kibbutz Studies at the University of Haifa, defines this adaptation:

> During the sixty years of its existence the
> kibbutz has been in a permanent process of
> change, trying to preserve its basic identity
> and the values of equality, direct democracy,
> mutual help and responsibility, by adapting
> the mechanisms and practices, the concrete
> forms of life to changing conditions.

The adaptations can become sweeping, as seen in Moshe (age 65) discussing a conflict between a member who wished to study and the Education Committee:

> I don't criticize our policies on education.
> I think they are ok. But if in a certain
> year when the total budget allows for 20
> people in universities, and one comes and
> says: "I want to study mathematics, not for
> teaching but for IBM or something." Another
> comes and asks for five years of education in
> art. Five years! And when we say, "Go and
> begin with two years," he says, "No I want
> all the five from the beginning." And an-
> other comes and says, "I want to study mathe-
> matics, just for my own knowledge, not to
> work in mathematics." And when we say to
> this 6 or 7 from the 20 that it is impossible,
> to the man who wants to study math, "We need
> engineers, we want to expand our industry, so
> why not study engineering for five years in
> the Technion," and he says, "I don't want
> that. My goal is to teach there some day."
> (What do we do?) I think he shouldn't get it.

The facts are that the kibbutz has given more and more to the individual tendencies of members and still tried to maintain its cooperative character. In the above case, and other conflicts over study and work assignment, usually some form of compromise is reached: the community weighs the importance of this member remaining, and the member's happiness, and the member weighs his or her very real responsibility to pull his or her weight and the ultimate desire to live or not live in the community.

Time after time the kibbutz has lost out on this method, probably because it did not have the ideological or religious fanaticism or the leadership fascism to sustain it. For example, some members thought that individual teapots in the rooms of each couple would "destroy" the fellowship of the community since no one would "have to" congregate in a common place to drink tea.

Another "norm" used to preserve this dialectic is the rule of thumb by which "profits" are invested in communal luxuries and facilities (coffee houses, culture halls, photo rooms) or branches to develop the communal economy. The individual's personal budget is allowed to increase and his or her possessions do become finer, but "profits" are not divided up into equal shares, large funds are not invested in building individual households.

It may be instructive to examine the state of the individual-community dialectic in Kibbutz Vatik and specific areas where it is being applied. It has often been said by social cynics that "no matter what a kibbutznik says about his or her life they just want more, more money, more material things, and more control over their lives. Their attitudes do not matter. Talk about social cooperation and then talk about cold cash and you have two different conversations." Many times this has come up in discussions with business people, or even middle-class ethnics who have worked hard to achieve some form of stability in the midst of a very competitive situation.

Investment Of Kibbutz Capital

Let us start here using as a criterion the notion that the average kibbutz member favors cooperation as a means to carry on life, including in the investing of community profits. [Question 21]. Kibbutz Vatik has several hundred thousand dollars available each year for investment, so the question is not hypothetical.

58% of the members favored investing new wealth in common projects which the whole kibbutz could enjoy, such as a swimming pool or more cultural buildings. 17.8% favored capital investment for further productivity as the source favored other sources, while 12.6% favored more private property for members according to the norm of equal distribution.* Indeed, if we are to believe

---

* Valid cases 119 - Missing cases 39.

the members of Vatik, increasing their living standard at any price is not their primary concern.

Work And Study Options

What is the general state of the individual-community norm? Two areas are relevant: providing greater options for individuals in the sphere of work [Question 26] and higher education [Question 24]. Tables 7A and B and 8 show the results.

TABLE 7A

Attitudes To Study Options

In your opinion what should be the limit of your kibbutz's consideration of individual inclinations and desires of the members regarding higher education?

All studies are ok, all requests should be positively accepted.	9.8%
All studies are ok, and people should go according to a line.	16.8%
All studies are ok, but the kibbutz should try to persuade people to study what it needs.	46.2%
All studies are ok, but those who study what the kibbutz needs should get preference	
All studies are NOT ok, unless the kibbutz needs them.	25.9%
All studies are NOT ok, since I am not sure a lot of higher education is a good idea.	.7%
Other	.7%

Valid cases 143 - Missing cases 15.

TABLE 7B

Evaluation Of Attitudes To Study Options

Do you think that your kibbutz is too flexible or hard regarding members inclinations about their education?

Too flexible	26.8%
Flexible	67.4%
Hard	2.9%
Too hard	2.9%
Not flexible and not inflexible	2.8%

Valid cases: 138 - Missing cases: 20.

TABLE 8

Attitudes To Work Options

In your opinion what should be the limit of your kibbutz's consideration of individual inclinations and
desires regarding their work?

All work preferences should be accepted.	3.5%
All work preferences are ok but the kibbutz must try to persuade people to do what it needs.	53.8%
All work preferences are ok but often a member will have to compromise for a year or two before he gets what he wants.	38.5%
The needs of the kibbutz are the main criterion of work possibilities.	4.2%
Other	0%

Valid cases: 143 - Missing cases: 15

In both regards there is very little support for positions that favor the individual or the community extremely. In work the members favor persuasion and compromise. Also, most members agree this situation is flexible and not unbalanced. Tobit, a nurse in her sixties and a founder typifies this opinion:

> Well, I think we should try to make people
> happy in their work. Too often we have to
> ask people to do things because of a lack of
> labor power. So someone who works with chil-
> dren may have to work in the dining hall for
> a while. Someone who has a profession, well,
> we try to let him or her work in that profes-
> sion. The person may temporarily have to
> work someplace else, but we try to please the
> member. But there are some people who never
> work out anywhere. They work two years here,
> two years there. But we have to try to be as
> flexible as possible. Look these are just
> matters of decisions. Most of the time it is
> just a change-over of positions. If someone
> cannot get along with poeple, and another can,
> you let the one work alone, and put the other
> one in a job with a lot of people. If some-
> one cannot work outside then we have to find
> a place where he or she can work. That is
> why we have a work committee. (And if some-
> one wants to work at one job) it's fine but
> the person would have to be willing to give a
> year or so to the kibbutz. After all, it's
> your home. You have responsibilities. If
> you go and study or go to the army you have
> to give something back.

More conservatism shows toward study; 25.9% of the sample favor giving priority to studies that the kibbutz needs. The dialectal nature of the process must be kept in mind. Two years ago the community laughed at people who spoke of studying program-ing. This year, they hope someone will come along since all internal (members' budgets) and external (purchases and sales and investments and taxes) accounts are being computerized. Now, they only laugh at those who want to study medicine, which would necessitate a seven year absence! Only 5.7% of the members think that the village is inflexible regarding studies [Question 25]; 67.4% think it is flexible and 26.8% too flexible.

The individual-community dialectic survives because it safeguards a subtle balance. For example, while the communal budget
mainly worries about the whole community before the individual,
most kibbutzim, because of greater affluence, believe it unfair
to pressure a member to work or study (except in temporary
crisis) in a branch not to his or her liking. Clear areas of
individual flexibility also exist in the variety of acceptable
member roles, cultural activities, and personal consumption.

Social Problem Resolution and Social Cooperation

Kibbutz Vatik adjudicates conflicts between the individual
and the community, attempting to compromise the positions of both
and preserve the basic features of the social arrangement. The
attitudes of the membership towards social cooperation [Question
56] and Social Problem Resolution [Question 55] acknowledge this
feature. Three approaches towards social cooperation were delin-
eated: cooperation for utilitarian or idealistic reasons, or the
difficulty of cooperation in any society. 52.3% agreed that "if
we do not cooperate and work together we could not attain this
standard of living." 40.9% saw cooperation as the main value in
life and 4.7% noted it was difficult in any society, kibbutz or
non-kibbutz.*

An additional 25 persons who had taken the utilitarian position changed the answer by adding that they also favored the
notion that cooperation was the main value of life. There is no
uniform attitude towards social cooperation. Possibly this stems
from the lack of an ordained spiritual or radical political
notion about the meaning of the kibbutz community. In a time of
normality, like Eytan (in Chapter II) the average member sees
the community as an alternative or better way of life. Attitudes
towards means of social problem resolution in Vatik can indicate
how committed the members are to their social arrangement.

_____

* Valid cases 149 - Missing cases 9.

TABLE 9

Means of Social Problem Resolution

How would you describe your attitude toward social
problems in the kibbutz?

Most social problems here can be solved by more money.   5.1%

Most social problems in the kibbutz are not paradoxes
and can be solved by planning, decisions in the
mazkirut, committees, and the sicha.   47.8%

The attempts to solve social problems here are games.
That life is better for some and less better
for others cannot be changed.   11%

Most social problems stem from problems between
people and groups in the kibbutz. Only by
honesty and discussion, not just plans will
they be solved.   36%

Valid cases: 136 - Missing cases: 22.

With 47.8% favoring decisions by community institutions and the
36% favoring resolution of problems by honest discussion between
people and groups, the population seems committed to a community-
oriented approach to social problem resolution.

Ordering Of Priorities, Group Involvement, Group Criticism

Where do members of Vatik stand when forced to choose the
group or the individual?

We examined the source of social control [Question 44], and
their attitude towards group involvement [Question 45], and group
criticism [Question 46] by offering clearly opposing orientations. 45.6% of the sample agreed, "It is better for the kibbutz
to agree on specific rules to regulate the behavior of members

than to leave this up to individuals. This will insure order."
36.1% felt "It is better for the kibbutz to be flexible and trust
individuals to decide on responsible behavior." 18.4% of the
members left the question unanswered. The margin is so close and
the amount of people expressing an opinion so high* that we may
conclude that the members of Vatik are clearly split on where
responsibility for regulating group life should be. Regarding
the social consequences of group involvement .6% agreed that,
"People who identify themselves strongly with some group usually
do so at the expense of their freedom as individuals, so social
life should be limited." 42.1% thought that "Individuals cannot
really find happiness unless they involve themselves deeply in
working with a group of people," and 43% favored a combination of
both approaches, with 24% of the sample not answering.** The
membership favors a middle path between the community and the
individual, although a sizable majority also see the importance
of group life as paramount.

Nevertheless, there is little support for the legislation
against individual diversity of the "first times" and the intimate commune. This view is supported by the attitude towards
group criticism. 79.1% feel obligated to criticize members of
the community when they break rules; 6.3% do not think it helps
and 4.4% do not care if it helps but thinks it not good; 9.5%
did not answer.*** Thus, despite the fact that group intimacy
has passed, a majority of the members feel group criticism necessary. The nature of criticism has certainly changed. Members
more often complain to committees, branch coordinators and community officers than to each other. Embarrassing a member to his
face before all is no longer considered respectable, but members
speak forthrightly in interviews, in their conversations with
each other, at coffee breaks, in general assembly meetings, and
in articles in the weekly newsletter. The community may lack
intimacy in comparison to its beginning, but involvement in
community issues is not a peripheral concern.

A division of attitude and approach exists that expresses a
division that has occurred in the history of the village itself.
One of the theoretical goals of this work is to understand the
nature of the individualist-communalist dialectic. Since we know

---

* Valid cases 132 - Missing cases 26.
** Valid cases 121 - Missing cases 37.
*** Valid cases 143 - Missing cases 15 [Question 46].

that members differ in their original motivation, and in viewpoint and individual expression, this division of attitude may express only the complementarity of the membership. On the other hand, it may express a real split in the community; this will be considered later.

The internal newsletter of Kibbutz Vatik shows that this issue is really a matter of many individual requests and arrangements before the secretariat whose decisions are summarized weekly:

Decisions of the Secretariat:

> Yisrael is leaving the kibbutz. He does not find the opportunity for study here and feels it necessary for self-determination.

> Yaakov will not return to teach at the high school since his courses were turned down by the committee. He asked to be given two years to study social psychology. We asked that he return and work on the farm first and left the issue for further discussion.

> Shira asked to return to her work in the hospital.

> It was decided to bring to a general meeting the problem of members who do not want other buildings built near the houses they reside in.

> Aron is going to spend some time living in Kibbutz Bet Kama (referring to a youth probably seeking to meet more young kibbutz women).

Decisions From the General Assembly Community Meeting:

> Tobit requested a refresher course in nursing and it was approved. She will study a course about Older Women and Children at Beit Styhaim Hospital.

> After much argument and discussion it was decided to erect our small hospital at the end of the Ulpan (Hebrew language seminar) building where the present artists' studios stand.

> Many members were concerned that the physical
> demands on older people working in the kitchen
> were too great. It was decided that men from
> the age of 55, and women from the age of 50,
> can, on the days in the middle of the week,
> take an hour off for rest. On Friday, when
> the large evening meal is being prepared,
> this can be two hours.

In conclusion, each member has an active role in determining
the balance between the individual and the community. One can
think of the many trends in the individual-community dialectic as
"schools of thought and action" that eventually create the social
matrix of decisions and behaviors which determines the quality of
life. Vatik's supportive, integrated, actively socially controlled and moderately geographically bounded community, with its
strong emphasis on the flexible social relationship between members and the institutional orientation toward protecting human
diversity, has a membership overwhelmingly committed to kibbutz
methods and gives a major role to group resolution of problems
and group planning within the community's institutional framework. There are, however, distinct divisions of philosophy,
whose implications are not yet evident. The social structure
of Vatik tries to maximize individual options and preserve the
kibbutz since circumstances of differentiation in the population,
in conditions in Israel, and in ideology have shaped its development as a communal village. Because changes in the standard of
material living and the economic structure of the village have
accompanied and encouraged this social arrangement, it makes
sense now to examine this sector.

CHAPTER III

ECONOMIC COOPERATION AND WORK

Section 1. Economic Cooperation

The kibbutz economic principle of social profit, its success
in practice, and its specific organization in Kibbutz Vatik is
explained, with a view toward the village's relation with larger
economic associations. Internal or practical kibbutz economics,
once the efficiency of the organization is established, is a
more salient quality of life criteria. Three internal economic
questions are explored: equality and inequality, attitudes towards affluence, simplicity and limiting the standard of living,
and the challenges of industrialization.

> It is different now that the kibbutz is not a
> commune of poverty....Some people say that
> the kibbutz will become more like a moshav
> shitufi (collective village in Israel with
> common production and individual shares and
> consumption).* In other words, once the
> influence of private income begins, it will
> continue endlessly. And there are other
> people who feel that this is sort of an added
> insignificant behavior; in other words,
> equality and cooperation here will continue
> and these (infractions or changes referring
> to money on the side a kibbutz member may have)
> will not substantially destroy or change--
> well, I would say change the kibbutz. How
> do you feel about that?

> Here comes the question of the private moral-
> ity of every member because (the more such
> changes occur) the quantitative becomes qual-
> itative. If somebody gets 100 Lira (approx.
> $12.50) or something (from a relative or
> other source) and he or she uses it and buys
> something, that is different from another
> who has a bank account and keeps thousands of
> Lira in it. This cannot be accepted. If it
> will occur this will destroy the whole belief
> between one and the other and thus the whole
> normative base of the kibbutz.

> *Author and a senior member in dialogue.

Kibbutz Economic Principles and Organization

The Principle: Social Profit

> You cannot measure the success of the kibbutz
> economic plant by profit alone. Financial
> profit is not an efficient or accurate measure
> of one's economic well-being. For example,
> you may make more money than I but live in the
> midst of a great deal of pollution. Maybe for
> me this freedom from pollution can be valued
> at $5,000 a year. What can you say to that?
> So profit is just one of the goals in the kib-
> butz. We are trying to minimize risk. We are
> trying to find a structure that will achieve
> 1) the promise of consistent and regular work;
> 2) the goal of settling the land agriculturally,
> and supplying the people with food and resources;
> and 3) making a profit. For example, say you
> compare two factories, one in a kibbutz and
> one in the city, and you find out that the
> profit of both is similar. Is it not meaning-
> ful that in the kibbutz the worker does not
> have to worry about being fired, or having a
> difficult situation if someone in the family
> gets sick? How can you say the salary of a
> city worker compares with this social situa-
> tion. Where is the standard of living?
>
> Conversation with Dov Peleg, Director of
> The Central Economic Department of The
> Kibbutz Artzi Federation, Tel Aviv, 1976.

Simply put, the kibbutz has a principle of social profit or integral profit that guides its economic planning. This profit includes the effects of the social and political milieu of work and
production on the worker; it includes planning for differences in
ability, differences in power, differences in position, differences in life crises; it eliminates totally dependence on central
Federal agencies for unemployment compensation, welfare, food
stamps; it organically connects the means (how the economic shop
is organized) with the ends (a high standard of living for all)
by applying the principle of cooperation. As a female member of
Vatik who was critically injured many years ago and feels this
concept personally puts it:

The basis of the commune is not only friends,
but here the basic principle is an equal and
collective way of life. And whoever agrees
with this can be a kibbutz member. So there
are some members who are more conservative,
some who are less...some work harder than
others, and sometimes this hurts, and you
have people that work hard and even spend
time in the evenings working out problems in
their work branches and this person gets the
same out of the kibbutz as someone who does
not spend as much time -- sometimes he even
gets less! But then you get into the fact
that maybe that one has a bigger family, so
more money is spent on the education of his
children...so it turns out that the quality
we are talking about does not mean that everybody is equal. People get essential things in
an equal way.

In short, one might summarize her ideas by saying that the kibbutz economic system is based on the premise that the complicated
social, personal, and economic factors balance each other out,
when members, whether the lazy ones or the aggressive ones, at
least accept the principle of cooperation and try as best they
can. For, how willing would the hard-working member be to pay
higher taxes for crime prevention and welfare programs for the
poverty and dislocation that the abandonment of the principle of
cooperation might ensue? Cooperation is the tax and the sacrifice.

These notions comprise the most frequently occurring definitions of what the kibbutz is by members of all ages, sexes, and
backgrounds: the security of basic needs in the context of a
relatively supportive and non-competitive social arrangement.
It figures as a central reason why members who could leave the
kibbutz for a better living standard said they chose to stay.

The early kibbutzniks did an interesting economic analysis
of society that seems relevant to the days of default. It was
simple: they decided they would plan a community where the
standard of living would grow equally for all members, where
there would be no unemployment, welfare, or poverty. The facts
do silence theoretical arguments. These problems and serious
crime, alcoholism and drug abuse are nearly non-existent in the
kibbutzims' population of 90,000, and absent in a startling way
when we look at a village such as Vatik on the inside over a year.
No example of serious or even moderately mischievous crimes or

alcoholism or severe mental illness were found. A few minor cases of pot smoking were the only drug-abuse (if one can call it that) found. This has been achieved through the economic principle of <u>social profit</u>. Kibbutz life is a web of educational situations in this principle. Although not identified as such, decisions in the kibbutz are made according to this principle, often summarized as "from each according to his ability and to each according to his need." This was an early movement motto.

Practically, the kibbutz does not connect the standard of living or "profit" of each member with type of work, amount of work, profession, training, family background, political beliefs, age, sex. One shares in the advantages of life as a member's right. This can be considered a socialist equation where one side is not proportional to the other. Before the individual standard of living goes up (for example, before television sets are bought or individual budgets increased for incidental expenses) the community budgets for all the needs covered by total social security: daily welfare, health, education, transportation, child care, cultural activities, and communal facilities. Basic economic rights exist. Along with this consideration, before figuring out the standard of living, investment for continued and expanded productivity in the work branches is definitively assured.

Vatik, like many middle-aged kibbutzim, has been breaking even or making a small profit using this criterion.

The Principle In Practice

The author examined the financial statements of Kibbutz Vatik for the last few years in order to confirm the general economic stability of the community. In addition, the community's farm manager was extensively interviewed. Good documentation on the personality of kibbutz members will aid little in understanding the quality of life if the village's economy is supported by government subsidies and not successful in its own right.

Two central facts of economic life in Vatik and other kibbutzim must be kept in mind when evaluating the advanced, profitable and, some would say, "capitalistic" progress of the kibbutz. First, the family is still not a recognized economic unit. The children's budget is communal. Their support and education is not an economic consideration of their parents. Also, while couples share a common house, marriage does not mean a large family budget, and members of couples get their funds and services as individuals in order to protect the individuality of each. Secondly, the kibbutz invests in raising the standard of living by improving communal facilities rather than by increasing the relatively small personal allotment for incidental expenses (only a few hundred dollars yearly) or by putting conspicuous consumption into the households. One must therefore not view kibbutz economic progress exclusively as individual "consumerism." In Chapter II this view was supported by a review of members' attitudes on investments. It is far from that.

Now we must consider the economic performance of the kibbutzim as a whole. We want to be sure Vatik is not just an exception. Such principles can be taught and practiced but if they fail, they will pass on. Kanovsky, (1967) in the Economy of the Israeli Kibbutz, a study done at Harvard University's Center for Middle Eastern Affairs, evaluates the kibbutz's performance. Briefly, the kibbutzim are more highly efficient productively, in comparison to all other sectors of Israeli agriculture, in almost all areas of agricultural commodities. This applies to yields per acre, productivity per worker, technical and innovative efficiency, advanced training, use of regional processing and distribution centers, and marketing. Kanovsky concludes that the collective structure is well adapted to the efficient planning of high productivity.

Kibbutzim have not, however, always made a profit. For every community the beginning is hard, paved with many years of long and short-term loans. This situation, common in the thirties, improved somewhat in the fifties when the kibbutzim reduced losses to small amounts. In the sixties most older communities showed small surpluses, and that trend is continuing with some communities showing large profits. The same productive efficiency and profitability is true for kibbutz industry. Melman showed that in fact kibbutz factories were more profitable than private sector Israeli counterparts. (1970) Peleg, head of the Economic Department of Kibbutz Artzi, agrees that while this may still be true for some kinds of factories the gap is narrowing because of the general upgrading of enterprises in the country.

The industry is highly developed. As in agriculture, the kibbutzim pioneered many of the most important sectors of Israeli industry and run some of the largest and most mechanized plants. (For a complete list of kibbutz industries see Criden/Gelb, 1974.) Because it cannot increase its holding of land or exploit its

existing fields more than is done now this is the only direction
for growth.   The farm plan (drawn up by a high-powered economic
committee and discussed at the general assembly meeting) is a
detailed plan and strategy for the farm's economy which involves
much work by the committee, public review, professional advice,
and branch and inter-branch haggling. In short, the kibbutz
economic principle is: planning and efficiency with moral
clarity.

How does Vatik fit this picture?

The Economic Plant In Vatik

        Vatik pioneered fish agriculture for the whole country
and has introduced new features to increase productivity through
research at its Laboratory For The Study of Fish Diseases. One
of the senior members invented citrus spraying methods that have
since been adopted around the whole country and have increased
productivity in this area. Only the plastics factory in Vatik
has been a near failure as an industrial enterprise. It was
originally started to give an easier form of work to older members, but the work roles and their fit with the machinery and
the noise was poorly designed. Labor is highly unskilled, and
workers there are not satisfied.   The metal factory in Vatik was
in this position but the farm manager credits the persistent and
careful management by a new coordinator with developing this
branch.   The farm manager explained that a high profit for every
branch is not the goal of the kibbutz system. He and other farm
managers use a figure based on comparing what each average worker
(these are never computed for individuals) produces per day and
what that brings on the market with what it costs to support a
member per day and provide overhead for the productive enterprise. Most farm managers prefer that a branch at least break
even and produce some extra profit (since by the usual definition
of profit the fact that a branch makes enough to pull its weight
in supporting the community shows profit). Only the plastics
factory in Vatik comes close to not breaking even. Most branches
however are moderate producers and profit-makers. The main profit of the community is made by the fish branch where 8 workers
produce 20% of the total community budget, and the turkey branch
where 15 workers produce 20% of the community budget.

Vatik, unlike many rich kibbutzim, has no industrial branch that is very successful. Members and economic coordinators complain that this situation causes pressure on the community since less money is available to alleviate problems of inequality, to upgrade equipment, and improve the community. They have been developing plans for such an enterprise for several years and are in the process of signing contracts with large electronics firms and the Israeli Ministry of Commerce to build a very large cable-making plant. A special members committee toured Europe and the United States on a fact-finding mission and drafted contracts. Later the author observed their report and aggressive cross-examination by the community's members before the plan was approved. A focal issue in approval was the affirmation that skilled and interesting non-assembly line roles for older members would be available.

Vatik is considered by its farm manager and the movement's Economic Department a moderately economically successful kibbutz with a middle income. According to our study of the efficiency of their farm plan most production goals by branches are met or nearly met, and the community has solid plans for upgrading productivity in its main branches.

The Wider Economic Sphere

Some further organizational information about Vatik should be filled in before moving on. Kibbutz Vatik does not achieve its economic success by sheer independence. It does not, as critics uninformedly accuse it and other kibbutzim of doing, get away without paying income taxes. The income is computed, divided by the number of members and taxes are paid. On the other hand, despite the fact it does not drain government resources at all for unemployment compensation, welfare, food stamps, law enforcement programs, old aged homes, social workers, it does as a municipality receive government benefits to which all municipalities in Israel are entitled. Dov Peleg, of the Economics Department of Kibbutz Artzi, enumerated them: (A) Health funds are received through the national health care system run by the government related Kupat Cholim (Sick Fund). Each kibbutz member as a member of the socially important National union, the Histadrut, pays into this fund. (B) The community gets education benefits from the Ministry of Education by which teacher salaries and building expenses are subsidized. (C) The same is true for various loan and grant programs made available

70

through the Ministry of Housing. (D) Every private industrial-
ist in Israel is entitled to Government loans and grants to
establish new industry. For example, in one of Vatik's $1.5
million productivity upgrading programs 30% was provided by the
Commerce Industry, 40% by low interest loans, and 20% by the farm
itself. The community was helped greatly by the Jewish National
Fund, the Jewish Agency and the World Zionist Organization, which
have helped to build many kibbutzim by low interest loans at its
inception, and have played a crucial role in the establishment
of the movement.

As a co-member of a kibbutz federation made up of 75 kibbutzim with a population of 31,055 (Criden, Gelb, p. 231, 1974)
the community gets substantial technical assistance in planning
and management. The Kibbutz Industrial Association of the Association of Kibbutz Federation provides a series of very important
technical services to the budding economic plants, as does Mercaz
Chaklai (Agricultural Center), the Economic Department of the
Kibbutz Artzi Federation, Bank HaPoalim (Worker's Bank) which
has a central lending role in village development, as has the
Kibbutz Economic and Agricultural School at Rehovot and the
Ruppin Kibbutz College of Agriculture. Communitarian attitudes
would be naive window-dressing without the backbone of good
organization towards a better quality of life.

On the negative side, Kibbutz Vatik is almost totally un-
aware of and disorganized concerning ecological effects of its
productivity and long-term ecological costs. No attempt is made
to replace biological control methods for spraying dangerous
chemicals. Solar energy is hardly developed despite the real
superiority of Israeli science and the intensity of the sun in
this area. Despite the potential of communal housekeeping to use
less energy the farm manager estimates that the community wastes
a large amount of energy both through lax personal consumption
habits and poor organization of capital equipment energy utiliza-
tion. While from the organizational standpoint of our analysis
one might say that small is beautiful in Vatik, the community had
better learn the lessons of Schumacher's post-industrial scarcity economics or it will be caught out in the cold. (Schumacher, 1973)

A serious organizational problem of Vatik is that with increased economic success it becomes more and more dependent on
systems of mass production, mass consumption, and mobility and
less self-sufficient as a community. Its participation in
regional cooperatives made up of farmers and cooperative

71

communities* in the area has helped it keep pace with the most advanced production and distribution methods without large capital investments. But the community does not raise its own food and does not build its own houses, and is not reflecting on whether there may be limits to increasing participation in an economic set-up over which it has little control. The regional enterprises and the always available support of the federation provide a buffer for trouble, but little has been done to explore ways of eliminating dependence rather than to buffering it. Last year, inflation alone increased the actual budgetary expenses by hundreds of thousands of dollars. This bell is now tolling even louder in Israel and around the world.

Let's look at the effect of all of this on the daily considerations of the member and his or her life. Truly, infrastructure, while important, cannot be considered the paramount issue of the economic arrangement.

Practical Kibbutz Economics

This part will cover the challenge of equality, the state of economic principles among the members, and attitudes toward individualization.

Turning to more specific aspects of the economy, Idit, a woman member of 30, gives us a view of the stresses in a cooperative economy caused by the tension between collective ownership and management of production, consumption, and individual needs:

---

* The most important is a consumer cooperative started by the movement and now one of the largest businesses (with the largest capital turnover) in all of Israel, HaMashbir HaMercazi. Tnuva, the producers' marketing cooperative, plays another infrastructural role for Vatik, along with the regional cooperative industrial center which Vatik and neighboring kibbutzim and non-kibbutz villages maintain for processing, packaging, and shipping. For further information see Viteles (1967).

You see the kibbutz does give you possibilities, many tracks to choose from. In the
city the smart ones become professors or even
if they are not so smart and only know how to
"get along" it still happens, they become
businessmen. Sometimes in the kibbutz they
are even more than professors, so in the kibbutz in a way, it is the same story. The
question is what is equality? Here a bright
person and a not so bright person are given
the same opportunities. But that has not
reached real equality because whoever is
smarter is really richer in certain unmate-
rial ways. And with this we finish off the
discussion of equality. In many kibbutzim if
someone gets a TV as a present from the outside they "open their eyes to it" and stop it.
Here there are at least 100 private TV's and
no one says anything about it. And so we
order one for everyone who does not have one
and wants one. As far as I'm concerned I'd
rather have a TV than a radio. There are
some kibbutzim where they have stopped buying
radios for the members and only buy TV's.
The point here is people do not buy things
in order to be "snobs" but because they
really want or feel they need them, not like
some simple workers we know who, as soon as
they get money, go out and buy a big American
car that they really cannot afford. I believe in the members here, for the most part
that they get what they need. Why should 100
people sit and watch the same TV. We'd like
to have one in our own room. Once it was the
same way with the radio, so when it came to
the point that you can have a radio in your
own room, you can have a TV too. The only
problem is the money to buy it.

When pushed for clearer criteria, however, many members
like Idit admit that the only problem is not the money to buy it.
Her attitudes represent a strong feeling, especially in Vatik,
that some social problems, are affected by available funds. To
prove this point members in Vatik point to a more prosperous
kibbutz where small infractions of equality are not as serious
a problem because inequality can afford to be solved.

73

Equality and Inequality

The problem of inequality ranks about third in a listing of the most serious problems of the community made by our sample of 158 members. The loss of ideology and a weak work norm were ahead of it. In the interviews which comprised several hundred hours of conversation and in the author's personal conversations with members it was the most persistent concern raised in terms of the amount of time and the degree of concern voiced by members of all ages and both sexes. To some extent, Kibbutz Vatik is <u>actively</u> aware of the problem. A few years ago a special committee was set up to examine the situation. Their report suggested that the community purchase television sets, cameras, stereos and other small luxury items for members who lacked them and that policy has been put into practice. It will take several years. What is important is not the amount of inequality, but the intense feelings and problems caused by the small amount of it that takes place.

A member of the hashlama puts his finger on the situation:

> We prayed to become a big kibbutz, a normal
> kibbutz and now we have the problems of a
> normal kibbutz. But we do not know how to
> solve these normal problems. All our lives
> we dealt with abnormal problems. I told
> you before that equality and cooperation
> cover 99% of our life, but you know, the
> one per cent left takes 99% of our atten-
> tion; it takes the attention of our com-
> mittees, and our members. You can go to
> bed and have a good sleep and never be able
> to dream about what in the morning these
> people will ask for. Therefore it could
> be useful to discuss the marxist formula
> according to which the material conditions
> of life determine value judgments and ideo-
> logical outlooks. From this point of view
> the kibbutz is a real society, an economic
> structure characterized by some features
> which are not capitalistic.

Let's look at those judgments.

The members were asked if they thought that it was possible to improve the situation of equality in their kibbutz [Question 34]. 32.4% chose the opinion that it was a problem to be solved by more money; 25.4% said it was a problem but no solution was possible; 17.6% saw the problem but felt greater rules and regulations as a solution were not possible to institute; 14.8%, however, felt more rules and discipline could improve the situation. Only 5.6% saw inequality as no problem. 4.2% had other ideas or did not answer the question.* Statistics can lie but they can also speak. There is no enthusiastic support for any position. Those who at least see a solution are as great in number as those who see none. Decidedly, however, a majority of the population (47.2%) see financial or regulational solutions to the problem as possible. In actual practice in kibbutz Vatik this is the frame of mind favored by members who work on this problem. The position is alluded to in conversations; specific proposals are mulled over by various committees, informal leaders, circles of friends, and coffee break "meetings" in the work areas.

Nevertheless, the truth is that the 22.8% who see no solution to the problem also represent an important trend in Vatik's population. For despite rational attempts to deal with inequality, there is never a basic full-dressed specific and serious discussion of the problem in the general assembly. The author has witnessed many meetings of the general assembly and noted that the discussion on this issue often abruptly comes to an end once the practical decisions are taken. On several occasions, a member who brings up the issue in a more general ideological framework is passed over and suddenly the assembly is discussing the next issue, dogs in the community! The point is that inequality is not only a major problem, and a minor phenomenon (in the context of all of the actual cooperation going on), but it is an important organic development in the communal village form itself; one gets the clear impression that with the commune of poverty gone the goal of the kibbutz today is to maximize economic growth and the over-all development of the village as much as possible without destroying the social milieu or establishing a competitive market. Yet members are unsure of the strains.

Affluence, Simplicity and The Living Standard

To understand this general judgment, the state of economic attitudes has to be more delicately explored. Let us examine the

---

* Valid cases 142 - Missing cases 16.

attitude towards economic affluence and simplicity, and the attitude of members towards limitations of the living standard in
general and the introduction of particular items like cars in
specific. Then, we'll conclude with a view towards the future;
attitudes towards the comprehensive budget and technological
development.

Table 10 summarizes attitudes towards affluence [Question
41].

TABLE 10

Attitude Towards Economic Affluence

Affluence causes disunity, social non-consideration, and less value agreement.	3.7%
Higher living standard brings less need for coopera- tion and more privacy and property and basic changes in kibbutz form.	35.3%*
No contradiction between high living standard and communitarian socialism, cooperation and mutual aid.	39.7%*
A crisis will occur and only kibbutzim that can deal with it creatively will continue to remain kibbutzim.	21.3%

* 7.4% of the members chose this in combination with the first
and fourth choices and this number was added here.

Qualified Answers	5.1%

Valid cases: 136
Missing cases: 22

_____

Very few members connect affluence directly with social disintegration, but most members foresee definite threats to cooperation at the hands of a higher living standard (60.3% of the
sample). Only 34.6% see no contradiction whatsoever. There is
obviously strong doubt in Vatik as to how far the living standard

76

can be expanded and how much distribution varied without hurting the social milieu. Just at that point where we observed defensiveness and repression at general assembly meetings, do some basic doubts arise.

Simplicity was the basic style of the early kibbutz. Members of Vatik remember how happy they were with a chair and a table "then." To the question, "Should simplicity be a basic value of the kibbutz way of life [Question 22] today?" they answered:* 30.7% yes, 54.7% no (with the qualifier that extravagance should not be allowed, while recognizing that poeple are different in their basic needs) and 14.6% absolutely not. There certainly is not a resounding value of simplicity that could limit the living standard, although when a rejection of simplicity was not qualified with "No extravagance" few chose it. The reality of everyday life in Vatik corresponds closely with this result. The 45 people interviewed were also asked about expanding their apartments if the kibbutz had enough money and very few would agree to that. The main reasons given were, "It is not necessary," and "I do not want to be bothered with more." Most of this group also rejected simplicity as a basic value.

One sees very little conspicuous consumption in Vatik such as closets full of clothes and shoes, cabinets of dishes and silver. Not one member was encountered who spoke about having the "finer things in life." In the interviews there was an emphasis on functional and comfort-oriented improvements: having a larger personal budget, having hot water heaters (_vs_. kerosene) in all the apartments, having a stereo, tape recorder and television set, increasing the number and variety of communal cultural facilities, sending more people to study, reducing the most difficult areas of physical labor on the farm, and upgrading machinery and technology to improve the structure of the work role in branches like the kitchen and laundry. As one member said, "We never thought we would be able to consider these things." These needs involve a rejection of earlier values and styles of simplicity. On the other hand, then it was food plus clothing plus home-made culture plus good agricultural productivity. Members argue that the new desires do not involve a running after luxury. Few students of the kibbutz understand the difference. As pointed out earlier, Vatik is still actively organized as a collective;

---

* Valid answers 137 - Missing cases 21.

members favor investing profits in the commune rather than in private homes; and less than 5% of the funds needed to support a member fully are received in hand as cash. Discussion and speculation aside, this is not the advent of a crisis because the goal is not simply conspicuous consumption.

But a look at attitudes as to whether the living standard should be limited, and why, does show a strong conflict in the population [Question 20].* 54.7% want to limit the living standard, 41% do not want limits, and 4.3% are undecided.** This group was asked why they wanted to limit the living standard; their responses are in Table 11.

TABLE 11

Reasons For or Against
Limitations to the Living Standard

A.	Only money is the limit.	33%
B.	Social responsibility to help others with less.	17%
C.	Materialism and bourgeois tendencies.	47%
D.	More possessions cause competition.	22%
E.	More material things mean the less time that can be devoted to ideas.	8%
F.	Other	6%

Valid cases: 104 - Missing cases: 54.

---

* Note, this question, like many other questions seeking a list of categorical answers, was constructed by reviewing answers to the question in the interview sample and then building a question which embraced most of the categories the population used. These decisions were then checked against previous questionnaires used in the movement and with senior kibbutz member researchers who were advisors to the project.

** Valid cases 139 - Missing cases 19.

The table shows to what extent the different reasons were favored.
A concern for materialistic tendencies and increased competition
similar to members' views of affluence shows up. However, a
strong minority (about one third) saw funds as the only limit.
Thus, the ambiguity and conflict that has typified this area of
inquiry in Vatik continues.

One specific issue which will aid in diagnosing the number
of people favoring immediate moves towards materialism is the
attitude towards the comprehensive budget. As noted previously
the members of Vatik's federation get a series of "closed budgets" for their personal and cultural needs plus various open
budgets for basic needs and a small personal budget received in
cash which gives the individual total freedom of choice. With
this arrangement a member can, for example, take as many shirts
as he or she needs out of the closed clothing budget until he or
she reaches the limit. However, if the member does not want or
need such clothing, this budget cannot be used for other items,
such as records. This budget reduces personal choice and some
members believe it actually works against the kibbutz ethic of
"each according to one's ability, each according to one's needs."
They won't say that the individual knows his or her needs best.
On the other hand, the Kibbutz Artzi Federation to which Vatik
belongs has long withstood introducing the comprehensive budget
since many (especially leaders) consider it a serious violation
of kibbutz ideology. They reason that it:

> runs the risk of opening the doors to inequal-
> ities arising from more skillful individual's
> better use of goods, and from the existence
> of external sources of income. "External
> sources" include presents and gifts from rela-
> tives and friends, and German reparation pay-
> ments, of which a kibbutz member may keep
> part according to specific decisions of his
> or her kibbutz.

(Shepher, 1975 p. 44)

While the closed system of budgets provides for fairly equivalent
growth in the living standard in different categories of items,
except for inequalities - the comprehensive budget, by giving
lump sums to individuals, provides that some people may develop
their standard of living considerably in certain directions and
not in others. Thus, the comprehensive budget reduces overall
kibbutz control of the standard. Opponents reason that this
introduces what would "look like" a greater economic difference

in the community even though it might not be the case. For example, one family may decide to have simple furniture and domestic habits but go to Europe each summer, while another invests a lot of money in dresses, another in books, another in giving it to a son or daughter outside of the kibbutz.

A majority of the members in Vatik are against this kind of budget (45.3% to 35.2% with 19.5% undecided)* [Question 38]. The most defended reason for favoring it was that 'People know their needs best' (75%). Fewer agreed that it was a better way to make socialism work (14%) or that what was over and above basic social and economic security in the kibbutz was unimportant (22%) or that they favored a trend towards privacy (37%). Thus the reasons for favoring it in Vatik were conservative reasons.** Those opposed, on the other hand, agreed with a broad number of conservative reasons. Of those opposed 52% felt private property would significantly change the kibbutz as a society; 54% felt it would open the gates wider for other sources of money; 59% thought it would give rise to more differences between people; and 21% thought that members would not be able to manage their funds well.***

Thus, despite the large problem and the minor phenomena that inequality involves, most of the membership in Vatik have a cautious attitude towards affluence, one that is unsympathetic to extravagant violations of simplicity, against expanding the living standard without limit, and narrowly favoring the continuation of the system of closed budgets. In each case however, sizable parts of the sample agree with the opposite attitude.

Two specifically emotional issues were chosen to clarify the nature of this narrow gap: the question of hired labor [Question 43], and the issue of personal cars [Question 17]. Personal cars are very expensive in Israel. They cost two to three times their amount in this country and the maintenance, insurance, and fuel costs are more than double. We theorize that if members favor personal cars they also favor many other attempts to try to push economic development and diversity in economic lifestyles to the utmost limit. This may be destructive

_____

* Valid answers 128 - Missing answers 30.

** Valid answers 48 - Missing answers 110.

*** Valid cases 59 - Missing cases 99.

to the social milieu and may represent the overriding tendency. In addition, hired labor is the very antithesis of communitarian socialism and the ethic of self-labor in the kibbutz. Vatik has only a few regular hired laborers and utilizes outside labor for only 7% of its work days, mostly in the branches and services that have little meaningful relation to the large profits generated in the fish, and turkey branches. The labor is usually seasonal when human and machine are at a loss to harvest all the grapefruit or olives, and in last year's economic report the farm manager encouraged reducing hired labor in the future. So while the trend may be away from hired labor, the membership may be a good indication of how far the community would go to maximize economic development.

Regarding personal cars, the members narrowly favor personal cars by 48.6% to 40.1% with 11.3% undecided.* Thus, the trend towards division over key economic opinions continues. Table 12 examines the opinions on hired labor.

TABLE 12

Attitude To Hired Labor

Eliminate it or stop calling ourselves a kibbutz.	10.7%
Opposed to it in principle but labor power problems in certain cases make it unopposable.	71.3%
No other possibility exists and no complaining about it should.	10%
Hired labor is not needed. The problem is that members will not work.	6.7%
Other	1.3%

Valid cases 150 - Missing cases 8.

---

* Valid cases 148 - Missing cases 10.

81

There is no strong acceptance of hired labor. While one possible interpretation of those who oppose it in principle, but make exceptions, is that they are really not supporting the principle, a examination of the facts in Kibbutz Vatik shows that the opposite is true: the farm plan for next year hopes to reduce hired labor, the new electronics industry has no plans to use hired labor, the farm manager has defended the point of view that hired labor increases production costs, and the Federation has produced rigorous research showing that factories with more hired labor (less self-labor) have less efficiency in productivity, and the difference is significant. (Kibbutz Artzi, 1976) The most cautious interpretation of the facts would be that before it became clear how disadvantageous hired labor could be, at least, a majority of the membership was willing to countenance turning the other cheek. Industrial attitudes represent the final acid test of economic opinion.

Industrialization

The issue of technological innovation pitted a concern for economic development against a concern for the social milieu [Question 27].

TABLE 13

Members' Criteria For Introduction of Technology

When the kibbutz has the opportunity to introduce technology what should be the main criterion?

A.	Economic advantage and increased production.	73%
B.	The possible positive effect on the members.	14.9%
C.	The possible negative effect on the members needs to be taken into consideration.	2.8%
D.	The investment capital needed.	6.4%
E.	Other	2.8%

Valid cases 141.
Missing cases 17.

Responses to this question in Table 13 express very little caution about technology, and a great concern for economic development. A female founding member who works in the kitchen after many years as a child-care worker explains:

> We're making progress all the time, new machines are introduced, more sophisticated ones. I have (in the kitchen) a cheese cutting machine and I have to move the lever. It is plugged in but I have to move the lever all the time. I'd be very happy if there were a machine that I would just plug it in and it would work by itself. Why not? It's very good if we could get to the point where we could work fewer hours, but it is still so far away in the kibbutz. I do not imagine that it shall happen so fast. If we could do more jobs in the fields more easily why shouldn't we? To the extent that we can cope with it financially, from the know-how aspect-it should be learned and people should understand how to use the machines-but the more we can (the better). I think we have too little, in the service branches, the kitchen, the laundry; it is possible to make improvements, but it is a matter of money. We need to buy all the machines, newer ones, better ones and it costs a lot of money, but I do not object to it. It can also help us work more easily. We work very hard.

While most of Western society suspiciously debates the meaning of technology here there is a striking degree of trust in the advantages of having more and more of it.*

---

*Menachem Rosner, a senior kibbutz researcher suggests that the kibbutzim have usually had only short-term economic and quality of life advantages from technology. It is usually introduced after much community discussion and obviously a community vote. Technology in agriculture helped the kibbutzim break into the modern world without drastically increasing their labor power, and industrialization accounts for most of their economic miracles. So a learned confidence is understandable. Rosner, however, along with other members has become concerned about the effect of technology on the job structure, the work itself and (continued on page 84)

When the opinions of Vatik's members on personal cars, hired labor and technology are taken together no crystal-clear tendency emerges. Personal cars are favored but only narrowly. Many members qualified their support for this by saying that while they would favor personal cars more communal cars (to relieve scheduling conflicts) would work just as well. No strong acceptance of hired labor emerged, although the willingness to compromise was strongly represented. Technology seems like the exception. There was hardly any caution about its effect on the social milieu. So no overwhelming move is on to have economic development at any price. On the other hand a strong division of opinion exists about personal cars and technology, the tension is repeated between conflicting opinions evident in the attitude toward correcting inequality, the effects of affluence, and the desirability of living standard limitations.

That there is almost a half and half division of opinion can now not be questioned. But what does this mean? First, it simply supports the notion - developed in speaking about the social arrangement - that a dialectic or active tension between individualistic/utilitarian and communal/communitarian opinions exists. From examining the motivation of early members we know that this tension is no recent arrival. In fact, the history of Vatik and the movement point to it as a basic dynamic of the whole system. So, concluding that the main problem is that all people do not agree is not a very creative insight. They have never agreed except when they were under extreme ideological pressure (and even not then) and had a totally different social form (the intimate commune). Another interpretation is that the individualists are slowly poisoning and ruining the communal idea and it is only a matter of time before the kibbutz is destroyed.

(* continued from page 83)
the way the worker relates to it. Extensive explorations of alternative ways to design the work place, the work task, and the work group are under way. This has involved far-ranging exchanges with Swedish colleagues since socio-technical design of the work and quality of working life is far advanced in Sweden. Naphtali Gollomb, another researcher working in this area, has posed the question "Why should the kibbutzim build and design a factory like everyone else? Why should we adopt lock, stock and barrel the American design of technology? Machines have to be fitted to our particular kind of society and we must begin doing this now." (Personal communication)

The problem with this explanation is that the individualists who did that with teapots twenty years ago brought about an important evolution in the quality of economic life that conditions deserved. They helped fulfill Rosner's touted adaptation of old ideals to new conditions. However, we have empirical data indicating this position is not valid. On the hunch that the people favoring individualistic/utilitarian notions in all the economic attitudinal questions in this section could be lined up against those with more communalistic notions, a correlation matrix was constructed to examine the differences. This hypothesis only was totally disproved; no opposing groups exist, rather when a broad set of economic attitudes is explored individuals show that the tension is inside them not between opposing groups. For example, although sometimes members thought affluence would destroy the kibbutz they also did not want to limit the standard of living, while remaining hard and rigorous in looking at technology. One possibility is that people were confused by the questionnaire but this must be ruled out since 45 people were personally interviewed on these same variables and no consistent pattern of individualistic or communalistic attitudes emerges from that sample either. The author was originally encouraged to use a few short measures of economic attitudes and to discover attitudinal differences from them; fortunately, that advice was not taken. Instead, as in this section, both attitudes towards principles and practical problems were explored, and now the complexity of economic attitudes must be recognized.

The best explanation seems to be this: as dual-culture bearers whose minds and attitudes have not been fixed for or against individualism and communitarianism, kibbutz members have both a real concern to guard the successes and advantages of their social milieu and also to improve the range of satisfactions and the economic security behind those satisfactions. Human diversity is too complex to be simplified to categories of communal and non-communal members. From the interviews, one cannot accuse the members of unpredictability. The development of thought is rather similar to that of Sarita, a female senior member (although the mixture differs in each case and some people do have remarkably consistent attitudes):

> Sarita is typical of one kind of founding
> member in that her eyes light up as she talks
> of the early intimate commune. She was and
> is very ideologically dedicated. She feels
> that since the founders many members came
> with a weaker ideology that hurt the communal
> nature of the farm, but she is not despondent

of depressed about it. After all, she keeps
reminding the interviewer, "Look this is a
kibbutz with social and economic security."
Sarita has a very simple house despite the
fact that her husband travels around the
world as a representative of a kibbutz branch
and could bring back much to make it elegant.
After a long career in education she works in
the kitchen in her senior years and makes
lunches for members working outside, and in
the agricultural branches. About more conveniences she says, "I am not against more
conveniences and improvements for the kibbutz.
I think it is necessary. In the youth movement we had an argument about silk dresses,
and now we have air conditioners." She is not
against a bigger apartment in the kibbutz
household, but she says that luxury should not
be the challenge and meaning of life. She
would favor personal cars. When asked about
limiting the standard of living her concerns
however are not consumerist. She is concerned
that profits be invested in developing the
consistent productive strength of the village;
she is concerned that equal distribution of
television sets be well organized; she speaks
about living standard issues money cannot buy,
then she finally agrees, once there is something to live on if you want to raise it why
not? On the other hand, she favors simplicity,
and self-labor and opposes hired labor. She
defines simplicity as living from what you do
yourself. She feels that the kibbutz is too
flexible in giving rein to individual inclinations in higher education and work that are
not related to kibbutz needs, and she is concerned that people not become soft. But she
favors as much technology as possible, theo-
rizing that it relieves people of the worst
and commenting that most work very hard. She
expresses a strong concern to insure equal
distribution of material things.

  As in the other conversations, there is a logic to Sarita's
words. She evaluates different parts of the village differently.
She colors in her own needs and wants, she emphasizes certain
principles in some areas but not in others. It is a mosaic of

individualist oriented and fellowship oriented concerns. She is talking about a whole life and how to make it better.

If this indeed is a plausible explanation, then the crisis Vatik faces is not disagreement, and not inconsistency.* The issue is how, in the final analysis, will all these diverse opinions, judgments, attitudes, and influences decide how much, how far and what type of economic growth can continue without destroying or altering the social milieu. A positive note is that most members do indeed take dual approaches. They are concerned both with maintaining the principle of social profit and increasing the satisfaction of their lives. They are not divided into attitudinal vigilante groups.

Section 2. Work

Work is the most immediate daily experience of kibbutz economics for the member. The following aspects of work in Vatik will be outlined: distribution of the work force; the kibbutz work style, the work coordinator, and attitudes towards hired labor; collective labor; the integration of work with public activity; specialization; community planning of work; the motivation to work; democracy in the workplace; the sexual division of labor; and work satisfaction.

---

* Some members in Vatik think they know what is coming; the moshav shitufi (cooperative village). Contrasted with the kibbutz or communal village this form has like the kibbutz collective production, work branches, committees, a general assembly, a local cultural life, a cooperative ideology.... but consumption is private. Yoram, a middle-aged member born in Vatik, says: "I think it is all going to end like that. The children will be together in school, but will sleep at home. You will get a budget for yourself (an equal share of the profits of the whole farm) to spend however you like. Each family gets an allowance once a month. There will be a general store to buy whatever you want. There will be bigger apartments. It would still be a kibbutz. If I get my own money I can spend it how I want to."

Work

        I do not think that you can really say that
someone is not suited for work in the kibbutz.
There is really no such thing. You can say
that the person who is in charge of the garage,
or the field crops is not the best person or
maybe he's not doing his best. It really is a
matter of the whole branch working together.
Maybe the organization is weak or there is not
a high level of planning; no one can ruin it
by himself. Everyone also has a say so that
one person cannot make a lot of monkey business. In certain branches, if you are working
alone, you can do stupid things, but if there
are five, and everyone knows what is going on.
So if you are responsible for the branch this
year well, there are others who directed it
before you and they will come and tell you if
what you are doing is no good. There are other
responsible people and they can see.

                   Yoram, a middle-aged male
                   member of Kibbutz Vatik

     Yoram's description of the interdependencies of work with
life in Kibbutz Vatik supports the popular kibbutz saying "Work
is our life." Work is the most important public activity in the
community. In the early days of the kibbutzim it was the most
significant objective behavior which showed that one was building
the community. Because of this and because A.D. Gordon, (Zobrow-
ski and Herzog, 1952), an early guru of the movement, viewed the
task of work as helping members to shed aristocratic middle-class
and "middle-man" and academic characteristics, work in the kibbutz village would be self-sponsored. It would be in a local
setting fit to the needs of the population and "the people" concrete and involved in real felt needs -- anti-intellectualism was
common -- and close to nature. Today much of this spirit of work
in the intimate commune remains although parts of the execution
have changed.

Distribution of Work Force

Figure 5 shows the distribution of Vatik's work force. This table accounts for 356 of the 360 members. 11.52% are involved in agricultural branches, 20% in industrial branches (plastics, the metal factory, and regional inter-kibbutz industry), 5.85% in other work branches, and 62.63% in direct and indirect community service branches. Included in community service branches are all non-productive branches. For example, carpentry and welding shops which mostly fix and build for community use and the support of productive sectors, and more obvious community service branches such as education, kitchen, laundry, plus members attached to the kibbutz Federation in Tel Aviv. 5% of the population are pursuing upper level studies at universities or technical institutes. This is usual for both Kibbutz Vatik and the rest of the movement since higher education is seen as a significant investment in the happiness of members and the future of the farm. Another 43 persons or 12% of the population work outside the kibbutz, in the government, in regional cooperative industries run by several kibbutzim, and in the Federation, plus several miscellaneous places (hospitals, semi-public sector firms, universities). Overall, 64 members (17%) are outside the community for educational or work purposes. Although the averages for the Federation are not known this is considered somewhat high. Members of Vatik explain that their community has been more tolerant of individual diversity in seeking outside positions and also more lax in creating proper positions within the community. It is this same group of outside members who are considered by many to be a prime source of inequality.

Despite the general tendencies towards balancing communal and individual-oriented economic considerations, the Vatik work force illustrates (as did our examination of the actual budgetary system in force and members' attitudes towards community investments) the radically communal nature of the village. The comparably high number of members employed in non-productive community-oriented work (service branches) and the fact that the main income-producing branches have only 8% of the work force evidences the extent to which the community as a whole is organized for collective welfare vs. the welfare different small groups could attain for themselves. This is a picture of cooperation, albeit less ideological, indeed, more oriented towards human diversity, but real cooperation just the same.

From the research sample more about the nature of the work force can be gleaned. 10% work alone, 36% work with others but in the last analysis alone, and 51.8% work in teams [Question 15B].

Distribution Of Members In Work Branches (1973 Statistics)

	Total In %	Workers In Branch Total (Actual #)	Younger Members 20-40 years old				Older Members above 40 years old		
			%	M+F	M	F	%	M+F	M	F
AGRICULTURE										
Fields	**	9		9	-	9	-	-	-	-
Dates		6		6	1	5	-	-	-	-
Citrus		3		3	-	3	-	-	-	-
Fishery	**	8		7	-	7	-	1	-	1
Poultry		15		7	1	6	-	8	1	7
TOTAL	11.52%	41	8.99%	32	2	30	2.53%	9	1	8
INDUSTRY										
Restaurant		3		1	-	1	-	2	-	2
Plastics Factory		37		15	3	12	-	22	8	14
Metal Shop		22		6	1	5	-	16	1	15
Regional Industry		3		1	-	1	-	2	-	2
Regional		12		3	-	3	-	9	2	7
Outside Workers*		15		6	5	1	-	9	4	5
TOTAL	25.85%	92	8.99%	32	9	23	16.86%	60	15	45
SERVICES										
Welding		2		2	-	2	-	-	-	-
Carpentry		2		-	-	-	-	2	-	:
Garage		3		2	-	2	-	1	-	1
Building		4		2	-	2	-	2	-	2
Electricity		3		2	-	2	-	1	-	1
Water		2		-	-	-	-	2	-	2
Storage		1		-	-	-	-	1	-	1
Committees & Store		14		3	1	2	-	11	3	8
Ulpan		4		2	2	-	-	2	2	-
TOTAL	9.84%	35	3.66%	13	3	10	6.18%	22	5	17
OTHER SERVICES		63		13	12	1	-	50	47	3
Kitchen		25		7	6	1	-	18	18	-
Children's Education		40		33	33	-	-	7	6	1
High School Education		16		11	6	5	-	5	2	3
TOTAL	40.45%	144	17.98%	64	57	7	22.47%	80	73	7
IN STUDIES OR SERVICE										
University		21		21	12	9	-	-	-	-
Kibbutz Artzi***		13		5	2	3	-	8	2	6
Special		10		4	2	2	-	6	4	2
TOTAL	12.34%	44	8.42%	30	16	14	3.92%	14	6	8
GRAND TOTAL	100.00%	356	48.04%	171	87	84	51.96%	185	100	85

* Government related and other.
** Main income producing branches.
*** Kibbutz Vatik is a member of the Hashomer HaZair Federation which has about 80 kibbutzim and close to 35,000 members. The federation was founded in April 1927. There are two other secular kibbutz federations with comparable numbers of kibbutzim and members: Ichud Ha Kvutzot Vellakibbutzim and Kibbutz HeMeuchad. A fourth federation is a religious movement with only 13 kibbutzim, Kibbutz HaDati.

FIGURE 5

Team work predominates in the agricultural branches, the children's education branches, the restaurant, and some support branches, like the garage and kitchen. Members in the laundry, plastics shop, metal shop, and administrative branches often work near people but mainly alone. From general descriptions of the early days of the community it certainly seems that team work was the order of the day. Now, 32.8% of the community is involved mostly in white-collar work (indicated in Figure 4 by "*") and 67.2% in blue-collar work (indicated by "+").

Work in the community still has many of the features of the intimate commune. They still work six days a week, taking Saturday, the Sabbath, off.

Work Style, The Work Coordinator, Hired Labor

While there are both lazy members and excited members who rush through their work, from the author's experience in working in almost all of the community branches the style of working expected can be explained so: One should work consistently at one's own comfortable speed. Working too fast will lead members to comment that you "eat your work" (a Hebrew expression) while under certain circumstances slow work may be commented on. There is seldom any attempt to quicken peoples' pace. For the work coordinator is just that, not a manager. One should be able to forget work during the coffee breaks and "fit in" when various informal periods of rest occur. For example, a news item on the radio may account for a five or ten minute work lapse. Some members talk when they work if those in the area can deal with it, and the diversity of how people can work well is widely recognized. Some say they can talk when they work, others say they cannot think when they work; some are glum, some look happy. The coordinator's role is to oversee the whole work branch. He or she prepares production plans and submits them to the farm manager and general assembly. He or she worries about the attainment of the plan, about morale in the workplace. This person is expected to consult with fellow workers about decisions and be open about what is going on inside the branch, and what plans are for the future. Since this person gets no extra pay or amenities, and can only demand respect, good organization and fellowship, the way he or she operates is a good determinant of how successful the coordination of the branch will be. This person also deals with the secretary of the kibbutz if personal conflicts rise up in the branch that require social attention. He or she will help bring in suitable members or even place branch members in other branches. This person will also be concerned about the planning of higher education for branch members to fulfill various goals to expand and upgrade production. Despite the fact that some kibbutz industries, unlike Vatik, are quite large and employ several top coordinators and specialists who may work in offices a lot or go on the road, remaining in the position requires an outward attempt to be one of the members of the branch since in reality that is all one is. Showing up at morning and afternoon branch tea is important.

The kibbutznik (Hebrew for a community member) pays deference, verbal or non-verbal, to no one. A uniform working class dress prevails even among white and blue collar workers. Members, however, live comfortable lives although they do work very hard eight hours a day plus public activity. While some kibbutzim do have large numbers of hired laborers (usually Jews and Arabs from nearby towns) the three main Federations of the 240 kibbutzim are trying to reduce this admitted error in socialist ideology. (Viteles, 1966)

In Kibbutz Vatik such labor accounts for only 4% of the yearly working days. (Yearly Work Report) It involves several workers at the community's small factory and citrus and olive pickers at the peak harvest season. The kibbutzim market most of their goods through cooperative economic institutions and thus avoid individual "middle-men." Work today, then, is still according to the central ideal of independent labor, although the problem of hired labor, while somewhat negligible in the largest federation of 80 kibbutzim of Vatik, is a serious problem for a few communities and the issue of much ideological conflict.

Work is an important norm in kibbutz life because the more the community has become a village and less a commune, and the more everyone is not directly intimately related, some form of behavior that is clearly observable and can be easily evaluated without "looking inside the other" needs to emerge as the mediator of public acceptance and prestige.

Let's examine further the components of the work force in Vatik and then look at several aspects and researches of kibbutz labor.

It is: collective, integrated with public activity, specialized, planned, socially motivated, democratic and sexually stratified.

Collective Labor

Labor in the kibbutz has a clear social and collective meaning, not mainly one that is economic. It is easy to understand how a blend of the importance of work, the absolute right to work, the ownership of means of production, and a social vs. a financial definition of labor gives kibbutz labor a special normative quality.

The fact that a branch manager, a University professor, a children's nurse, or the community's farm manager do not get different rewards ties work to a social and cooperative definition of profit, a radical departure from the way the rest of the world operates.

While work in Vatik is collective because of the kibbutz structure, the extent to which it is a communal demand varies. In the early days of the community, older members comment on how members were asked to leave Vatik because special work more suited to their personal needs would not be created. Today, however, as noted in Chapter II, only 3.5% and 4.2% of the membership respectively are willing to grant all individual requests for work or force kibbutz needs on individuals. A spirit of compromise prevails while kibbutz needs have to be taken into account. Talia, a middle-aged woman, now work organizer of the women comments:

> Look, we cannot send a member to go out and
> work in this town nearby, and then go and
> hire somebody to work in the chicken coops
> from outside. And I think this has to be one
> limit. And I think in general the boys under-
> stand this very well, they want to work within
> the kibbutz. But I think if the same person
> were to come and say he wanted to study soci-
> ology for five years, I think we should let
> him even if there is a shortage of people to
> work.

This is the state of Vatik today. The farm manager pointed out that there was a slight shortage of workers two years ago. Since then the number of members studying has been increased to deal with tensions expressed by middle-aged women about lack of opportunities. Currently, in Vatik there is pressure on the women remaining to staff the children's houses and kitchen and laundry with fewer people. But Vatik clearly has made the trade-off Talia speaks about. On the other hand, members do not believe

93

that the work norm is strong in Vatik. It is considered one of the most serious problems of the kibbutz, but the community wants to encourage more individual choice in work. This situation has caused sure conflict. One younger member comments:

> I think this problem derives mainly from two
> points. First, there is no central strong
> body that can exert strong moral pressure and
> a strong demand from the people that they'll
> do what they should, and there are all sorts
> of different problems like that: work, night
> guarding, and there are some workplaces where
> you must find people to work in them for there
> is no choice.   But there are places no one
> wants to work in.

The out-going work organizer agrees. While years ago a refusal to do a night guarding or take one's turn in the kitchen meant communal recall and castigation and discussion before the general assembly or a committee, today, the work organizer says that a small group of people get away with this, and there is a new style prevalent whereby you do not talk about people personally (i.e. by name) at the general assembly or the sicha about such matters. While he complains that the number is small, his concern is that it means a break in the norm. If the situation with a certain member becomes serious the work organizer will take him or her before the executive committee and talk about it. But, he like others, does not desire to make personal conflicts where they can be avoided. So, often many appropriate situations do not reach this level.

Recently, a member refused to coordinate the supply part of the kitchen, and the whole kibbutz and executive committee decided to force the issue. In this case, the member had been receiving studies and special time for outside research, and there was a strong feeling that refusing an important public coordinating role was a serious affront to the community and insulted a sense of balance about that member's relation to the group. On the other hand, less serious infractions like refusing to do kitchen duty often seem dwarfed in importance when that member's whole participation is considered in community life, or as when, in the case of one member who has worked outside for years and really should have returned long ago, the community perceives that only bitterness and possibly a departure would result. These particulars of work go to illustrate the high degree of integration in kibbutz life. Whether a member refuses to work well or in a public role or coordinate branches and volunteers for many positions, the member's work involves a dimension beyond the limited economic task it is. But, how do members perceive their work relations in actuality?

Relations between the members at work is a more accurate guide to the collective function of labor than the work ideology itself. The centrality of social support at work has already been described in Chapter II.

We asked members to evaluate their work relations. Their opinions follow in Table 13.

TABLE 13

Work Relations Attitude

Category Label	Absolute Freq	Relative Freq (PCT)	Adjusted Freq (PCT)
Very friendly and friends	37	23.4	28.0
Very friendly not friends	38	24.1	28.8
Proper relations	53	33.5	40.2
Bad relations	1	0.6	0.8
Student	3	1.9	2.3
Valid cases 132			
Missing cases 26	26	16.5	Missing
	158	100.0	100.0

While very few members have bad relations at work, relations are generally friendly but not oriented towards friendship. A young female member who works in the kindergarten describes relations in her work group:

> There is tension at work when one says one thing and the other thinks the other way (in the education of children), and sometimes when there is friction, when it seems that one of us did not speak properly to the children, we discuss it among ourselves, not during work usually, but after work, and together we reach a common denominator, or we try to

know the direction of things...We really try
to reach a uniform way of thinking because,
look, the child can get confused when one
says this and the other says that, and the
child needs to know where he stands.

The author found that tensions in work branches did not stay sub-
strata for long. Because members must live with each other and
live with public knowledge of their situation, serious tensions
are brought to the fore. Usually, the gossip circuit will tell
you that two people have argued at work and recently made up, or
are now not talking and a meeting is being arranged, or so and so
has been refused entrance into a certain branch and the social
secretary is trying to place that person. One's job is in the
public domain.

Work and Public Activity

Kibbutz work is mixed with public activity. (Golomb, 1963)
As noted, in Vatik 70-150 people can be involved in the diffuse
policy and decision-making and management bodies of the kibbutz
outside of the general assembly itself. Work in the services
itself is actually public activity also since community services,
like the kitchen, are often strictly looked over as one looks
over the community economic manager. Some participation in
public activity (committee, kibbutz office) is necessary every
few years for a member to maintain a high degree of status and
prestige. While sanctions such as complaints, gossiping, snub-
bing and ultimately expulsion will result from laziness or extremely poor work, non-participation in public activity would
more likely lead to a lower amount of esteem.

Joseph Shepher's excellent study of public activity outside
the kibbutz (1966) thoroughly analyzes the advantages and problems in a member's participation in such outside jobs as:
university professor, nurse, Federation or government worker,
Parliament member. Shepher found that while much competition
between the kibbutz and the Federation or Government exists for
very skilled members, outside work can be a solution for certain
problems involving members with family difficulties, senior age
and experience who are beyond physical work, or special skills.
Nevertheless much role conflict and difficulty is experienced by
such workers.

Specialization

Specialization is a larger part of the work scene than before. In the early days of most kibbutzim the branches were
agricultural and tasks were interchangeable. It was hoped in the
beginning that this "simplicity of training" would also reduce
inequality. As occurred with the kibbutz attempt to have a more
unstructured family and to have mostly direct intimate relationships, the demands of continuity and the construction of a complex efficient cooperative organization, the resistance to specialization did not remain. Today, many members and branch
managers (including household services, education and the kibbutz accounting office) require special training. In Vatik's
industry the metal factory requires an engineer. Specialization is now accepted but an array of "safety valves" has evolved
to prevent it from threatening the community. The majority of
branch coordinators are still rotated (some few blatant exceptions exist for good and bad reasons); rewards economically
speaking still do not vary with training; a specialist finds
that the critical community's questioning and ultimate vote goes
along with his or her prestige and dampens it. On a branch level
a specialist is not allowed to "dictate" the branch policies
either because of the branch members or the diffuse interests of
different parts of the decision-making structure in his or her
activity (the budget committee, the members committee, the planning committee), or the fact that another member is probably
completing training and preparing to replace him or her. In
Vatik they are training several engineers so rotation can occur
in the factory.

In spite of this, specialists and technicians are listened
to more than in the past (although they try to explain and not
mystify members with details of technical decisions) and do
wield special power. An ultimate test of kibbutz life will be
to see if they gain undue power.

But the possibility of specialists taking over is not a
central concern in the kibbutz. A branch coordinator still has
too many diffuse decision-making and social influence units (like
his or her childrens' roommates' parents' questions or the decisions of several committees may affect the branch) to deal with,
and this wide array of interference factors, plus the openness
with which even technical information is available in the kibbutz,
makes pontification difficult. And should one succeed in managerial pontification it may be at the cost of social status.
Vatik, unlike several other kibbutzim, has no strong managerial

types and no coordinator of any branch "runs" the branch through a finely knitted system of social and personal nets. There are several examples of this in a few other communities. Levitan and Eden, (1970), however, in comparing farm and factory workers in kibbutz have found equivalent psychological satisfaction in both groups but a sense of being "lonely in a crowd" in the factory.

Thus, the advantages of working life in the kibbutz may be clear, but the effect of greater specialization and industrialization is altering the nature of work in Vatik, and the overall superiority of kibbutz industry may mask a subtle loss of work satisfaction when agricultural and industrial sectors in the same kibbutzim are compared. Only strict vigilance will prevent a crisis. Such vigilance will of course partake of the tradition for planning kibbutz labor.

Community Planning of Work

The community plans its work. A work committee makes up detailed plan of probable needs and resources and regularly evaluates efficiency of the planning process. They consider issues of worker satisfaction and the appropriateness of present work branches to members' needs. A work organizer handles daily work assignments. Most members have regular jobs, but usually some temporary switching of the regulars and the assignment of the "floaters" must occur daily. This takes place after dinner and usually involves extended discussions, arguments, and compromises between the organizer and branch managers and individual members. Even temporary volunteers from abroad in the kibbutz spirit haggle and argue with the poor work coordinator. It is, as one might guess, a very unpopular and often rotated job.

In addition to the work organizer a work committee and the farm manager and economic committee work with various branch coordinators to plan as exactly as possible the work days needed to satisfy their next year's production plan. They also work on personal and branch problems on a branch-by-branch basis. This is one of many time-consuming events where the complexities and interdependencies of kibbutz life are probably uncountable. Economic needs, production ceilings, feelings of branch teams, absences of various members for education, funds for social needs and many other factors must be taken into account in both these consultations and the preparation of final production and labor

power plans. These matrices of social planning and involvement
also criss-cross Vatik and along with our statistics on attitudes
of members need to be recognized at every turn!

TABLE 14

Comparison of Labor Power Plan And Actual
Use of Labor Power For 1973*

	Planned	Actual
Joint Programs For Adults	20.76	20.975
Educational Services	17.400	17.460
Children	38.160	38.435
Service Branches	7.710	8.460
Agricultural Activities	18.570	18.390
Industry and Outside Jobs	22.650	23.300
Army Reserves	1.5	1.69
Kibbutz Federation	4.2	4.3
Sabbaths	27.38	28.0
Holidays, Vacations	19.345	19.0
Total of General Committees	5.4	5.49
TOTAL	144.915	

Comparison of Total Days:	Service Branches	7.71	8.46
	Agriculture	41.22	41.69
	Industry...		

Table For Work Days According To Type of Workers*

Members	131.260
High School Students (from kibbutz)	1.500
Soldiers	100
Ulpan	2.640
Work Camps (youth groups)	3.000
Hired Labor and others	7.200

* days figured in thousands

Table 14 shows Vatik's labor power plan and the actual use of
labor power for 1973. The plan, as one sees, is closely followed.
In actuality, figures are prepared monthly, and army reserve,
educational leave, and vacations are all carefully figured in.
This plan, which was fairly successful, represents the rule not
the exception in Vatik and established kibbutzim like it.

Nevertheless, the labor infrastructure would not function if members were not motivated.

The Motivation To Work

Value is placed on the <u>social motivation</u> behind employment. Rosner (1963) in studying difficulties and rewards of the branch manager, Cohen (1963), and Shepher (1968) pointed out that the relational and social rewards become more emphasized in a kibbutz since economic rewards are granted in complete equality and are not given to variance. This quality of kibbutz labor has often puzzled the Western entrepreneur: Why would people work unless they knew their exact pay per hour and took a check home? One would respectfully point out that in the U.S. now 40% of that paycheck goes for taxes to support poor social programs to pick up the pieces of a disintegrating mass society! The gossip and prestige process whereby a member's abilities and dedication are recognized and reacted to accounts for the normative importance of work. The ability to cooperate and function on a team (as most community work is organized) is also important here. If anything, kibbutz research has unveiled many of the subtle factors that account for small cooperative community success.

Thus, in this area, (Etzioni, 1957) looked into the relation between motivation and prestige generated by the closeness of kibbutz workers to their "clientele." He found that workers in the field and factory who were not actually face-to-face in providing service to other members were able to achieve more prestige and were, in fact, more "protected" in their probable motivation than workers in the kitchen and children's education whose exposure to others and their negative reactions was much higher. The predictable stability in agricultural over service jobs was verified by this investigation.

Members in Vatik constantly complain about service, staff, and switches in the service branches. (For this reason, more research comparing service and production workers in the kibbutz should be undertaken.) Our research found a particular dissatisfaction with the service work branches by female members, which will be discussed later.

Democracy in the Workplace

Congruent with the inter-dependence of collective life and the involvement of all in the work of each, work has an important democratic quality. All work branch teams are expected to meet regularly to discuss decisions. In practice, this varies from team to team and is usually replaced by the open-ended leadership view of many coordinators or (and) the real sense each member has that he or she does not work for the branch coordinator. Rosner (1965) analyzed changes and processes of direct democracy in the kibbutz, and his general conclusions apply also to workplace democracy: despite the tendency to institutionalize and formalize decision-making (which the greater decision-making responsibility of the coordinator seems to require at present), the kibbutz is still anti-bureaucratic in character, utilizes general meetings as the main agent of democracy, and is one of the few organizations in modern society which embraces so many decisive aspects of its members' lives. Clear empirical data exist for this claim. In a recent NSF-sponsored study, Rosner worked cooperatively with Yugoslavian, Austrian, Italian, and American researchers viewing the hierarchy in factories in those countries. Using the same procedures of investigation, the kibbutz outshone even the worker-participatory Yugoslavian factories in being less hierarchical, less alienating, more participatory, more contributing to psychological adjustment, and in offering members most possibility for advancement. (Tannenbaum, 1970)

Practically speaking, the execution of these principles varies in Vatik. The traditional kibbutz mechanism for self-management is the weekly work branch meeting. Only in the agricultural branches are these meetings held weekly, almost daily. One sees the branch members haggling, arguing, and planning in a swirl of dialogue almost every day what to do next, what to do next week. Possibly the fact that these are the main income-producing branches and that they are manned by middle-aged and young men who worry about the kibbutz economic plant is the reason. Such meetings occur maybe only once a month in the metal shop, and only occasionally in the plastics factory. They are rare in other service branches, except in the educational and children's branches where they are considered a regular part of the work itself. It is not known how the situation is in other kibbutzim when all branches are considered (not just self-managed industries as in the kibbutzim where most of this research was done), but in Vatik, workplace democracy is more dependent on the free flow of information, the social camaraderie of the branch, the lack of punishment for raising issues, and the ability to

101

rotate and change managers easily. Formal meetings are in the minority.

In fact, the rotation of management and public service jobs (farm and social manager, committee members) is, however, the mainstay of kibbutz democracy. Cohen (1974) looked into rotation and found less rotation then we find in Kibbutz Vatik: rotation usually occurs yearly or bi-annually in managerial positions which in all Federations were rotated at a rate of 55%.* This compromise is explained by specialization in the economy. Nevertheless the main full-time public offices are rotated bi-annually along with committee members since limitations on the pool of possible coordinators are less tight for these positions. Our research has not uncovered opposition to this situation except with regard to the Economic Committee of Vatik where some members feel that long-term economic planning and technical considerations are tending to limit the pool of people who can participate seriously in this committee's deliberations.

It is significant that the basic preservation of the kibbutz's diffuse and fellowship-oriented decision-making system seriously undercuts the possibilities of wholesale "takeovers" of power prevalent in many other cooperative community ventures. (Viteles, 1966) Since power is shared, issues of stratification in the work place are more prominent when referred to different groups in the community.

Sexual Division of Labor

Of the seven important aspects of work under discussion the sexual division of labor has undergone the most dramatic changes and was, in fact, quite central to the normative ideology of early members, who regarded it as one of their most important aims. Critics of the kibbutz's obvious failure in this area unfortunately do not emphasize the very radical and comprehensive steps the kibbutz took to eradicate sexism. Formal equality was established but they did not stop there. All ties between sex and economic remuneration were disconnected. In addition the economic security of women, like that of men, was associated with their membership rather than with their marital status or number of children. There was complete formal political equality and the possibility and actual opportunity to hold central offices and seek educational advancement. All the usual work of the housewife was carried out by educational institutions, communal

---

* Recently, more carefully collected data indicates that this figure is much too low (Shepher, 1977).

kitchens laundries and purchasing institutions. Nevertheless Shepher's recent book <u>Women in the Kibbutz</u>, written with American anthropologist Lionel Tiger (1975) documents exhaustively that after embracing these changes in the early years, women progressively chose not to take advantage of this situation and today are almost totally involved in community services (the kitchen, laundry, education), and defending in most areas of the kibbutz family-centered values, and are almost totally passive in political decision-making (except for a few young women and old-timers). Thus, in Vatik there are 130 women, or 90%, in community services and of only 41 workers 3 women, or 7%, in agriculture. They make up 26% of the factory staffs (mostly the disliked plastics factory), but only 4.3% of the more interesting support roles (such as plumbing and carpentry). Except in service branches there are no women branch managers.

The fact that in Vatik and other kibbutzim women serve as social managers, chairpeople of important committees, and important community spokespeople does not evidence a negative feeling in the community towards their abilities. If anything the absence of such "inferiority typing," reward discrimination, and the egalitarian and non-sexist nature of the kibbutz economic structure is part of the revolution that has taken place. But the days when women worked alongside men in production branches, and men worked equally in the kitchen and laundry, are gone.

Rosner, (1967) whose research on the changing status of kibbutz women showed an egalitarian attitude with regard to which traits members felt were characteristic of the sexes, found also that the changing status of women was but an aspect of familistic tendencies at large in the kibbutz and was connected to what is here called the tendency from the communal kibbutz (less sex-differentiated) and the tendency towards the communal village (more sex-differentiated). The very strong communal village trend, however, has not put this issue to rest.

The situation is not static. While no vocal women's movement exists in the kibbutz (possibly because some of the organizational goals have been achieved) women in Vatik, for example, are very uneasy about their service-oriented jobs. They are seeking greater opportunities for training, personal fulfillment and work outside the community. The situation is clearly very complex, but in Vatik their demands are being met. But structurally we cannot avoid the fact of rampant sex role polarization.

Leaving considerations of the structure of working life what are the consequences?

Work Satisfaction

Let's examine the ways members evaluate their work experience. First, in order to get a general idea if persons felt ade-
quately prepared for their jobs they were asked if they worked in
their profession (Question A) and if they were satisfied with the
professional aspects of their work (Question B). 63.5% said they
worked in their profession while 36.5% said they did not.* There
is clearly a sizable group of members who do not feel matched to
their work. 82.3% noted they were satisfied with the professional
aspects of their work, which 17.7% were not, so evidently the
situation is not wholly unsatisfactory to those who do not work
in their profession.**

Members were asked how much they enjoyed their work [Ques-
tion 11]. Their responses follow.

TABLE 15A

Work Enjoyment

Very much enjoy work	30.9%
Enjoy work a lot	58.3%
Never enjoy work	5.0%
Hate work	2.2%
Other (students...)	3.6%

Valid cases:	139
Missing cases:	19
Mean:	1.98

More than 90% of the members enjoy their work, while a minority
of 7.2% strongly dislike it. In order to understand some of the
components of enjoyment and lack of enjoyment members were asked
to evaluate various aspects of their work [Question 12]. A more

---

* Valid cases 126 - Missing cases 32.

** Valid cases 124 - Missing cases 34.

TABLE 15B

Aspects of Work Enjoyment Or Non-Enjoyment

Enjoy work itself	53%
Not enjoy work itself	13%
Feel I achieve something	58%
Do not feel I achieve anything	4%
Have a professional feeling	38%
Do not have a professional feeling	8%
Enjoy personal relations at work	40%
Do not enjoy personal relations at work	3%
Other reasons	5%

Valid cases: 142
Missing cases: 16

---

realistic picture emerges when the percentage of members who considered any reason is viewed. Still, a majority evaluate their work positively. On the average about 46% of the sample refused to answer the question with one or more of the pairs of attitudes. Thus, the amount of satisfaction that was found when members were directly asked must be further questioned. A more straightforward expression of this phenomenon occurred in the interviews. Many older members spoke of their work as a duty and obligation and, despite what was at times aggressive questioning, would not say more than that, and seemed unable to evaluate the job from different points of view. The weakness of the kibbutz in the area of designing the whole job has already been noted. In the days of the intimate commune "doing the job" was more important than "being the job," and some members do not know how to evaluate whether or not they like their work. An indication of this is the relatively low number of members who actually make a crisis of their work situation and demand attention. The social secretary, branch coordinators and other administrative coordinators might do more if a greater awareness were encouraged on the part of individual members.

To study further the complexity of work satisfaction, members were asked to answer the following two questions: Do you have responsibility in your work and do you enjoy having it [Question 14]? Can you use your talents and potential in your work in a way you like [Question 13]?

TABLE 16

Responsibility In Work And Use Of Talents

Work Responsibility		Use of Talents	
Not enjoy responsibility I have	13.9%	A Lot	39%
Enjoy responsibility I have	70.1%	Somewhat	41.9%
Have no responsibility but would		Very little	13.2%
enjoy some	9.5%	Never	3.7%
Have no responsibility and would		Student	2.2%
not enjoy some	4.4%		
Would like responsibility but			
would not enjoy it	0%		
Valid cases: 137		Valid cases: 136	
Missing cases: 21		Missing cases: 22	
		Mean: 1.97	

With regard to responsibility, a great number of members would like to see their situation changed, and as far as can be told 16.9% have little way to use their talents. As only 22 members out of our sample of 158 did not answer these questions, these opinions are certainly accurate.

Work satisfaction is certainly not determined by simple questions of "liking your work." When a wider set of issues is taken into consideration in judging the quality of working life in Vatik, dissatisfaction changes from a matter of 5% of the population to an issue involving 15-30% of the membership. This was not done to confuse the reader but to illustrate that if social motivation is spoken of with regard to kibbutz work, it cannot be pontificated as theory. Consideration of the complex factors of the social role called work that may motivate people is necessary and goes much further than simplistic questions in explaining a variety of complaints, a tendency to avoid the question, and a lack of interest in evaluating the work situation. When a work satisfaction index is constructed from the data one individual gives us about his or her work situation a wide distribution occurs. With a score of 1 indicating very low satisfaction and 12 indicating very high satisfaction, the mean for the whole sample is 9.244, indicating that a fairly high percentage of the population consistently evaluate their work positively. Nevertheless, about 20% of the population give consistent low evaluations to many sectors of their work (scores of 7 and under).

A reasonable interpretation is that about a fourth of the population of Vatik have moderate to serious claims about how their work is organized. There are many members who are not satisfied at work but are generally hopeful in other parts of their life. Low or high work satisfaction does not predict general satisfaction (see Appendix I for a description of the Satisfaction Index). The correlation between the two is highly significant (.001) but the strength of the relationship is only moderate (.34). Essentially that means that knowing one only explains about 13% of the population's position on the other. Possibly, this accounts for the poor work norm members criticize since members can be generally happy but unattended in this sphere. Maybe it indicates that a greater awareness of work organization is needed.

In conclusion, work in the kibbutz can be most clearly defined as community effort. It involves levels of meaning foreign to modern mass society, yet involves comparable options for individual development which are, in some respects, because of the unoppressive and flexible nature of kibbutz society, at times, probably greater. On a day-to-day basis many small problems arise in each of these seven aspects of work. However, a high degree of acceptance of the community values makes work the collective experience it is. Thus it represents one of the most significant learning situations. The problems can be understood by an examination of the organization of work itself, the tendency toward specialization and the complexity of social motivation which interconnects many aspects of the job. Changes in the social organization of Vatik have been paralleled by the breakdown of egalitarian sex roles in work, formal direct democracy in the workplace, and the demanding and limiting tendency the kibbutz used to exercise toward individual work options. But in another sense these changes complicate the achievement of work satisfaction.

Several advantages of the structure of work life in the kibbutz were put into perspective by widespread problems of work organization which are not being actively and consistently dealt with. The community's decisions concerning technology will affect work in the future; this is a key issue. So far the tradeoffs and balancing of tensions in Vatik have been emphasized in an attempt to describe how a middle ground between extreme communitarianism and extreme individualism is worked out in real life. Now, the energy of "working out" itself must receive focus, and the nature of the desire to participate in shaping its structure needs to be understood. This is a function of communal politics.

CHAPTER IV

POLITICS AND CULTURE IN THE COMMUNITY

In order to comprehend the actual functioning of democracy in the village the following subjects will be discussed: changes in the style of kibbutz politics, the necessary conditions for direct democracy (which will be evaluated in the case community), leadership and differentiation between political role-takers, the patterns of public participation in kibbutz institutions, the interdependence of democracy and culture, the cultural life of the community, the sense of political participation felt by members and the political/cultural problem of Kibbutz Vatik.

Politics And Culture

Changes In The Style Of Politics

> In each group there are "speakers" of the group. They are perhaps the better public speakers, or they have more common sense than the other fellows. Anyway when they speak twenty other fellows identify with their views. I can speak in the nicest way, but if I cannot express what the public feels, I will not get any support! That is not a matter of influence. You see, you feel, you express, in fact what others feel. If you do not people will back other opinions. There are sometimes discussions about light shades of opinions and positions. Sometimes one side will get the support of the public, sometimes the other side will get it! True, there are people who take the discussion very seriously. They ask for support from the public. There was once a discussion and each speaker got the support of the fellows; that means in that specific moment about this specific matter that the people were ambivalent.
>
> --Zalman, a senior member of Kibbutz Vatik

Zalman's thoughts about "personal influence" point to the centrality of common identification within the kibbutz group when considering the question of political power. The early kibbutz viewed itself almost as an elite school for democracy (Viteles, 1966), as a way of functioning that people would learn more about as they continued to understand the meanings of the structures they set up to encourage public participation in decision. From Newsletter Number 5, January 1936, a member of Vatik puts it this way:

> Democratization is the principal basis for
> the process of development in a continual and
> optimal way for the people who carry the bur-
> den of social building and responsibility,
> and the economic and ideological development
> of the kibbutz to the best of their ability...
> The question of democracy and demand for it
> does not have to stop at the establishment of
> normal rights and equality among kibbutz mem-
> bers, but must accompany a perpetual investi-
> gation and questioning of these principles.
> In a society where a member does not receive
> direct monetary or materialistic reward for
> his work, it is necessary to reward him with
> a substitute--non-materialistic, non-individ-
> ualistic--a collective reward for his contri-
> butions in helping to build the collective
> life of the settlement, and that is the re-
> sponsibility in helping to direct and develop
> its way of life.

> --Archives of Kibbutz Vatik

While direct democracy as defined by the member quoted has remained, many changes have occurred since the early days of Vatik. Developing a way of life and learning to pursue common goals is the function of kibbutz democracy. It is not, as in a mass society, simply a matter of voting, tabulation, the majority, or various representative mechanisms. It is integral; like the fingers of a hand, public participation goes together with economic cooperation, collective work, the individual-community dialectic, and a common ideology. Such a highly community-oriented society as the kibbutz could not function without it, for the whole matrix of mutual responsibilities would be paralyzed.

In the early days of Kibbutz Vatik decisions were made mostly by consensus. Since the form of the society was taking shape concurrently with the evolution of specific decisions both processes occurred hand in hand. Long ideological discussion and argument dominated a decision about the placement of a dairy. For a dairy, like any new part of community life, influenced many other factors of life. For example, some issues were: how such a new branch would affect other branches, whether a sufficiently skilled coordinator could keep the branch organized, whether the treasury could handle the investments, whether the location of the buildings would disrupt the layout of houses and if the noise would bother other members, whether other kibbutzim could be counted on to lend a hand. Oftentimes, these discussions were personalized to the extent that group decisions came to be identified with the arguments and speeches of different members. With regard to ideological decisions the early commune at Vatik emphasized the notion of collective ideology (collectiviut raionit).* That meant that once a decision was made members, despite how much their argument beforehand, were expected to support it enthusiastically. Thus there was a curious combination of encouraging the open and often raucous contribution of different members, but having all toe the group line once a decision was made. Older members of Vatik report that many members left as a result of disagreements at meetings, or of their inability to accept group decisions. Many times these decisions dealt with allowing such members to study or work outside the kibbutz, or to change their place of work. Senior members in large number expressed the sentiment in the interviews "We lost a lot of good members then. Many who left are now skilled and respected individuals.

While the awareness remains that political decisions involve a matrix of responsibilities in the community, the degree to which ideological discussion enters the general assembly has drastically decreased. Today, matters of principle are debated only occasionally - once every few months - and this is done in the spirit of necessity. "We are debating a matter of principle because we cannot make clear decisions of a practical nature until we do this." In addition members are no longer expected to be personally supportive of all decisions. True, they must go along with the decision behaviorally, i.e., do concretely what it recommends, but that is all. Today, nevertheless, a small number of members

---

* This was not an important element of democracy in other Kibbutz Federations.

do not go this far. One foreign woman who married a young member
would not agree to let her newborn baby sleep in the childrens'
house. In the old days, a crisis would have been forced between
the individual and the community on this point. Vatik today has
decided to let the situation continue and attempt to have members
persuade her informally over a period of time. She is a good
member; they do not want to lose her; dealing with her diversity
will not destroy the community. The lesson learned by this example is that consensus and collective ideology can cause personal individual crisis (and in the old days crisis after crisis
would occur) and departures that the membership will no longer
tolerate because of the social tension involved and the possibility of losing good members. However, such exceptions are
made infrequently, and few members can for long behave against a
decision without an attempt to resolve the situation.

But as in the recent case of a member who was raising dogs
and selling them privately, instead of being ideologically ac-
cused, personally attacked and discussed at the general assembly
he was gossiped about extensively and was told before the smaller
secretariat (executive committee) that, "This is against the way
of the kibbutz and you must stop it." The kibbutz simply ap-
proached him through a non-personal and unexcited political
medium to preserve a less limiting but still clearly defined social arrangement. In the light of these changes of sentiment
and style (often unanalyzed by social research), let us examine
the still functioning system of direct democracy in Vatik.

In reviewing research in this area, let us examine four
issues: the conditions for direct democracy in the kibbutz,
leadership and differentiation, patterns of public participation,
and the relationship between culture and democracy.

Conditions For Direct Democracy

Menachem Rosner's research analyzes the five conditions for
direct democracy in the kibbutz. (1965) (A) It requires a
small scale organization allowing members proximity to decision-
making centers and an awareness of events without the need for
formal means of communication. Up until 1948 kibbutzim usually
did not exceed 200, so today increased social density (populations usually from 400-600) reduces the visibility in social
relations somewhat. Nevertheless, the kibbutz organization of
Vatik and other communities still remains small-scale. Instead

111

of increasing the size of existing kibbutzim, new communities were founded. Cultural reasons exist for this. Vatik, like many kibbutzim, brought in large and small groups of new members gradually over the years. After the trauma of absorbing the hashlama in 1948-50 absorption continued more gradually; smaller groups grew into the society slowly. Also, while social relations are less intimate and visible to all members, the diffuse decision-making system of interrelated committees, branches, informal leaders and groups still exists. There are more committees and their functions are more specialized. Politics is more spread out over a variety of consultative and executive groups that have become the new decision-making centers.

(B) Also necessary is an <u>awareness of members</u> about the life of the organization, an active interest in it and a willingness to take part in executing the community's functions. This is directly related to how greatly the functions of the organization appear to be <u>essential</u> and integral to the members' lives. While there have been greater trends towards heterogeneity, specialization, some transfer of decisions to individuals, and greater influence of the external society, our data on social, economic and work attitudes show that the integrity of function has been maintained. But the awareness is nowhere as acute and intimate as it was when the kibbutz was a communal homogeneous group; apathy has increased.

Noticeable differences regarding such awareness are identifiable in Vatik. The meetings of the committee on the members (which deals with personal problems, members' requests, conflicts) are well attended. The economic planning committee meetings draw a high degree of participation; even non-committee members, unwilling to wait for the report to the general assembly, show up to follow developments. Because of the centrality of children in the kibbutz, the education committee meets regularly and most members attend. But the cultural committee of Vatik has been languishing for some years. Members constantly complain about passive culture (movies twice a week). One member active in this committee comments:

> "I can tell you about myself. I was in charge of the culture committee already three times before this year. The last time was a year ago. Now they want me to do it again next year; there is not anyone else to do it. So that is how I go, a year yes and a year no. That is how it will always be in the kibbutz, a year yes and a year no. So that

> is how we solve the rotation problem with
> that. I change with myself. That is what
> it is like here. I change with myself."

A subtle neglect of culture in Vatik confirms most members' lack
of real awareness of guarding and making vibrant the least tangible things that unite them. As a cooperative village much is
integral and essential to the now more diverse and more private
lives of members. Having movies, celebrating the Jewish feasts,
marking changes in the seasons - all these still occur. But
vibrant, home-made, non-ritualized cultural events do not happen.
What use would they serve? The more such awareness is concentrated on the necessary activities of the community, slighting
the less tangible and less necessary ends of cultural sustenance,
the greater the risk that while Vatik's arrangement of fellowship
and collegial decisions will remain, the sense of it may be lost.

Fortunately, because of the close socially integrated environment of the village, Rosner's third condition of direct democracy blossoms: (C) an environment for non-formalized public
opinion, the direct exchange, airing, "cooking" (in kibbutz
lingo), and resolution of views. This should be in the absence
of or together with formal legislative and supervisory functions.
The general assembly today still integrates the legislative,
executive, and the judicial functions of the political process,
since social relations are still frequent and personal between
members. Internal telephones between apartments do not exist and
members deal with each other by "going to" the other's apartment
or meeting at meals or paths. But this is not the case for all
members. Heterogeneity of opinion, differences in ages, and background means that all members are not comfortable in dealing with
each other (see Chapter II). So, there is more institutionalization, with rules and codes regulating behavior; for example, the
right to a free university education is now specifically defined
regarding the member's age, interest, special needs, and prece-
dent. Unlike the early commune, where cultural activities seemed
to emanate from the group itself--lots of spontaneous dancing,
singing--it is formalized now: a cultural committee plans more
activities.

In Vatik, as in many kibbutzim, the increasing materialism
of life led to accusations of favoritism or inequality in the
nineteen fifties and nineteen sixties, so the community rationalized many kinds of distribution. In the intimate commune one
could take the care when one needed it - "each according to one's
needs" - but this dictum actually became a cause of inequality
and lack of clarity in the collective village. The amount of
clothing each member can take each year, the number of kilometers

for auto transportation each is entitled to, the number of vacation days based on age and years of membership, are just a few
examples of such rationalization. When non-formalized public
opinion governs most of life, power accumulates in unpredictable
people and groups. So along with the notion of mutual obligations Vatik has clearly defined specific mutual rights which do
not have to be discussed; they are written and clear.

A frequently heard phrase is "lesader inyanim" (to settle
matters) with a certain member, committee or administrator. Today, the Constitution of the Kibbutz (1976) safeguards the rights
of members who leave to have proper resources to start a new life
and defines all rights and obligations. As a community of mutual
obligations, the limited institutionalization of many matters
rationalized problems of distribution, and reduced petty
arguments.*

Members' attitudes to political participation indicate the
extent of awareness of Vatik's problems and the efficiency of non-
formalized public opinion and the non-formal political system in
dealing with individual needs. Members were asked which form of
participation described their lives most [Question 54].

TABLE 17

Degree of Overall Participation In The Kibbutz

I am bothered about kibbutz problems and involved a lot
  in public life. (1)   15.5%
I am concerned about kibbutz problems and involved in
  public life but not a lot. (2)   69%
I am more involved with my family and comforts than
  with kibbutz problems. (3)   15.5%

Valid cases: 142. Missing cases: 16. Mean: 2. Median - 2.
Adjusted frequencies used.

---

* Contract solutions deal with use of resources and all the contracts (except for issues of age) are equal. Obviously, a contract governing how much money members got by how much they produced or where they worked, or what they originally contributed
to the community, would break down if fulfillment of basic human
needs (food, shelter, social support, health, education, right to
work) were to differ according to how one filled the contract;
the system would self-destruct.

This confirms the description of the system of involvement as being diffuse. Few members are more involved with their family than with the kibbutz.

How satisfying is this involvement vis-a-vis achieving individual goals? Members were asked how they viewed the planning of their lives [Question 59].

TABLE 18

Degree And Cause Of Achievement And
Non-Achievement Of Goals

What happens to me is my own doing and I reach my goals.	39.3%
What happens to me is my own doing but I do not reach most of my goals.	25.9%
I do not feel that I have enough control over my life but it is not the kibbutz that interferes.	31.9%
I do not feel that I have enough control over my life and it is often the fault of the kibbutz.	3%

Valid cases: 135
Missing cases: 23
Adjusted Frequency

While the number of persons who perceive problems in reaching life goals is very large, the small number blaming the kibbutz is startling. The members of Vatik generally seem to be involved in community life and not suffering loss of personal goals specifically because of it.

Communal democracy does not make leadership obsolete. (D) Direct democracy requires a reserve of potential cadres for a wide range of duties with the personal qualities and the experience necessary to carry them out. This reserve, as Rosner notes, is larger the less specialized the functions and the less specific the knowledge needed to carry them out. In Vatik most duties were originally interchangeable and easily learned; many jobs now require vocational or university training. Because of the "safety valves" which prevent the monopolization of skill by a group -- especially the right to education and training and the principle of rotation, which avoids pockets of elite leadership, this personnel reserve expands rather than declines.

115

One indication of this reserve in Vatik is the percentage of members who report political involvement in the last ten years. This is an approximate criterion since members frequently alternate periods of involvement and non-involvement so the participation index of a member cannot be judged on one or two years. On the other hand, other members tend to forget their involvements so the author has good reason to believe that under-reporting has to be figured into these results.*

TABLE 19

Participation In The Last Ten Years By Percent Of Total Membership

In Committees:	34%
On the Executive Committee or Secretariat:	15%
As Branch Coordinators:	15%
As Committee Coordinators:	22%

This certainly indicates a broad amount of political involvement. Holders of main administrative positions do not often repeat their political role. Thus, from our population sample of 158 members in 40 years:

10% served as work coordinator; only one person had the job twice. Given these figures (while we take into account non-reporting of additional roles), given a two-year term for this office, Vatik had a new work coordinator every two years except during eight of the last 40.

3% report having been farm manager; one having the job twice. It did not rotate in nine out of 40 years. No member has repeated this job twice, the last 12 years. While farm manager has the highest rate of repetition from these figures, today, with a central kibbutz school for farm managers, the community plans to have a new person in this role every three years and constantly has two members in training courses.

---

* We, however, report the results as tabulated without any adjustments.

10% have been mazkir or social secretary; a few report
having the job twice. With a two year term this means
that for 34 out of 40 years a new person was social
secretary every two years. Two to four members did
hold the office twice.

Only 3% or six individuals report holding the position
of treasurer. In Vatik, this is a fairly powerless job
of complicated accounting that is not frequently rotated.

Thus, despite interviewees' complaints that Vatik lacks a lot of
competent leaders, many members have functioned in positions that
have been rotated substantially during most years.

In Vatik today, all economic branches are coordinated by a
member of the second generation (middle-aged). Older members
decided that they had worked hard in building the kibbutz, and the
turnover of roles should take place while the senior members were
still capable of coordinating the branches. Younger members coordinate many of the committees, although more experienced older
members coordinate the economic committee and the committee on
inequality. In this regard Vatik is not different from other kibbutzim in the movement. Rotation must be planned for. The spread
of higher education is increasing the reserve of young political
cadres. Several members are capable of coordinating the metal
factory and the plastic factory, and a few engineers are in training to deal with the coordinator of new industry. The branch and
committee coordinators are rotated every year or two on schedule.
This condition for democracy seems to be intact.

(E) Closely related to this large reserve is the equality
in living conditions of the officials and the members of a society, such that privileges do not exist which make it advantageous
to hold offices for long periods. Rosner postulates a relation
between the equality of members and the change-over of officials:
if officials are not especially rewarded they will not want to
guard their positions. This criterion for direct democracy in
Vatik is also intact. Any slight inequality here is to the disadvantage of the administrators, who work longer hours, get in-
terrupted more often at home, have upsetting confrontations, and
get blamed by part of the kibbutz no matter what they do. If rotation and a diffuse arrangement of political responsibility did
not exist, economic power might easily gravitate to a particular
community group. Structural characteristics like this which prevent such circumstances are important in quality of life considerations. With the increasing complexity of kibbutz culture it
has become more complicated for people to live a common life.

Of the conditions Rosner lists only the members' awareness of their connection to the essential nature of activities in their community seems to be weak. Not participation but a sense of participation seems to be the political problem of Vatik. This is a matter more of culture than political structure. A trade-off has occurred. Homogeneity, group unity, collective ideology, control of individual choice and expression were traded to achieve a flexible social arrangement, capable of adapting to human diversity and encouraging its participation. The political structure runs smoothly without police, courts, and legal fights over contracts. Goods and services are distributed according to a set contract but the contracts are the same for everybody and do not change according to human diversity, except for extenuating circumstances like poor health.

Thus, it would be naive to say that there is far less social cohesiveness and fewer eqalitarian arrangements in Vatik. Nothing is further from the truth. There is less unity and less agreement and less uniformity. Certainly, this is also the stuff of which endless group joy is built. (Zablocki, 1971) But this was never the goal of the Kibbutz village. Their goal is to create the least coercive conditions that find a middle road between concern for basic human rights and respect for human diversity and fundamental social, political, and economic obligations between one and the other. Few social statistics measure this endeavor. The kibbutz really is a community school. Yet, we wonder how many people learn and to what extent? Vatik alters the conditions for and the possible consequences of stratification, but is stratification eliminated? On page vii the reader is referred to a far more extensive analysis of power, prestige, and opinion as they vary with demographic group.

Leadership And Differentiation

Auerback (1953), Rosenfeld (1951), Talmon (1972), Etzioni (1958) and Schwartz (1955) have essentially come to similar conclusions: The kibbutz has more and more developed functional differences between its members regarding influence, but these differences are neither rewarded, encouraged, or created by material rewards (payment for services, better housing, better standard of living). Differences in the kibbutz are real according to age, sex, family status, state of health, and seniority. Regarding leadership, however, social prestige leads the list in determining differentiation. One indication that this is the case in Vatik is that members who have a stronger sense of political participation in the village do not report greater satisfaction in their lives, greater work satisfaction, or better mental health.

118

Persons do differ significantly on their Actual Index of the Present Sense of Political Participation when it is related to both
Satisfaction and Work Satisfaction (p=.002, correlation -.20),
(p=.009, correlation -.26) but the correlations are very weak.
And persons do not differ significantly when their Historical
Index of Political Participation Throughout The Years is related
to work satisfaction and satisfaction. High scores on neither
index have any correlation to better mental health (Composite
Mental Health Index) or increased social support (Social Support
Index, or more communitarian economic attitudes (Economic Index).

    Still, this does not mean that no differences in social
prestige exist. Prestige is a combination of a member's skill
(which may be related to age and experience), past achievements
or previous reputation as a leader, efficiency in working on past
projects, whether the member is personally liked and respected,
and the member's current participation in managerial positions,
committee roles or less clearly defined social roles, such as the
"cultural leader" defined by Etzioni. Talmon, and Rosner (1965)
whose related research is probably more reliable because of the
number of communities they studied, found that kibbutz society
cannot be divided into social strata by virtue of the functions
performed. True, strata of social prestige can more or less be
made explicit but age, family status, country of origin, or community friendship clique do not predict such differences well.
When the amount of political participation is cross-tabulated
with varying types of human diversity (except sex, which will be
dealt with in the section on personality), such strata do not
emerge. The kibbutz is not mainly competitive; the society is
mainly a fellowship oriented society and all groups overlap significantly. Several central mechanisms reduce stratification:
foremost is the collective system of reward. Members are nomi-
nated to public offices, not elected; thus "influence campaigns"
seldom occur. Power in such offices and committee posts is coordinating and executive, not definitive. People persuade, relate and direct. The General Assembly, however, defines, decides,
and sets the limits and policy for officials. Officials receive
power from the community, not from the people who held power
previously.

    The following layers of political participation can be de-
scribed. First are the informal leaders. These members find
themselves speaking for the people. Sometimes they hold offices,
sometimes they do not. But their influence continues and their
desire to formulate trends in the community exists quite indepen-
dently of offices. Next, come those members who constantly fill
public positions in the kibbutz. For example, in the political
participation index of the membership of Vatik, a low level would

signify a participation in several minor or major roles and a
moderate to high participation in the general assembly. But about
a third of the membership far outdistance this kind of participation. They have been consistent holders of offices and also
identify themselves as having high participation in general political institutions. These high participants fit with this group
of informal leaders.

Third are members who participate to some extent in the
general assembly and identify themselves as having some or no
actual influence; they are "average members" in kibbutz terms.
They are concerned about membership and are involved to some extent. Members of Vatik describe the moderate participant as a
good worker, a member who discusses kibbutz affairs but does not
seek a high degree of involvement. A member of this group who
goes to some general assembly meetings, sits on some committees,
and is very talkative and active in the dining room describes
herself:

> I do not have any influence at all. Person-
> ally, I just do not have any. The fact that
> I may raise my hand and vote in a certain
> way in meetings, that does not mean that I
> have influence. You see if you are not
> really involved in the decisions that you
> have not (personally) worked for then I
> do not think you can influence anyone. You
> see, I do not think of myself as being such
> a strong person that I could go and organize
> something about the kibbutz...maybe there
> will be something.

She would be in the middle group of political participation.
This group, one might say, has participation without influence,
if influence is defined as organizational ability, involvement
and being a spokesperson.

The fourth group can be divided into two kinds: the occasional participants and what are called in Hebrew the "schulaaim."
Occasional participants get involved in decision-making depending
on situational factors. This can be a request by the nominating
committee that the member is ashamed to refuse, or a specific
interest in a particular issue. Idit, the young woman quoted
above, for example is interested in photography. She wrote
several articles and spoke at several meetings about issues of
inequality regarding camera equipment. Talia, middle-aged woman,
gives more detail:

Look, it depends very much on the person. If
someone wants to influence a decision, so he
or she can go to a committee...for example,
because I am on the counseling committee, I
know that I have influence on all of the social problems and decisions...if I'm on the
work committee, so I have influence on matters
related to work. I would not say that I have
an influence on any specific aspect all the
time.

In general, in the Kibbutz if something bothers
you enough, and you care about it, you can go
to various committees and try to influence
them. Someone who believes in the kibbutz
and has the energy and wants to change something, can simply do it. And that is
what I like about the kibbutz. If I were
living in the city I do not think that I
could influence the ideas of the mayor, but
on the kibbutz, yes. And I think that it is
good for a person to feel he is capable of
influence and change. (emphasis added)

The last layer of political participation can be called
"Those on the fringes" ("schulaaim"). These members do not even
get involved in public issues concerning them. Their greatest
involvement will be to settle a matter of personal concern with
a committee. The lower third in the political participation
index, approximately 10-15% of the membership, fall into this
category, characterized by infrequent participation at meetings,
having held one or two roles during their whole tenure of membership, and a low sense of participation in the community. The
following table illustrates the Political Participation Index.*

---

* Appendix I explains the construction of the political participation index. The division of the population into three groups is
made by decision. The descriptive categories approximate a good
definition of the range of members' participation which our statistics illustrate. The important point here is to define the
nature of the diversity in participation and attempt to understand
and categorize it. It should be made obvious that the author is
eclectically using both empirical data on political participation
that defines actual behavior and anthropological data "prestige
groups" which suggest how these facts may be interpreted. Alternate forms of interpretation are conceivable.

FIGURE 6

Suggested Model For Political
Participation in Vatik

Informal Leaders Constant Public Servants	High Participation	27.7%
Moderate Participants	Moderate Participation	37.5%
Situational Participants Peripheral Members	Low or Very Low Participation	34.8%

Understanding the conditions for democracy and the kind of political differentiation in Vatik we will now find a straightforward
reporting of political data of some value.

Patterns of Public Participation

Patterns in leadership do not present the whole picture.
What are the actual patterns of public participation? The General
Assembly reflects kibbutz character well. Its emphasis is on airing of issues, free-flowing discussion on principles along with
specific action on detailed proposals. The weekly meeting serves
the function of communication of the main issues in the community
(though it is by far not the only or main conduit).

TABLE 20

Frequency of Reported Attendance
At General Assembly Meetings

Every one (1)	33.8%
Sometimes (2)	37.2%
Seldom (3)	11%
Never (4)	17.9%

Valid cases: 145. Missing cases: 13. Mean : 2.083.

The results appear to support the interpretation of the index of
political participation. Close to 30% seldom or never attend
these meetings. Yet the results are misleading for two reasons:
first, random observation showed an attendance rate of about 20-
30%. Thus, many members who say they participate in all or some
meetings are actually switching off with each other.* Second,
because of the diffuse character of all formal and nonformal participation these data do not justify a conclusion that direct
democracy is not functioning in Vatik.

Examining the reasons for participation and non-participation in the assembly will provide an explanation of what conclusions are justified.

TABLE 21A

Reasons For General Assembly Attendance

Participation is an obligation of members.	63%
Desire to influence decisions.	57%
Meeting is interesting.	38%
Meeting solves problems.	8%
Enjoy meeting.	-%

Valid cases: 105 - Missing cases: 53
N.B. Percentages express number of all who answered who chose
that reason in their group of reasons.

_____

Members participate mostly out of obligation and a desire to influence decisions, not because they enjoy the meeting or think
it solves problems. Actually, because of the diffuse character
of decision-making, the perception that the general assembly
meeting does not solve problems is accurate. Possibly the social
forces of the intimate commune that once made meetings of the
assembly cultural events and sessions in ideological education
account for its fall in popularity. Members who do not participate in line with the above interpretation do not see the assembly

_____

* In other words some come to one meeting, some to another, so attendance remains the same in percentage while the people change.

123

TABLE 21B

Reasons For No General Assembly Attendance

Participation is not an obligation.   5%
Sense of member that she-he lacks influence.   11%
Meeting is boring.   34%
Meeting does not solve kibbutz problems.   48%
Meeting is personally enjoyable because of tensions.   8%
Other   11%

Valid cases: 35 - Missing cases: 123
N.B. Percentages express number of all who answered who chose
that reason in their group of reasons. No ranking was used.

---

as solving problems. A large percentage of them are bored. A
sense that one has no influence or that participation is not an
obligation does not have a place. This strengthens the interpretation that a participatory ethic in Vatik still provides
concrete opportunities for different kinds of members.

Participation in the General Assembly declined considerably
when the kibbutz changed from a small commune into a collective
village. In Vatik, the changes in the conditions for direct
democracy Rosner suggested have taken their toll. The number
participating in the assembly increases if an important decision
is up. "Routine" meetings involving university study, general
community announcements, and voting on uncontroversial codes attracted about 25% of the membership. When issues were the stand
on national politics, the right of younger returning members to
use their Army pay for their year abroad, or decisions about the
standard of living or the education of the children, attendance
rose sharply. This agrees with the research of Peres (1962) and
Rosner. While participation has declined generally this does not
necessarily represent a surrender of responsibility. Rather,
many members do not consider it important to be present at every
point in the political matrix. The fluctuation in attendance depending on the substantiveness of the issue suggests that members
are more likely to delegate decision-making to the diffuse system
of committees. Recently, some kibbutzim have experimented with
novel organizational approaches to increase the effectiveness of
the assembly and redesign the political matrix. The democratic
structure is intact. Work on process is required.

Democracy And Culture

This raises the question of democracy's relationship to culture. Direct democracy, while it has changed perceptibly in the kibbutz organization, is still a reality. The collective, integrated, and fellowship-oriented nature of kibbutz life makes the cooperation and consultation of all members a necessity if the community is to be a success. Our extensive interviews at Vatik suggest a strong common identification among all kinds of members with the norms of the community: the individual-community dialectic, work, cooperative living, participatory democracy, and ideology and national service. While not shrouded in the ideological (often socialist) language of their mothers and fathers, the second generation clearly espouse these concerns as their own. We interviewed fifty members representing different ages, sexes, and levels of participation and prestige in the community.

One impressive trend in these interviews is the tendency for all members--even the most peripheral and "isolated"--to view their lives as criss-crossed with mutual responsibilities, and to appeal to kibbutz norms and values in analyzing their personal problems or community issues. This is not to say that there are groups of members who are not alienated from decision-making. Zalman's discussion of children's toys and bicycles illustrates this:

> Interviewer: You said that years ago there were no bicycles here? How is that handled today? In other words, what is the limit nowadays between what I am allowed to do and what is considered good for the kibbutz?

> Answer: Do you confuse the situation! It (having bicycles) was not bad then and it is not bad now. When I am speaking about values that is not the materialistic aspect which matters but the social aspect. It is quite evident that no kid had a bicycle then but that was the result of a low standard of living. Of course, the question of the price of an object was not the issue mainly, although who could afford even fifty pounds for his child then? Maybe you could have afforded half a pound or a pound. You would buy a toy and that was a big affair, and as a matter of fact people bought toys, but imagine what

would have happened if someone suddenly appeared with a bicycle!! First, the attitude of our collective education was different, so its object was to give the property of the whole group of children, and a schedule would soon have to be defined: I can ride from two o'clock to two-thirty and you from two-thirty to three and so on...The children then would never agree that a bicycle belonged to one person. What...yours? This has changed with the standard of living and that means other problems. People think that the poor have a headache because they have nothing to eat, but a rich man also frequently does not sleep at night! I think we worked very hard. We invested all our power and energy in improvements. We wanted to produce more. By the same token, our living standard goes up and there are no more problems about bicycles: every child now has his own. The question now is how do you go along with it. Now you have another problem underlying all the questions and developments. That is the problem of equality and that's a function of ideological values.

Every kibbutz member to an extent serves as a social and political philosopher attempting to guard and speculate about the village. The kibbutz is structured to encourage such thinking, since the sharing of common social developments and identifications is matched with a diffuse and decentralized fellowship-oriented political community which allows each member to share power in determining the direction of such developments and the importance of such identifications. Without the cooperative small community life of the kibbutz the freedom of choice, the possibility of representation, discussion of issues, and common agreement would occur in a vacuum. Democracy then is isolated, burdensome, mechanical, and to an extent devoid of meaning. Because of this the future of kibbutz culture is where the worth of its democratic structure resides.

Cultural Life

Life is not all work and ideology. After work members do not go to the city or to neighboring villages for entertainment or friendship. The kibbutz, not just a base or a home, is a world, and from the beginning its founders felt it must have a wide variety of cultural activities.

Kibbutz members, intensely concerned about new ideas, new books, new political developments, are considered among the most culturally inclined of all the Israeli population. The absence of excessive pressures of materialism gives members time for hobbies such as pottery, carving, painting, music, reading, research, photography. Conversation, the tentative and serious banter of ideas, goes on throughout the day, especially at coffee breaks, meals and afternoon tea. The afternoon tea is a cultural institution of special importance. Food is shared, feelings explained, letters read, children played with, newcomers entertained and to some extent socialized, and current issues in the community, the country or the family discussed. There is also ample time for meals; members do not only eat and run.

During a usual week in Vatik almost all residents attend movies once or twice. During the summer everyone brings folding chairs and snacks and watches films on a large lawn outside of the common dining hall. The cultural committee invites lecturers on various intellectual or political subjects almost every week. Each group of regional kibbutzim cooperates to bring in orchestras, dance companies and other groups; often Vatik's large modern auditorium is the setting for such affairs. Members from different kibbutzim with common interests participate in "chugim" or study circles during the winter. Each kibbutz has several chugim organized by its own members to study philosophy, to listen to and study music. These groups are now sometimes connected with outreach community college centers where, after hours in their own locality and in a kibbutz setting, members can work on degrees. One evening a group presented a series of skits and a living newspaper making fun of different things the community took seriously. Transcendental meditation and yoga courses are offered. There are music and art rooms and dark rooms, and a discotheque open every night especially for the younger members. Older members use the coffee house and reading room which offers a wide variety of reading material and special treats on certain nights to attract members.

Some events are celebrations of skill of achievement and of the community. The community basketball team draws big crowds during the summer when they play neighboring towns and kibbutzim in their league. Informal games of basketball, football and soccer are organized within the community and last summer an informal softball league was organized with some neighboring kibbutzim.

The many Jewish festivals are excitedly celebrated, devoid of their religious significance and emphasizing themes of harvest and nature and kibbutz values. Much preparation goes into such celebrations: special food, new clothes, decorations, dances, group singing and other programs. These festivals serve to integrate Jewish cultural values with the kibbutz values of community. One Jewish custom is the weekly celebration of the Sabbath. On Friday evening, the members dress up and eat together in the large dining room which is formally set for the occasion. At this time the spirit of the community actually changes. People are more at ease. They seem friendlier. As there is no need to rise the next day, which is not a work day, some activity usually occurs afterward. On Saturday, time is devoted to reading, resting, receiving visitors (many times from family outside the kibbutz), and spending extra time with one's children. While the traditional Sabbath usually ended with a religious service, in the kibbutz the weekly General Assembly meeting is held.

Another kibbutz celebration is the day of remembrance. The whole kibbutz celebrates the death of its members by gathering to remember that person in a personal way. Often the person is an older member known intimately by all for many years. His or her life is talked about in a matter-of-fact way. No attempt is made to make the person seem better than he or she was, but time is given to remembering his or her uniqueness. Usually, a small book is printed with the person's writings, life history, pictures. The person's foibles or characteristics are talked about appreciatively and with understanding, and his or her personal contribution to the kibbutz described. With the death of a young son in a military action, one views a deeply shared sadness and loss amidst the somewhat paradoxical but devoted understanding that national defense is an important national commitment of the kibbutz member.

Weddings and births are celebrated in differing ways. In the smaller community we studied the whole community attended them, while now in Vatik's they tend to be family affairs with special planned hours for community participation. This decision is due to the increased size and cost of such celebrations, their

128

increased occurrence, and the general trend of familization in the kibbutz. Some large kibbutzim, unlike Vatik, still have large community affairs for such events.

Thus, identification of kibbutz members with each other extends far beyond the collective structure of their lives and community norms. Bien (1973) documents the preference of the kibbutz member over the average Israeli for community-oriented activities. He compared preferences of members and Israeli citizens over a wide range of activities and found kibbutz members to favor more family, collective, and intellectual forms of recreation.

Television is a counterforce for this view of kibbutz culture. In two years every apartment will have a set in Vatik. Private sets came gradually, first as a result of inequality, then as a result of members' scrambling to get one as quickly as they could. Everyone who does not now have a set will get one out of the community budget. All this occurred with little or no collective debate about the meaning of television for kibbutz "culture," and it indicates the often bland and blind absorption of outside trends in Vatik. Gurevitch and Loevy (1972) emphasize an inherent contradiction between the social collectivism of the kibbutz and the diffusion of television as a cultural innovation. They see the rising number of private sets in kibbutzim as just one symbol of the threat cultural disintegration poses to democracy:

> Television will cause the atomization of society by increasing the tendency to gather in private rooms into which (it) has infiltrated. Following this gathering, interest will wane in...fulfilling the social functions which are the main foundations of democratic life. One fears the increasing passivity among the kibbutz community which will prefer--like the entire Israeli community-- to enjoy a television program instead of making an effort at independent cultural creativity, which has prime educational, social, and cultural value.

Gurevich (1972), pp. 182-183.

Communities are just now beginning to recognize that passive culture may help to destroy the democratic conditions of kibbutz life. While familization and the collective village (vs. the radical communal) trend have given kibbutz life more extensive, more stable, and more flexible communal structures, the resultant economic progress and diversity this trend has allowed threaten the foundations of the kibbutz itself. Many members felt it was neither possible nor desirable to return to the earlier organic and spontaneous culture with avid group singing and dancing and freer sexual mores, yet mentioned that there were not enough in-novative cultural activities in the community.

The Sense of Participation: A Political/Cultural Issue

With information on the state of culture in Vatik, the sense of participation (vs. the type of participation) can be further explored. Members were asked to evaluate their influence with regard to making decisions in the public life of the kibbutz [Question 36] and in areas relating to their personal matters in the kibbutz [Question 35].

TABLE 22

The Sense of Political Participation

Influence in Kibbutz Matters		Influence in Personal Matters	
Very Much	.8%	Very Much	14.2%
Much or Somewhat	63.2%	Much or Somewhat	66.9%
Little	21.6%	Little	12.6%
None at all	14.4%	None at all	6.3%
Valid cases: 125		Valid cases: 127	
Missing cases: 33		Missing cases: 31	
Mean 3.4		Mean 2.6	

The bottom third of kibbutz Vatik's membership feels little polit-ical potency. The membership seems more able to feel influence on personal matters. A problem clearly exists regarding public participation in Vatik. It is not serious, since the basic condi-tions of direct democracy are intact, the spread of leadership fairly wide, and the degree of participation diffuse. It is worrisome because the low degree and low sense of participation among such a large part of the population indicate areas of weak

identification. The membership complain, at times bitterly,
about the lack of cultural activities and of a vibrant cultural
sense in the village. Most members consider the relationships
among the membership as the single most important criterion for
a high quality of life, yet the maintenance of a rich cultural
life, which is the expression of such a sense of relationship,
is treated as an unimportant criterion. Kibbutz Vatik seems somewhat puzzled over the competing trade-offs of its social structure. On one hand the members see that the passing of the
smaller, collective community brought great advantages. On the
other hand, they do not perceive the connection between a sense
of political participation and providing an ongoing sense of
cultural development.

These considerations suggest a problem that is circular. A
strong creative culture is needed to provide the depth of involvement from which common identification springs and direct democracy
is experienced as community vs. mechanical participation. However, kibbutz members need to confront their society's problems
through participatory democratic meetings that will allow them
to shape the culture they are building. (Arian, 1966)

Abiding common identifications must arise from deeply shared
concerns. The cultural shape of the democratic problem of the
kibbutzim means that working every day, showing successful economic cooperation and having a democratic collective village
(in structure) is not enough to insure the kibbutz's survival.
To abide by general norms is not enough. Common concerns require
concrete and deeply felt form (ideology) and methods of learning
and development to insure their continuity. Possibly, searching
out the advantages and crisis of collective education will put
one of these factors in greater perspective.

131

CHAPTER V

EDUCATION IN THE KIBBUTZ: CREATING THE COMMUNAL
ENVIRONMENT FOR FURTHER GENERATIONS

This chapter's opening perspective is that the collective
educational system is only part of the broader kibbutz learning
environment. The fact that the second generation has indeed
inherited Kibbutz Vatik is established. Then, four aspects of
education are explained: the wider meaning of learning in the
kibbutz; the similarity between educational and social-economic
principles; the actual structure of child-rearing (for the
younger ages) and "schooling" (in the kibbutz high school) and
problems in each sphere; and finally, a review of research
findings on the consequences of this system.

Some Orienting Remarks

The kibbutz is a voluntary society which hopes to change
behavior by encouraging the value of cooperative experience. The
description of various areas of the village's life illustrates
the seriousness, the extensiveness and the intensity of this
learning process. In considering education in the kibbutz, we
emphasize that learning about the common concerns of kibbutz life
is an important aspect of the life of each member. Ideology is
not simply a matter of radical statements made forty years ago.
The values that have been described (the individual-community
dialectic, work, economic cooperation, political participation
within the original zionist and pioneering context of the early
founders) are the practical kibbutz ideology. (The early forms
of this ideology and how it differed among individual members
were considered in the discussion of Zionism and the early
countercultural motivations of the original kibbutzniks.) But
the kibbutz has consistently changed itself over the years in a
dynamic process which has sought to put each of these values in
terms of changing conditions and its evolution as a society, for,
after all, the community is not controlled by some external force
such as a government or a religious system. In considering ideology and education a kibbutz norm, we mean that in its development the community places important emphasis in its value system
and its daily activities in coming to terms with the principles

which should guide it. In other words, the process of "learning what we believe in" is central in kibbutz life. Vatik has had to transmute this practical ideology into an educational structure created for the young.

This factor ultimately affects the community's structure of its educational program. Making some kind of peace with what they believe in and the kind of life they want to live is the challenge of every member and every kibbutz institution. But especially, for the second generation it is central in their decision to remain and make their lives in the kibbutz, for membership is not automatic. It must be requested. So far, the motivations and the ideological strength of these generations has been compared with the founding and "hashlama" groups. Now, in treating ideology and education, the discussion will focus on a description of the learning of children and youth and a review of research of the second generation and the educational program, with particular emphasis on the kibbutz high school, and an overview of learning in the kibbutz.

A serious review of education in the kibbutz must include the attitudes of the children and youth to many of the issues discussed in other parts of this work. Ample space is not provided for that project. Rather, the educational approach will be described and the attitudes of the membership toward it elucidated. The description of the children's houses and lower grades is based on interviews with child-care professionals and workers in Vatik plus observation sessions conducted by the author in the houses of various age groups. In addition, the author taught part-time for a month in the kibbutz high school and interviewed various members of the staff there.* In order to put the situation at Vatik in perspective with the rest of the movement

---

* The Research Project On The Kibbutz at Harvard School of Education, funded by NIMH, conducted a study of the attitudes of high school youth in Kibbutz Vatik and five surrounding communities in cooperation with Menachem Rosner of the Institute For Kibbutz Studies, University of Haifa and the teaching staff of Kibbutz Vatik and its neighbors (Rachal Aharoni is principal of the school). This study surveyed students' attitudes in all of the areas covered in this thesis, plus additional measures presented in later chapters on mental health and philosophy of life. Attitudes toward studies and the kibbutz educational group were also researched. Unfortunately, it will be some time before this material is available for use, as a substantial amount of evaluation is necessary before the completed computer analysis can be properly interpreted. At that time, a most interesting comparison between adult attitudes and student attitudes on the same measures can be made.

133

interviews were conducted with Menachem Rosner, expert on the kibbutz second generation, the coordinator of Kibbutz Artzi Federation's education department, and with various staff members of the Kibbutz Educational School at Oranim. By a satisfying research coincidence the regional kibbutz high school is the same school described in Melford Spiro's The Children Of The Kibbutz. The kibbutz, however, is not Spiro's Kiryat Yadidim, and his book actually, in presenting data on the students there in the nineteen-fifties, deals with students who are now the middle-aged members of Vatik.

The Second Generation

It would seem that with one very critical exception the collective moral ideology of the collective (kibbutz) settlers differs from that of the non-kibbutz settlers in Israel (The Moshava or villages). The collective moral ideology includes a heightened sensitivity to injustice, cruelty, and to the sacredness of human life. It includes a stricter orientation to self-labor and a stronger de-emphasis of the nuclear family and religious workship. These aspects of the collective ethic were apparently successfully institutionalized in the kibbutz and forcefully transmitted and preserved in the value orientation of the second generation. In fact, it appears that in one aspect--that of national identity and societal responsibility-- on which both types of original settlers felt existentially insufficient (or inauthentic), the kibbutz was able to implant deep roots in its second generation whereas in the moshav this trend was somewhat reversed.

These points argue strongly in favor of the success of the collective (kibbutz) system, at least insofar as its second generation is concerned.

Thus do Passamanick and Rettig (1963, pp. 165-178) summarize their findings after comparing the moral ideology of first and second generation members of kibbutzim and moshavim (plural of moshav). The moshav is the non-collective village settlement in

Israel similar to American farmers' cooperatives. As a community learning environment the kibbutz has succeeded in developing common concerns in its children.

One of the main criteria for the success of the kibbutz way of life is its ability to succeed in socializing its second generation and, as Joseph Shepher has pointed out, "the ability of the second generation to enjoy kibbutz life and find roles and satisfactions in it." Few precise data exist concerning this success, which we wish to assess and put in perspective before considering the youth educational system in the kibbutz. Rosner studied the status of the several thousand members of the second generation of the Kibbutz Artzi Federation which was founded after World War I. This Federation includes some 73 kibbutzim and is the federation to which Vatik belongs. 16.1% of all the second generation born in the communities left the kibbutz for good, 2.1% died, mostly in the wars, and 11.3% left for other kibbutzim, mostly because of marriage. Therefore, 70.5% of the 2,904 second generation members born in the kibbutz still live there. This is a very high percentage and there is no reason to believe it is different for the other federations. In Vatik, according to research conducted by the Social Department of Kibbutz Artzi under the supervision of Menachem Rosner in 1976, the number of departures, higher than the average, is around 40%. (Schlomo Rosen personal communication.) Now, the average percentage of departures in the rest of the Federation is about 30%. Shepher has pointed out that this success of kibbutz socialization is impressive when we consider how unsuccessful many utopian communities have been in achieving continuity. When put in the context of the emigration that occurs from normal communities (be they cities or villages) in a time of increased mobility and diversity the figure is even more meaningful.

The ideology of the remaining members of the second generation puts them well on the way to taking over the economic, public, and social direction of the kibbutz.

This is the case in Kibbutz Vatik where an almost complete transference of responsibility has taken place in the last ten years and more than half of the adult population not members of the founding generation or the hashlama are below 50. Despite the expectation that this group would be less devoted to kibbutz values than their elders - which is what the elders predict in their interviews - all our attempts to cross-tabulate the attitude results in previous chapters and find significant differences between these layers in the membership have not been successful, except in discovering that the founding and the second generations

135

differ in the influence of the pioneering ideology of socialism and Zionism on their original motivation to join the kibbutz. On one hand, older members at times berate the middle-aged members for not being concerned about socialism and what they call "ideology," but the fact is that they are no more unconcerned than their elders, when their attitudes toward practical kibbutz ideology are examined. Our interviews show more a difference in language than in concern. The following characterization of the "middle generation" by a male member of the old is accurate in describing their motivation but untrue in interpreting their ideals vis-a-vis the old today:

> What disappoints me is the lack of ideals in
> our life. Let me put it this way. In the
> later years, when the second generation
> started to become members of the kibbutz,
> their ideology was that the kibbutz was their
> home. It is not a way that they want to live
> because it is their theory that they want
> to build up a new society. They did not talk
> about a new society. They say, this is the
> way, I was born here, I like this place, the
> way of living here even, and therefore I want
> to live here. If you switch over to this ap-
> proach there is no background of ideology, so
> today your home is good and you like it. To-
> morrow you do not like it, you take your pack
> and go. And this is what happened. This is
> what is happening today.

The older generation defines a lack of ideals as not defending one's motivation in terms of Zionist socialist theory and movement lingo. The facts, however, are different. In fact, as we have seen in Chapter II, there was a great deal of ideological diversity among the founders and hashlama, more than the myth of "one mind" is willing to note. In fact, today, the elders are nearly as non-ideological as the middle-aged members of the second generation. The differences we pointed out between the age groups in Tables 5A and 5B were not supportive of the assertion that the young have no ideology.

In fact, preliminary analysis of the high school students of Vatik and surrounding kibbutzim show them to be more ideological than the older members, just as in interviews.

They criticize violations of equality among the older members bitterly. In fact, most of the outside workers who are criticized for bringing in inequality are members of the generation of the founders and hashlama. There are two dynamics at work here: first, the older generation have clearly not achieved utopia, and second, in an attempt to make peace with their high expectation of bringing about a utopia and a "new human being," they find it necessary and convenient to blame the middle-aged and the high school generations. On first examination their reasons are persuasive; the younger and middle generations live here because it is their home, therefore they have no ideology. It is the last phrase that does not follow. Indeed, our results suggest that while the middle-aged and the young are not socialist or Zionist ideologues, they are at home with communitarian society. Also, just as their elders choose the kibbutz despite the fact they did not have to come to Israel as pioneers, out of persecution and a radical counterculture, the second generation did go through a process of screening. And some of them left just as some of the initial group of elders left. Thus, the elders, most of them, fail to grasp the nature of the actual choice the new generation has made.

The second dynamic at work here is that the context for weeding and screening out human diversity has clearly changed in Vatik. As the study of kibbutz structure documents, the basis of membership today is more the middle road between individualism and community than the path of the intimate commune, denying individual diversity and personalized options and specifying a rigid group identity. The kibbutz, then, has changed, along with the generation. The elders spearheaded this change, and it is understandable that they have trouble perceiving its effects on new layers of membership.

The second generation is guided by a strong concern to live in, take over, join, and normatively support the kibbutz as a cooperative community, but this is not cast in ideological terms, nor is it easily perceived by their elders for the reasons noted.

Rosner and Cohen analyzed the differences in perspective and experiences between the first and second generation in a similar fashion. Spiro's study The Children of the Kibbutz basically agrees with this conclusion. Thus, it is important to note that the number who stay or leave is not so crucial to this discussion as the actual ideology and quality of life of the children who remain. Sarel (1959) pointed out that the second generation was caught in a dilemma. Should they accept the revolutionary values transmitted to them and adopt the lifestyle of their parents, which would seem conservative, or should they revolt against those values, and thus end up returning to the individualistic values against which their parents revolted? The question is often

137

asked: How is it possible to inherit a revolution and not revolt
against it? He found that the second generation in the kibbutz
took an intermediate position: they were not as radically communitarian as were the radical founders of the communal kibbutzim
nor were they as open to more individualistic arrangements as the
founders of the older kibbutz communities. His investigation was
concerned with institutional spheres of consumption and family
life and work. Rosner has completed a definitive study of the
second generation of the largest kibbutz federation. He, however,
is finding that while the newer members do not express the concerns in the same way as their fathers and mothers, they do indeed
have a kibbutz ideology. What is it in kibbutz education that
accounts for the evidence of generational continuity?

The Kibbutz Educational Program

Four aspects of learning in the kibbutz may account for this:

the wider meaning of learning given a society
like the kibbutz;

the similarity between social and educational
principles in the community;

the actual structure of "schooling" and child-
rearing in the kibbutz;

the consequences of the kibbutz educational
system.

By developing these aspects we hope to illustrate the unique stand
the kibbutz takes on creating common ideology for the members of
its society.

The Wider Meaning of Learning in Kibbutz Society

In Vatik, as in other kibbutzim, the economic sphere is not
neatly divided from the sphere of social relations. Fellowship
and cooperation mutually support each other. One does not make
money with one crowd, make friends with another, and make decisions with still another. The community nature of the society

means that most of its members are constantly interacting around developing the goals of the society. These interactions in the communal economy, in the political arena, in the family and in the cultural life have resulted in many clear behavioral changes in the kibbutz when we compare the 240 communities with other societies. Because as a society the kibbutz is a deliberate attempt to structure experience such that relatively permanent changes in behavior occur it is a learning society. This is actually the definition of learning. The whole community can be considered a "school of living," centering on the norms discussed above: the individual-community dialectic, work, economic cooperation, political participation, ideology and national service. One can say that life in the kibbutz community prepares the person as much for the school as vice versa.

The "school" is not loaded down with the burdens of providing magical solutions to survival, happiness, justice, fitting in, and finding worthwhile work. The community itself creates the appropriate conditions which instruct members how to increase the strength of their ability to succeed in community. Thus, the "life is collapsing around you and so try to figure it out in school" phenomenon is not the way the kibbutz operates. Despite the obvious problems of Vatik, the cycle of life of the community is intelligible enough and predictable.

Without entering the argument of how learning occurs we can identify several ways of changing behavior as a result of experience. Events can take place independent of the individual's behavior that are related or connected and come to influence quite permanently the hopes, fears, or attitudes of a person (association). A member can be rewarded for certain behavior or punished for other behavior (reward). A range of behaviors can be purposefully manipulated in practice to induce skills (acquisition of skill). Things can be repeated over and over again (repetition). The "world" can be organized in different ways which make sense and these relations in the environment can effect a perceptual reorganization or restructuring of how one perceives and hence interacts with the world (gestalt). Every area of kibbutz life presents intentional arrangements which are oriented towards actively shaping behavior. Community/school lines cannot be rigidly drawn.

This attempt to define learning specifically helps one to see that the goals of learning in the kibbutz (community norms) can be "taught" in a series of different situations. How, for example, is the half-hour story which a kibbutz kindergarten teacher reads to the children about economic cooperation different from the economic cooperation the child may see for hours each day? Why should the parent's rewarding of a child for sharing toys be distinct from the cooperative behavior of the childrens' play group which is rewarded by the teacher-member? How does the knowledge that each Saturday night one's parents go to the general assembly meeting differ from the more direct emphasis the children's nurse puts on group consultation before decisions? In fact, it would be quite accidental to arrange educational language and plan life in such a way that what happened in a school was called learning and what happened in other areas of life was not included in the construction of the educational program. Small community life in Vatik avoids this difficulty and thus constitutes a total learning environment where school and living broach a common set of real issues in coterminous areas of life.

It is true that adult life is not the life of a child and learning is not just living. It is not letting children simply participate in community activities without planning special activities or organizing their time to aid them in getting the experiences they require to live in the society. This presumes that they are developing, have special needs, and require a certain amount of reserved attention and guidance. The free school or extreme de-schooling approach is not accepted by the kibbutzim which organizes itself quite seriously for the special developmental exigencies they consider the issues of children. A review of the principles of educational organization will illustrate this.

Similarity Between Social And Educational Principles

Bertha Hazan in Collective Education In The Kibbutz says,

> Collective education is a product of kibbutz
> society, which bases every aspect of its life
> on mutual aid and unlimited reciprocal respon-
> sibility, as well as on equality and sharing.
> Collective education has grown organically
> out of the social milieu. The relationship
> between the educational system and the social
> essence of the kibbutz and its aspirations
> has endowed collective education with its
> form and content. (1973, p. 4)

140

A check on factors of kibbutz education considered most advantageous by the members of Vatik confirms this theoretical position [Question 30].

TABLE 23

Advantages Of Kibbutz Education

Childrens' society. Education of children in groups.	70%
Training of children's house staff.	41%
Training of the high school staff.	18%
Relationships between children and metaplot (Hebrew, children's nurses).	43%
Early education of children.	25%
Relationship between parents and metaplot.	23%
Children without fears and worries.	30%
Seriousness of the high school students.	9%
Separation between children and parents.	19%
Other reasons	10%

Valid cases: 116
Missing cases: 42

Members see the relationship among the children in a communal learning situation and the relation between the children and the child care workers as most significant. Even in the interviews praise for the fellowship character of education took precedence.

Education is collective and communal. The children live to-gether in small groups in children's houses. In the early days of the kibbutz this meant quite a separation of parents from the children. Those who had the first children were vehemently op-posed to their own form of child rearing which they considered possessive, controlling, and oriented to individualist values. The kibbutzim later found that such extremism as limited visiting hours for parents and the priority breastfeeding by mothers of others' children before their own did not improve child rearing. It stifled the parent-child relationship and caused parents a great deal of unhappiness. (Viteles, 1966)

Dealings with children were not immune to the radical nature of the intimate commune. A mother from the hashlama recounts with some bitterness:

141

Twenty years ago visiting hours for
parents were strictly controlled. I
have a daughter who tells me straight to
my face that she does not want to live
the way I lived, or to work as hard as
I did. And I cannot tell her what to
do. She wants the children to be with
her and not in the children's house.
(The daughter left the kibbutz.) She
wants to educate them herself. And she
wants to be able to see them whenever
she wants. I think I understood her.
I can give you an example. In the
children's house when I put her to bed,
the metapelet (nurse) would have to run
from house to house to be sure that all
the parents had been there and put their
kids to sleep. So if I would be the last
one, she'd tell me to hurry up so the
rest could get to bed, and I'd have to
leave my daughter in a state of crying,
and it was hard for her--and she did not
know how to express it or get it out.
And this kind of thing stays inside.
I can understand her decisions. I think
the changes have been very good (in
eliminating this kind of child-parent
relationship). It used to be that when
a mother came to visit her child she
would get lecture about how she is dis-
turbing everyone.

The smallness of the village makes parents and children
accessible to each other. The nurses in the childrens' house
are chosen by the educational committee, which is heavily
influenced by the parents' evaluations of each particular
nurse or child care worker. Parents can visit the children
during the work day and often give special attention (that
would be impossible in another place) to a child with particular physical or emotional problems. They consult with the
child care worker at any time or with the parents of other
children in their child's play group. (Shepher, 1969) In
addition, a resident child therapist and a member experienced
in child care counseling are available for consultation. The
children go to their parents' houses from 4 to 8 p.m., cherished
in the community as time for children. Now, in Vatik, the
children come to the communal evening meal in family groups.

The communal childrearing system of today does not separate
children from parents but rather safeguards child care and
uninterrupted time for the parent and child.

There are strong sanctions (supported mostly by gossip)
for parents who do not devote much of the "childrens' hour"
to their children. The individual-community dialectic informs
this system: the kibbutz today seeks a balance between a diversity of child-care patterns and parental relationships to
their children and to community sharing of child care responsibilities.

The parents' special relationship as central agents
in their child's socialization is not allowed to take total
control of a child's life. As one member at Vatik put it:

> You cannot choose your parents and usually
> in society it is a result of accident.
> The kibbutz tries to recognize the family
> but provide a minimum set of healthy con-
> ditions for childhood, since we can
> choose the people suitable for education
> and we can make those conditions.

If a certain child has emotional problems or requires
special attention the child care worker takes the initiative
to work with the parent. This total learning environment is
a unity of the factors influencing children: parents, teachers,
the children's own groups and the social life. The school
is run on principles congruous with those of the community.
It would be contradictory for parents living in a cooperative
community to pay tuition, child care, or counseling costs
for their children. Child care and education would then be
stratified. Communal child-rearing means that each child has
an equal opportunity for the physical and emotional conditions
and resources necessary for development. These resources
are a right, not a privilege.

Consonant with this is the attitude of economic cooperation that imbues collective education. Learning opportunities
and goals do not depend on the economic status of the parents
(savings, wages, profession, training, managerial status,
quality of work). Learning and economic power are not pro-
portionally related. According to research conducted by Tel
Aviv University Psychology Department, the kibbutz is the
one place in Israel where there is no statistical difference
between the IQ's of children born of parents from a European
or American background and those born of parents with an Asian

or African background. (Kerem, 1973) In Israel's non-
kibbutz sector there are clear differences in economic power
between these two groups. The Jews from Asia, Africa (Arab
Countries) and the Middle East (Iran) have organized black
panther movements and complain rabidly of Israeli discrimination. Economic equality then is applied from birth through
adulthood in providing opportunities for kibbutz children.

Education through communal work leads the children into
the community not away from it. As soon as they are able
children in their small children's society begin to help
clear the house and do chores. Older children begin with
a short period of work per day. High school students have
regular work responsibilities from 2-3 hours daily. In Vatik
they participate in many different branches. One student
drives the giant, mechanized, specially conditioned tractor
ploughing fields each day in the hot desert sun. This
tractor is one of the largest machine investments of the
community. Young children tour the farm and learn about
different branches. They also maintain a small farm of their
own, patterned after the kibbutz farm.

The children's society is unique to the Israeli kibbutz
but children do not "go to it." The child does not confront
an alien educational bureaucracy but other members who work
in the "educational branch" who are also the child's neighbors,
parents' friends, school-mates friends and relatives. The
term "school" is a misnomer especially in reference to elementary school in the kibbutz for it may suggest principles
and structures totally alien to this collective village.

Structure of the Children's Society Educational Program

Education in the kibbutz is social change. The early
educational system was formed out of a desire to create a
"new person" who would accept the values of a just society.
Viteles (1966) outlines the source materials for this
original concept of education by the early kibbutz members.
In the beginning, Degana Aleph (the first kibbutz) established
collective child-rearing and education as a utilitarian necessity so that more women could work. Only in the nineteen-
twenties, around the time of the arrival of Russian immigration,
did more ideological kibbutz members begin to root the
communal learning system in a radically new social ideology.

Rabin and Hazan (1973) present a detailed summary of these principles.

Two books have helped to form our main attitudes about kibbutz education. Spiro's classic empirical work, The Children of the Kibbutz can be considered the basic text for attaining a realistic day-to-day picture of kibbutz education and child-rearing and an assessment of the "psychological price" it exacts.

Unfortunately, many aspects of the book are out-dated today.* (Spiro, 1958) Although it would be unfair to read his work without sufficient understanding of the society as a whole (as this work does) and the ideological antecedents and goals of the educational system (as presented by Viteles and Hazan), it is an excellent review of actual kibbutz educational practice.

Bettelheim's The Children of the Dream, while well-known (1969) has distinct problems. Kibbutz educators have leveled serious criticism especially at Bettelheim, but also at Spiro for his often harsh evaluation of the second generation. Both authors consider that the second generation has paid a high price for their unique kind of learning by developing an in-ability to get involved in intimate relationships and a certain flattening of affect (distance from emotions and deep feelings) in their personalities. Bettelheim is persistent in his claims despite the fact that his findings based on six weeks short-term participant observation were totally disproved by empirical research. (Jay and Bimey, 1973) None of the empirical psy-chological and psychiatric research done by clinicians from outside of Israel and kibbutz members in the country supports Bettelheim's conclusion. It is unfortunate that many of the popular conclusions about kibbutz education are influenced by some of his unsubstantiated criticisms; however, the Children of the Dream has introduced kibbutz education to the public.

---

* They are: changes in kibbutz education as a result of general liberalization in society; greater understanding of the place of the second generation in kibbutz society; the psychological consequences of kibbutz child-rearing about which we know much more; greater influence of Western culture on the kibbutz high school; the debate whether kibbutz education should be more practical or return to its roots.

It cannot be concluded from Spiro's (1965) view of the second generation member's personality that kibbutz adolescents exhibit "negative features" more than people from other socialization systems, nor should the psychoanalytical perspective lead one to believe that a social system eliminating all emotional conflict or tension might be devised.

The following summary of the daily structure of kibbutz education is presented in the context of two issues: first, that this alternative educational system should neither be over-idealized or presented in a way not giving ideology and the quality of learning in kibbutz society as a whole sufficient emphasis; second, that one must beware of seeing as special to kibbutz education problems that may be general problems of youth everywhere and of socialization.

The structure of child-care and learning in the kibbutz has three goals: to shape development, providing resources and conditions for the kind of development the kibbutz considers important; to watch development, providing special guidance and care for children's needs, and to adapt development to kibbutz society and achieve cultural integration.

Baby Houses And Younger Ages

In shaping development the kibbutz gives the very best of resources in creating the children's society. (Rapaport, 1958) Child-care nurses for young children and teachers are trained in specially designed programs. (Rabin and Hazan, 1973) Each individual kibbutz gives priority to the children's budget, providing them with the very best care facilities. These conditions are scrutinized especially by the various branches of the Education Committee. Each kibbutz has infants' houses for children from birth to one-and-a-half with four to six children to a room, cared for by a nurse (metapelet). Children from one-and-a-half to four live in the toddlers' house, with toys, a play area, and other amenities geared to their physical development. The childrens' group formed in the babies' house will continue as a unit until the beginning of high school. At the age of three to four several groups are combined to form a kindergarten group of 15 - 18 children which lives in its own house made up of bedrooms, a playroom, a dining room, and an outdoor playground with suitable equipment. In the time from

146

approximately eight to twelve years the junior children's community is formed. It consists of four educational groups (third to sixth grade) of 15 - 20 children providing a wider choice of companions.

Each group has a full-time educator and child care nurse (responsible for guidance in the childrens' home, personal care and training). The young child's society is made up of 50 - 60 children. (Abel and Diaz Guerero, 1961)

The community is finely attuned to the developmental exigencies of each child or age-group. In early child-care the nurse (metapelet) is specially trained in baby care and mother-infant relations. During the first six weeks after birth the kibbutz mother spends full time with the child.

The mothers breast-feed the children together in a relaxed atmosphere in the babies' house. During the first year the mother gradually begins to resume the normal work schedule (six hours for women, eight for men). The metapelet does not attempt to form an intimate bond with each child. She is considered a child-care professional who assists the mother, attempts to supervise and provide special assistance to the child's early development. Answering charges that kibbutz children suffered from emotional difficulties because of this pattern of child-rearing several researchers (Rabin, 1958; Neubauer, 1965; Spiro, 1958) found that the term "hospitalism", resulting from maternal deprivation, could not be applied to kibbutz children.

In the toddler's house, ideally, the metapelet who began working with the children continues to be their nurse. The nurse working with a small group can give extensive individual attention and guidance, creating a direct, loving relationship with each child. The children from babyhood have an increased awareness of each other and the nurse gives special attention and guidance to the forming of these relationships. The metapelet is responsible for much of the training given to the children (toilet training, eating, dressing), and organizes daytime activities for the small group.

At the age of three several metaplot begin to merge their groups in preparation for kindergarten. The metaplot support the parental relationship with the children rather than confusing the children or depriving them. As Hazan and Rabin (1973) point out,

147

>One individual cannot possibly fulfill
>all these needs (of the child) ade-
>quately as every mother who has raised
>a child in the kibbutz will confirm.
>Greater success is assured when the mother
>and the permanent metapelet work together
>to create an environment that will afford
>the infant many forms of contact.

(Rabin, 1974, p. 25)

A tenet of the child care program provides support for parents so that their relationship with their children is not in constant competition with the demands and tensions of a busy life, but occurs in more relaxed, pleasurable encounters when the parents can give children great attention. The kibbutz hopes that by relieving some of this tension better mental health for children and better family life is possible.

The parents visit the kindergarten at different times during the day; sometimes the children may visit their parents at work. They observe their child in the group and share reactions with the kindergarten educator and the nurse. They participate in presentations of the group's art and help prepare for holidays and other occasions. In addition individual and group therapy for children and parents are provided where needed.

A concern for providing ample affection and physical care is significant with infants, a concern for providing training and directing the instinctual drives of the children into positive activities is foremost in the toddler stage; providing increasing variety of activities, educational resources, chances to create new and different relationships, and individualization of instruction is most important throughout the elementary years.

In the junior children's community the emphasis is on the formation of the peer group, a common concern for children at this age. Children begin increasingly to care for each other's development with the guidance of the nurse and the educator. They try to guide the tendency for the group to pressure its members and consolidate its identity by encouraging the group to set positive goals and experiment with what "gang leadership" patterns that emerge in a variety of different settings requiring different abilities. Some group activities are: preparation of plays, investigating branches of the farm, sports, camping trips, gardening. The parents and educators encourage the children to create their own society; group meetings are held and a farm committee is elected to supervise work. Rabin and Hazan summarize the developmental priorities of this stage of the educational program:

> Kibbutz society is based on the free
> education of the individuals living
> within it. The children's community,
> is a sphere in which they learn correct
> social behavior in the course of ex-
> periences while at the same time
> satisfying their need for play, work,
> and enjoyment. It is not an organizational
> framework, but one of essence, in which
> the child molds his or her personality
> and learns to impose limitations on him-
> self or herself and to respect the rights
> of others. Above all, the children's
> community assures the children a happy
> childhood.

> (Rabin, 1974, p. 60)

Problems in Early Collective Education

Problems of the younger ages in Kibbutz Vatik are of three types: planning, staff-parent relations, and the special needs of certain children. The education committee must plan children's trips, work out budgets, make sure that new baby houses are constructed if new children are expected, plan ahead for adequate new staff (which must complete courses of several years), make the schedule for the present staff of nurses. Today, members are critical of what they perceive as a staff shortage. Many middle-aged women have chosen to study, and there is inordinate pressure on the remaining educational staff. This problem is particular to Vatik; the kibbutz did not plan for the sudden resurgence of professional goals among young and middle-aged women.

A middle-aged father comments on its staff-parent relations:

149

In general I think that the educational
system is good. You see how kibbutznikim
come out - all healthy and strong. But
there are some problems with the education because of the relationship of the
adults. The metapelet or the teacher
may not get along or there may be compli-
cations with the parents. Now there is
a trend that the kids will be together
all day, but will sleep at home at night.
I feel that even with the system the way
it is now, the parents influence their
children most in the evenings and also
on weekends when the children are with
parents all day. In the city kids are
influenced greatly by their parents.
Whatever mommy and daddy say, that's it.
Here, it is different. Most of the time
your child is in a different house, and
it is greatly influenced by his or her
metapelet. If she is stable and a good
person then it is fine. But if the
position is constantly being changed or
filled by new people, then the children
become wild. And I feel that parents
have to have a bigger influence. They
should be able to say that this is my
child and I want him or her to be a certain
way. The child does not belong to the
metapelet. The child is mine. She works
with the child, so that I can work, and
so that I can be a little freer and that
is it. Look my older son has a metapelet
who just came back from the army. She
never studied anything. She's just a
young kid herself and she has no background.
In the city that would never happen. You
need a license to be a teacher and to
work with children. So what will happen,
she'll find a boyfriend and maybe go to
another kibbutz, so we will have to find
someone else. Next week she is going on
a trip so we will have to find someone else.
All the time it is like that...always
changing...Here we are filling holes. So
who suffers from this? My son. One is nervous.

150

> Another one's boyfriend is coming so
> she does not pay attention to the kids;
> another one is a little nuts...so it is
> hard. On the other hand, the kids are
> happy; they are with their friends and
> they always have someone to play with,
> and they have plenty of space to run
> around in. They are freer, and they do
> not have their parents hanging down on
> them telling them to do this or that.
> So there are advantages and disadvantages.

This long exerpt illustrates a feeling widespread among Vatik's parents: "The system is good but we often do not run it well." Many members like this father have a fundamentally positive evaluation toward the system but begin to talk conservatively--taking more control over their children's education--because of repeated inefficiencies. Confrontations and arguments at times occur between parents and metaplot which exacerbate the problem.

A third problem with early childhood education at Vatik is dealing with the diversity of children and their special needs. A full time psychologist, constant meetings and conferences, a counseling committee, and observations of visiting psychologists, psychiatrists, and senior kibbutz educators provide attention for children who are gifted, disabled, disturbed. Several families participate in family therapy at child guidance centers run by the kibbutz movement. An elder educator at Vatik also has the role of informal helper to many kibbutz mothers and fathers and metaplot, and she often can be seen conducting completely confidential family conferences.

No criticism was made of this aspect of the educational program in our interviews.

In order to get an overview of the educational situation members were asked to point out the disadvantages of collective education: [Question 33].

TABLE 24

Disadvantage Of Collective Education, Kibbutz Vatik

Children's society. Education of the children in groups.	8%
Training of the children's house staff.	33%
Training of the high school staff.	17%
Relationships between children and metaplot.	17%
Early education of children.	4%
Relationships between parents and metaplot.	44%
Children with fears and worries.	12%
Seriousness of the high school students.	36%
Separation between children and parents.	25%
Other	28%

Valid cases: 78
Missing cases: 80
N.B.   An inordinate number of people did not answer
     this question.*

---

* Many older members refused to discuss collective education
because they said they were "out of it" and did not think
about it much anymore.

Taking the problems that relate only to younger children, it
is obvious that the feelings of the kibbutz father quoted

earlier were representative. The main concern is with staff
training and parent-staff relationship, with a fourth of the
sample concerned about parent-child separation. This confirms
the conclusion that only a minority really are interested
in reverting to non-collective sleeping arrangements (having
children sleep in parents' apartments) and that this attitude
may stem from non-ideological concerns tied more to inefficiency
in collective education in Vatik rather than to a challenging
of the system's principles.

In conclusion, the educational program for the young is
well integrated into life at Vatik and serves as an intelligible
extension of the whole kibbutz learning environment. Many
members have moderately serious questions, not about the
principles of collective child-rearing but about specific planning
and staff problems in Vatik.

The High School

From approximately the age of 13 on the children move
to the youth society of the high school made up of about
150 - 200 children. It is a society of educational groups
(containing the original group of six and the elementary school
groups which by now have set group identities).

Groups from individual kibbutzim--the same group of
children one was with from babyhood--live and learn together
but all the groups cooperate in social and cultural activities.
The high school is located about a mile from the community
near another kibbutz. It is a regional high school, whose
budget and staff are cooperatively shared by several neighboring
kibbutzim. This distance enables the group to remain in the
kibbutz movement yet outside their own with a larger and
more diverse group of persons (usually including 18 - 25
children from cities and villages not kibbutzim). It also
discourages, as Hazan and Rabin note, "premature imitation
of adult life and safeguards the value of studies and youthful
activity." (Rabin, 1974, p. 23) The high school community
is unlike the smaller childrens' houses which have much adult
supervision, and are contained in the middle of the kibbutz.
The high school community is actually a "little kibbutz" with
its own common dining room, meeting rooms, work branches,
committees. The children live with one or more roommates in

dorm rooms scattered in one-story structures around the community dining room and study halls. The youth society has shops, hobby rooms, music rooms for common use.

The older high school kibbutzniks live in rooms at their home kibbutz during the summer and on vacations, and use these as their "base" when they return home each afternoon to work in their community. The younger high school students must stay at their parents' houses when they visit during the day and during the summer live in semi-private quarters.

The first high school at Vatik was radically unstructured. Members made no excuses in explaining that the only education worth occurring happened as a result of the natural interest of the adolescents and the ability of the high school staff to command their respect. Today, Vatik's high school has almost totally put aside the project method. A structured curriculum with many courses and specific disciplines is set and pre-conceived choices by the student are required.

The emphasis on the group's importance in the development of its members continues, despite these structural changes. Adolescents in Vatik mentioned repeatedly and forcefully that a few members in each group felt that they did not fit in, had low status, and were hurting because of this. It has not been determined if this problem is integral to kibbutz group socialization or to the peer group centrality in adolescent socialization everywhere: it was voiced as a hard criticism by students today and members looking back on their education.

Another adolescent of Vatik criticizes the group about evaluation of diversity:

> When one lives all one's life with the
> same people, and for seventeen or twenty
> or how many years you have seen that
> person, learning their strengths or
> weaknesses, their characteristics in
> a very basic way as a result of living
> so closely, one develops a rude or
> vulgar attitude. People have had it
> with one another. In this closed society,
> people stop caring, stop paying attention
> to one another. It is as if they figure
> that it would not make any difference to
> them if they acquired different habits
> of relating. You do not change your

society, it is not like changing air
(when you breathe), it is human. This
is a problem here that people are bored
and have had enough of each other. I
think it is that way in every kibbutz.

This opinion points to a strain on high school society in the
kibbutz: childhood is over. Adult life is creeping up
and this fellowship-oriented collective society does not
seem to have removed the pains, the angry immediate and
sweeping evaluations, the bitter social accounting of
adolescence. (Erikson, 1950)

High school in the kibbutz is mainly a social experience. As mentioned, the youth society is even more like
a mini-kibbutz than the little childrens' farm. It has
its own organization and cultural activities, but does not
deal with its own budget, security and curriculum. Planning of social and cultural activities and work is done
through a general assembly meeting with the advice of adult
representatives. (Shepher, 1971)

Each group has a counselor-educator who is the full-
time advisor and educational coordinator and who directs the
development of the group by intervening with various individuals,
conducting weekly group discussions on personal and organizational problems, and mediating individual-group conflicts.
The educator is carefully chosen by the educational committee
and the parents. At this stage the group's metapelet provides
for the living quarters of the adolescents, cooperates with the
educator and works with the parents.

Kibbutz adolescents generally criticize the kibbutz
community and consider actively its pros and cons. Probably
because they are not forced or brainwashed into membership,
they are in a frustrating position. Developmentally they need
to give their society a "good going over," but for the long
term many of them will find it to be the place where they will
live. The three-and-a-half years in the army and a year or
two travelling abroad plus the usual university study before
the age of thirty for some members of the second generation
give ample time for the balancing of the accounts and the
decision about membership. (Eisenstadt, 1956)

155

Problems In The High School

The high school in the kibbutz is not <u>only</u> a high school.
Kibbutz educators and the children themselves admit that the
main events during this period are social and developmental--
i.e. people are changing and growing in interaction with the
unique communal environment. Four special problems of the
kibbutz high school are: generational tension and its
relationship to the attitude of students to the community,
authority, ideology, and outside educational norms.

There is definite tension between the elder members
and the high school students as Gideon, 18, describes:

> Socially I think this kibbutz is not
> good. This is because the relationships
> between the older kibbutzniks and the
> younger kibbutzniks are very bad. The
> attitude of the young person to the adult
> or older person is generally aggressive,
> impatient, occasionally sarcastic or
> mocking. In addition, the older members
> also have occasionally impatient, not too
> comradely attitudes toward the youth.
> In day to day life when the interactions
> between members are frequent, the most
> typical example is the insulting relation-
> ship. Impatience, not listening, or
> when people make fun of or relate to the
> weaknesses of others. Among the older
> people it is the weakness of growing old,
> for example with all of its characteristics.
> This appears in many places in kibbutz life,
> practically in every area of the life.

Surely, there <u>are</u> close relationships between high schoolers
and elder members, the ability to listen and to refrain from
critical condemnation are the most valued characteristics,
younger students look for. Clearly, however, many younger
members perceive that they need to explore other alternatives
to the kibbutz, and often scare the older members who know
they have not built any foolproof way to have a free education
and insure that a free choice to life in the kibbutz is the
ultimate result. Gideon continues:

> The best example of this is that a lot
> of people when they finish the army,

156

> instead of coming right back to the
> kibbutz, go to the city, go abroad, taking
> what is called a year's vacation, because
> they want to breathe new air, to see a
> new society. And it even begins in high
> school. They need to meet new people,
> not all the time the same funny faces.

The influence of Americanization is a real factor here.
America represents the height of individualism and the boon
of human diversity without community. In the last few years
Vatik has allowed young members go on one-year leaves of
absence after the army. They did this conscious that otherwise
they would have forced a desire to explore to become a decision
to leave.

Thus, the struggle between the individual and the community,
a basic tension of kibbutz life, hovers in the high school.*

Learning is only possible through intellectual interest
and motivation. Spiro reported that classes were often
disruptive, while the teachers were unwilling or unable to use
personal authority to bring order. Youngsters at Vatik
reported that each teacher had a different evaluation with
their group and his or her ability to interest them and relate
to them was a central dynamic in determining the nature of
that particular class.

A related problem is that of authority. Spiro noted (1958)
the primal issue of alternative schools: should the teachers
exercise more authority in dealing with the youngsters for
educational goals or is the appeal to conscience, to the
responsibility of the group enough? While Zvi Lavi, a former
director for the Educational Department in the Shomer Hatsair
Federation of Kibbutzim recognizes several prominent free
school experiments as influential in kibbutz educational

---

* The kibbutz high school program includes precious little
information to give the young person an appreciation of the
conflict between the individual and the community throughout
history. For example, students know almost nothing about the
history of the kibbutz movement, especially the influence of
the European counterculture. They know nothing about communal
and cooperative experiments around the world. Material in
these areas may be a central part of any attempt to face
squarely the tension about individualism and community many
kibbutz adolescents feel.

practice, (Rabin, 1974) Kibbutz Vatik is clearly not using
a high school approach which favors spontaneous learning in
unstructured situations with substantial control by the children.

There is an organized educational program and students
are expected to participate in it, but because it is an
organic part of the children's society it has not the same
quality of being the authoritative place where one fails or
succeeds as has the high school in modern society. Rather,
learning is a function of the person's interests and motivation,
the goals set with the educator and teachers, and the ability
of the educational staff to be responsive to the student's
needs. Lacking educational enforcement structures (no expulsion, no marks, no ability to ruin the future work career)
the kibbutz high school cannot force its member-students to
participate. Thus, "educational performance" is not a closely
measured statistic. It depends more on life experience,
personal goals, and development. Many a "poor high school
student" in the kibbutzim has later become quite creative.
The success correlation between high school and later life is
not a forced issue. (Ortar, 1967)

Adolescents sense at Vatik that intellectual learning is
a hit or miss phenomenon. When questioned about how they relate
to the intellectual (vs. social) goals of the Mosad the
responses are: it depends on who the teacher is, how interesting
the material is and if I feel motivated. Some are motivated
and most just go along with it. This presents a frustrating
and ambiguous situation for students and teachers alike.
There is not strong support for embracing a system of voluntary
learning. On the other hand, the idea of introducing grades
and pressure (supported by some parents) goes counter to
kibbutz educational philosophy. As one member said, "how can
you throw a student out of a kibbutz school? It's impossible
and ludicrous." In [Question 58] an attempt was made to gauge
attitudes about this dilemma in Vatik:

TABLE 25

Education of High School Youth: Parental Attitudes

Following are some ideas about education
of the young. Mark all those with which you
agree.

1. A youth needs to be free to make up his
    or her mind, to work for what he or she
    considers personally right.   28%

2. I really believe that education in the
    kibbutz shows the young the best society,
    in which many different people can find a
    place.   33%

3. I am not yet convinced that kibbutz educa-
    tion can both encourage our children to
    think freely and at the same time educate
    them so they will want to live in this
    kibbutz.   31%

4. Young people need direction and concern or
    they will get confused. Parents and teachers
    in the kibbutz must explain and show them
    and let them try to live our life.   70%

5. Kibbutz education must become more strict
    and academic. If we have good students
    who can go to the university they will
    stay in the kibbutz.   13%

6. Kibbutz education must become more like
    it was in the past: more freedom, for
    the children to learn through doing, to
    decide on their own what to study. We must
    resist packaged education.   32%

Valid answers: 136
Missing answers: 22

159

While most members answered this question few made more than one choice. Possibly, that indicates some problem in choosing. A desire to give direction and example (3 and 4) drew the strongest agreement. This has always been a traditional part of the educational ideology, but the community is both unclear and split on issues related to more or less freedom (1 and 2) and more or less structure (5 and 6). Vatik needs to clarify this situation. It is the author's opinion that in the kibbutz high school the issue of restriction or how to encourage diversity, is in another guise, the tension between communal identification and individual freedom. Here, we will see the real creativity of Kibbutz Vatik or its fatal division.

Another problem with kibbutz high school education is ideological education. At the time of Spiro's study in 1951-52, membership in the kibbutz political movement and weekly ideological meetings were compulsory for high school students. Adults taught the younger members about socialism and kibbutz ideology. Now ideological education occurs in an emphasis on Zionism and Israeli history but no attempt is made to recreate the young vibrant Movement that the original kibbutz founders tried to pass on to their children. Some senior members deeply resent the Movement's passing, but it occurred in response to young kibbutz members' radically different formative experiences. Spiro spoke of this situation:

> The Movement in the Mosad (high school)
> is not successful. The students seem to
> be apathetic to its program and display
> only a perfunctory interest in its meetings.
> The Organizer attributes its lack of success
> to the absence in the Mosad of the usual
> motivations for participation in youth
> movement--camaraderie, group belongingness,
> social activities, the opportunity to meet
> people of the opposite sex--since these
> needs are already filled by other aspects
> of Mosad life. It has been his experience
> that a successful youth movement is based
> on rebellion against parents and the latter's
> way of life; and in the kibbutz the movement
> is supported by the parents.

(1958, p. 303)

Many high school students in Vatik said that they liked or disliked the kibbutz for emotional and personal reasons.

"It is my home," "All my friends are here," "I like the actual environment of the village," "Kibbutz life is less pressuring, more cooperative," were common responses. The educators, however, feel that it is "impossible to maintain attachment to the kibbutz solely on the basis of such motives; it must also stem from ideological firmness." (Rabin, 1974, p. 110)

The challenge to kibbutz education now is to figure out how early learning experiences can encourage common identification among their youth with important vital criteria on which to judge and build the social life of the kibbutz. For just because the kibbutz is dynamic and changing, just because it must be continually shaped and re-formed by its members "learning what we believe in," this issue must be faced.

More than the other sectors of the educational program the kibbutz high school is affected by educational norms of the outside world. The Israeli Ministry of Education made various demands for the standardization of the kibbutz curriculum with national norms, and in fact, hinged the kibbutz's receipt of municipal education aid on this process. The desire on the part of the youngsters to go to the University has meant that they must study to be able to pass the national matriculation exam, a rigid requirement for university admission.

These developments have raised cries that high school education in the kibbutz is losing its unique original qualities. After the war of 1972 when high school students ran many communities while their fathers went to the army, some students asked why they need high school when they proved they were able to take responsibility in the kibbutz. While in the University the kibbutz students work harder and achieve as well as or more than others, this is not connected with the formal aspects of the high school program but with their unique socialization and motivation. One prominent kibbutz sociologist (Joseph Shepher, personal communication) in fact called kibbutz high schools "factories that prevent free thought and creativity" because of their increasingly pre-structured nature. The issue is complex. However, high school is not the central structure for learning in the youth society, and the organic fit between "school" and community still reduces the degree to which the kibbutz high school can become bureaucratized.

The author, who has taught in an inner-city alternative high school, recognized that these problems were not the fault of the kibbutz alone. On the other hand, one wonders if

adolescence is so full of questioning that no suitable
structure can be grown to contain it. In the end, kibbutz
adolescents do develop considerably through their high school
experience, which eliminates many stresses found in mass society
high schools, and eventually take over the operation of the
society. They exhibit less mental distress than children in
the rest of the population but this period of their lives is
replete with other problems notably attempts to assess kibbutz
life and their possible membership. The outcomes of this
educational program need to be examined, for we cannot form a
good judgement based on its functional problems alone.

Outcomes Of The Kibbutz Educational Program

Existing research shows that the kibbutz educational
program achieves many of its broad cultural goals. Data on the
second generation, already presented, indicates their fairly
responsible position in the kibbutz community. Because we
lack specific data on Kibbutz Vatik a general overview of
psychological research on kibbutz children will be considered.

In addition, it is clear that kibbutz childhood is quite
healthy. Rabin (1965) found that kibbutz children
lagged somewhat behind non-kibbutz children in intellectual
and ego development in the first two or three years of life;
this was attributed to frustration because of the temporary
withdrawal of the mother. Nevertheless, he established that
these difficulties were overcome after the first few years, so
that kibbutz children at ten were as well or better developed
intellectually as non-kibbutz children. They showed greater
emotional maturity, less sibling rivalry, less selfishness,
and somewhat more anxiety and hostility towards their parents
than non-kibbutz children. Seventeen-year-old kibbutz children
functioned somewhat better intellectually and were as emotionally
adjusted as their non-kibbutz counterparts. They had fewer
conflict problems and less hostility towards their parents.
Rabin found kibbutz young men to be strong in ego, less aggressive and less rebellious toward society than their non-kibbutz
counterparts. He discounted Spiro's hypothesis that maternal
deprivation produced social immaturity or that kibbutz adolescents were more hostile than non-kibbutz children. He also
concluded that the childrens' personalities were quite variable
in their differences from one another.

162

Kaffman (1965) found that kibbutz children were less prey to mental disturbances and had no clinical entity of mental illness which was prevalent among them. He also noted that out of 3,000 emotionally disturbed kibbutz children which his child guidance clinic treated not one case of early childhood psychosis was found. This was attributed to the unique aspects of the educational and child-rearing program in the kibbutz. He also found that kibbutz children had fewer mental problems than non-kibbutz children.* (1961)

Other researchers have taken these hopeful facts further. Kohen-Raz shows how emotionally-disturbed children are actually introduced from the outside into the kibbutz program and are greatly helped. (1972) Saar (1975) and Posnik (1975) have made two excellent proposals to effect a change in Israeli education using the kibbutz. Continuing to pin down the possible reasons for the increased mental health and ability of kibbutz children, Kohlberg (1971) and Reimer (1972) found that they had higher stages of moral development and were more finely attuned to and responsive to justice than lower and middle-class Israeli children, American working and middle-class children, and children of several other nations.** Drug abuse and juvenile crime are so rare that there is general agreement that it is almost non-existent. Yet, Spiro and Bettelheim and others generally agree that the kibbutz has not created the "new Person." The utopian dream of unbridled and fully dedicated humans, if it is even desirable, has not come true. Nevertheless, in certain critical areas, the kibbutz has proved that childhood and society are deeply related, and that many positive experiences can be encouraged and negative outcomes eliminated by kibbutz child development.

In conclusion, this examination of the educational program in the kibbutz and of issues creating a common ideology illustrates how deeply learning is a part of the larger environment in the society and how the special features of Vatik's program work. An honest assessment of advantages, strains, and problems of this program has been given in the context of

---

* Nevertheless, far more careful comparative research is necessary.

** These conclusions are now being questioned and re-worked.

describing the areas and norms of community life. While from
a structural point of view the clearest advantage of learning
in Vatik is its broad and diffuse cooperative character,
in school and in the larger learning environment, the same
tension between individualism and fellowship that is the
creative struggle of kibbutz life is also a central issue here.
The final survey of life in Vatik will deal with personality
and life philosophy in the community. These issues bear a
continuous relationship to the creative struggle under
question. What are some of the ultimate beliefs and personal
outcomes for individuals that life in Vatik leads to amidst
its struggles and its cooperation?

CHAPTER VI

ISSUES OF PERSONALITY IN KIBBUTZ VATIK

Introduction

Section 1 begins with the claim that a "kibbutz personality" as such does not exist. While the kibbutz in question has a distinct effect on persons through its unique arrangement of their lives, the fact that the community is organized to accept a wide diversity of attitudes, personalities, and philosophical styles without the control of a rigid religious or philosophical system is viewed as a quality of life advantage, albeit involving a trade-off. Data on how members report their own personal traits, and their attitudes towards personal development are reviewed and analyzed in terms of the kibbutz as a whole. The effect of life's shifting stages on social roles in the community, particularly the personal problems of the aged, is considered. The meaning system of members is described and related to the structural characteristics of Vatik. Section Two describes patterns of life satisfaction, mental health, social support, and mental health services in Vatik. The purpose is to make a reasonable estimate of the kinds of dissatisfaction in the community and to determine if particular groups in the population are disenfranchised, in terms of some psychological outcomes of their lives.

Section 1. Some Aspects Of Personality In Vatik

This section will treat several aspects of personality in Kibbutz Vatik to gain a general picture of "the underlying motivational structures or overt behavior patterns that characterize individual humans" in the community. (Oliver, 1976, p. 98) Kibbutz institutions which act as the social context for individual development have been examined. Before proceeding, the limitations of this particular section must be understood, since our questionnaire data is at most impressionistic and tentative.

Is There A Kibbutz Personality?

The dynamics of personality formation, the processes
by which personalities change and manage tension, the definition of the "kibbutz character" (if indeed any exists in
the special sense of that term) will not be analyzed or dealt
with. Because movement researchers have been more concerned
with practical problems of the kibbutz social structure, and
visiting researchers have been more concerned with the personality development of kibbutz youngsters, this is the most
neglected area of kibbutz study. Possibly, the widely
recognized fact that no "new person" has been created by the
kibbutz movement and the lack of extensive personality
research has led to the supposition among researchers that is
accepted fact among the members of Vatik:

> When someone asks why the kibbutz is the
> way it is, then my opinion is that
> there are things that happen during the
> life-cycle which are brought out by life
> itself, the life of human beings. You are
> young, you get older. It is the same in
> the kibbutz. It's the same in New York,
> in Tel Aviv. And you also marry someone,
> create a family, in New Delhi as well as
> Moscow and then you have children there
> as well as Africa...That has
> nothing to do with the kibbutz. That has
> to do with life. Nevertheless, the way
> the kibbutz solves or faces these problems
> belongs specifically to kibbutz society.
> You have to make a distinction between what
> belongs to life in general (and what is
> particular to the kibbutz). Everywhere
> human beings love, hate, feel jealousy.
> You know someone likes stamps, another
> pictures, drawings, or music. That is the
> rule all over the world, including the
> kibbutz. Where is the singleness of the
> kibbutz? In the kibbutz, people are able to
> feel the joy as well as the pain of their
> fellows, and it is different from the city
> and from other places. That is not the very
> meaning of the kibbutz, only its expression,
> the expression of something deeper, the
> solidarity, the reciprocal responsibility...

> I am not a psychologist nor a sociologist,
> and if I am asked whether the character in
> the kibbutz has changed, I'll answer by
> another question: Is it possible for a
> character to change? Let the psychologist
> come and explain if it is possible for
> character to change. As for me I think not.
> I reached this conviction since we live in
> this kibbutz. Sure, there are problems that
> the kibbutz creates, but there are also
> problems that the kibbutz succeeds in easing.

In personal interviews kibbutz members were questioned
about personality, personality development and change. This one,
Zalman, quoted above, comes closest to summing up the wild
stares, the halting answers, the "Why is that important in
talking about kibbutz?" attitude many members tried to communicate.

The kibbutz is a societal arrangement that tries to ease
various human problems by applying principles of cooperation
and community. It does not require conversions, it does not
require radical experience of change, it does not even require
a uniformity of ideology since, as we have seen, the diversity
of human viewpoints (once the centrality of the value of
community and cooperation is recognized) seems to be the very
stuff out of which the "middle-road," the historic "urban-
rural compromise" is formed. That fuels an ever changing
individual-community tension. True, the original intimate
commune of Vatik and other kibbutzim did require these things
to an extent, but those days have long passed, and another
generation is in firm place.*

---

*This is not to deny the special insight of Rosabeth Kanter
that communal societies depend on commitment which includes
a particular definition of the self which helps to bind
members together as a community. The difference is that the
kibbutz's commitment demands central agreement on secular
arrangements which mediate between individual and community goals
vs. radical religious ideologies, extreme attempts to alter human
nature or mortify the flesh, perfect the individual, or build
relationships, all of which are the stuff of the Shakers, Oneida,
and other utopian communities. In this sense, it is difficult
to call the kibbutz a utopia in spite of the fact that compared
to mass society it does seem like "no where." See Kanter
(1972) for further understanding of this issue.

Perhaps, the additional fact that second generation members of the kibbutz have unquestionably good mental health and the society has almost totally eliminated violent crime, suicide, juvenile delinquency and drug abuse, is a further reason for little interest in studying personality. The desire to reflect on personality seems uniquely tied to the need to figure out what is wrong or find methods to rectify gross social and psychological ills.

All of this left the author puzzled for some time. First, it was decided not to mythologize the "kibbutz personality" (honest, hard-working, outdoorsy, educated farmer) since enough diversity has been met that such a task would not be fair. On the other hand, reading of the interviews has not led to enough material or "sense" to use a case study approach. Possibly, if the author chose only two or three interviews, like Freud, he would have been able to construct a tighter theoretical framework. Again, this seems unfair. In addition, it was early decided not to use interpretative tests (such as Rorschach, MMPI) or try to superimpose theoretical frameworks on innocent conversations. Technically, many of these measures are not sufficiently validated in Hebrew, and if they were, substantial comparative data would be necessary to know if the "found character" was kibbutz or Kalamazoo. Also, kibbutz members and researchers advised that this form of testing would not be welcome or understood.

It was decided to use self-report measures as the main approach. Members reacted quite well to the approach and no serious drop in the desire to participate in the research resulted. The goal is to consider personality in Kibbutz Vatik in terms laid out by the members themselves. It is hoped that in the context of a larger body of ethnographic data this will prove helpful. Four aspects will be examined: (1) diversity and similarity among the members regarding personality characteristics and their attitudes towards personal development; (2) re-definition of social roles persons fill in different life stages; (3) the meaning system of the member; and (4) some psychological outcomes of membership, such as mental health, ego development, and life satisfaction. (Section 2)

The wider theoretical framework in which these four aspects are considered come from the writings of Erik Erikson. In his book, Insight and Responsibility Erikson notes: "I would posit a mutual activation and a replenishment between the virtues emerging in each individual life-cycle and the strengths of human institutions. In whatever way we may learn

168

to demonstrate this, virtue in the individual and in the spirit of institutions have evolved together, and are one and the same strength. We must fortify the concept of ego with insight into the nature of social institutions." (Erikson, 1964, pp. 152, 156, 148) He continues to define identity as "a persistent sameness in oneself and a persistent sharing of some kind of essential character with others" (p. 192) and to speak about stages of development whereby humans achieve greater integrity in their lives, so that social experience achieves satisfaction and significance for the person. (pp. 148 - 156)

Having examined the kibbutz as a social institution, certain aspects of identity and integrity will be explored as Figure 7A illustrates.

FIGURE 7A

Examining Identity And Integrity In Vatik

Identity, by examining:

A. Diversity and similarity in personality characteristics.

B. Diversity and similarity in attitudes to personal development.

C. How the kibbutz deals with significant identity changes (e.g. age).

Integrity, by examining:

A. Diversity and similarity in the meaning system of the members and how that fits with the nature of the kibbutz as a social institution.

B. Outcomes of kibbutz identity: life satisfaction, mental health, ego development.

The goal here is to describe some aspects of personality in Vatik and not to explore the dynamics of personality in the community. But another question immediately comes up. Shall we lump our descriptions together and imply that a kibbutz character exists? Oliver provides us with a pivotal guide-post:

> A central tension in any human society
> is the fact that culturally defined or
> general rules, ideology, or roles must
> be channeled through diverse human be-
> ings. Wallace has described this tension
> by suggesting that there are two ways
> of looking at culture and society: one
> as the "replication of uniformity," and
> another as "the organization of diversity."
> From the point of view of the "replication
> of uniformity":
>
> > the society may be regarded as cultur-
> > ally homogenous and the individual will
> > be expected to share a uniform nuclear
> > character. If a near perfect corre-
> > spondence between culture and individual
> > nuclear character is assumed, the
> > structural relation between the two
> > becomes nonproblematical, and the in-
> > terest of processual research lies
> > rather in the mechanisms of sociali-
> > zation by which each generation becomes,
> > culturally and characterologically, a
> > replica of its predecessors.
> > (Wallace, 1970, pp. 22-23)
>
> From the point of view of the "the organization
> of diversity":
>
> > Culture...becomes not so much a super-
> > organic entity, but policy, tacitly
> > and gradually concocted by groups of
> > people for the furtherance of their
> > interests, and contract established by
> > practice, between and among indivi-
> > duals to organize their strivings into
> > mutually facilitating equivalence
> > structures. (Oliver, 1976, p. 148)

Our viewpoint is that of the "organization of diversity."
While accepting Erikson's position that similarities will
probably be evident when aspects of the ego and aspects of

the kibbutz institution are compared, the stress here is
that the most plausible reason is that a wide diversity of
individuals in the kibbutz have some similar interests, practices, traits, ways of behaving, and reasons for acting.
The social agreement or the web of contracts we call "the
kibbutz" simply organizes this diversity.

The examination here is of statistical trends gleaned
from many kibbutz individuals, and it would be invalid and
wrong to call such statistical trends "the kibbutz character,"
since in practice it is very difficult to look at a variety of
human beings in Kibbutz Vatik and say, "These statistical
trends mean that they have underlying ways in which they are
constructed that are similar because they are kibbutz members."
The author doubts that kibbutz research (for the reasons noted
above) would ever find this since the kibbutz gave up trying
to produce a "kibbutz character," and anyone who actually
lives in a kibbutz for a year or more (vs. looking at measurements from a distance) could be expected to have as difficult
a time finding it. Nevertheless, our data are only suggestive
and require much further study before we really understand
personality in the kibbutz.

Personality Characteristics And Self Development*

Let us turn directly to the first aspect: diversity and
similarity among members regarding personality characteristics
and attitudes towards self-development. A semantic differential
self-description method involving 25 traits [Question 62] was
used. Members were asked, using the following scale, to "mark
the place closer to how you see yourself and not how you would
like to see yourself."

Friendly____ A   B   C   D   E ____Unfriendly

_____

* The self-report semantic differential measure was that of
Sherwood (1962, 1965). A few descriptive categories were added
to accommodate the population. This measure was used descrip-
tively and not as a measure of identity perception or mental
health. It is found in (Shaver, 1969).

To explore how characteristics are shared, the following approach seems most appropriate to the overview of Erikson and Oliver:

>Highly Shared Characteristics - where less than 5% of the population view themselves at one extreme (for example, position D and E) and 95% see themselves in a neutral position (C) or at the other extreme (D and E).

>Moderately Shared Characteristics - where less than 10% of the population view themselves at one extreme and the rest see themselves neutral or at the other extreme.

>Diversely Shared - where 20 - 40% view themselves at one extreme and the rest see themselves as either neutral or at the other extreme.

The outcome is shown in Table 26.

TABLE 26

Clusters of Personality Characteristics In Kibbutz Vatik

Highly Shared Characteristics

	A	B
Friendly	99.3%	.7%
Cooperative	99.3%	.7%
Fair	98.6%	1.4%
Responsible	98.6%	1.4%
Independent	97.2%	2.8%
Self-insightful	97 %	3 %
Affectionate	96.3%	3.7%
Happy Life	95.6%	4.4%

Moderately Shared Characteristics

Self-confident	94.3%	5.7%
Value myself highly	94.1%	5.9%
Skillful with others	92.5%	6.5%
Optimistic	91.9%	8.1%
Flexible	91.6%	8.4%
Have basic life beliefs	87.3%	12.7%
Decide on goals and achieve them	86.4%	13.6%
Democratic	85.9%	14.1%
Relaxed	83.9%	16.1%

Diversely Shared Characteristics

Does not care what others think	79.7%	20.3%
Active in social relations	77.2%	22.8%
Closed about inner feelings	73.4%	26.6%
Intellectual	73.2%	26.8%
Enjoy routine life	66.9%	33.1%
Express anger openly	65.5%	34.5%
At times not fully honest	62.4%	37.6%

A: Percentage of population identifying with characteristic
      or in middle position.

B: Minority percentage.

In one characteristic, that of Follower/Leader, a judgement was
difficult to make. 17.6% identified themselves as followers,
32.4% as leaders and 50% in the middle position.

Valid answers: Between 130 and 143 on all characteristics.

Missing answers: 15 - 28

While it would be unfair to call this distribution random, since all traits but one are shared by 60% or more of the population and two thirds of the traits are shared by 80% or more of the population, a substantial number of interesting traits are shared (as defined for the purpose of this description) according to human diversity. Analysts of kibbutz personality claim a "group mind" exists in the kibbutz, yet 79.9% of the members point out they tend to not care what other people think. The order of kibbutz life and the honesty of the perfectly poised kibbutz member are also commented on, yet almost a third of the population claim not to enjoy a routined life, while (62.2%) report not being fully honest at times. A fifth of the members are not afraid to admit they are not the kind to be active in social relations. Members seem to rate themselves higher on the best traits (being friendly, cooperative...). If it is true, this shows agreement on how the members think they should be. However, many of the traits which members diversely share would have to be distributed more widely if this interpretation is followed, i.e. one would expect members to rate themselves as more honest, less closed, more intellectual. So, regarding Oliver's concern that superorganic unities not be blindly defined, it is clear that substantial diversity exists in the population of Vatik.

The most meaningful way to look at these data is in the context of the large amount of diversity in attitudes and valuations already noted in the area of kibbutz institutions.* With this perspective, (and since wide diversity in attitudes was found there) the concept of Kibbutz Vatik as basically a social agreement "concocted by groups of people for the furtherance of their own interests" (Oliver, 1976, p. 148, p. 99) tends to make more sense. Similarities are evident when personality characteristics of members are compared. Given the strong lack of emphasis on uniform personality formation in the community, there is no reason to ascribe such similarity to "a kibbutz character." Further evidence in parts of this chapter will confirm this particular evaluation of the data. People are

---

* Because persons describe themselves similarly, that is no basis to claim that the underlying psychic dimensions and dynamics of their selves are also similar. Yet the author is aware that one could plausibly contend that Table 26 supports an opposite conclusion of greater uniformity in kibbutz personality.

different in some significant ways, despite strong tendencies
to favor certain traits; they tolerate and encourage diversity;
they avoid institutional mechanisms which would severely limit
human diversity (fascism, fanatical religions, ideological
purity) and they try to make the best of this mutual arrangement.

"How (are) the immense differences in humans along such
dimensions as age, sex, temperament and talent orchestrated
into reasonably constructive roles in common social settings?"
(Oliver, 1976, p. 148) This question is central for further
research. Now, we examine its relation to personal development
attitudes.

One difficulty with the "replication of uniformity" point
of view is that one has little reason to explore how different
people do in the social setting, for either everybody is
thought to be the same, or one posits that everybody should be
the same. (Oliver, 1976, chapter 7)

This leads directly to a consideration of the attitudes
of the members in Vatik to self-development, which further
confirm the "diversity" position. Donald Oliver states:

> There are two kinds of utopians:
> those who would create perfect social
> arrangements where various fallible
> human beings of different types and
> qualities will somehow live in harmony;
> and those who seek to perfect people who
> can live happy lives under almost any
> conditions.
> ...The underlying assumption (of the
> second position) is that within some
> relatively narrow range of ability and
> a large number of various human talents,
> people should all be pretty much the
> same. (p. 147)

Despite the fact that Kibbutz Vatik has distinct egalitarian goals, the members definitely do not accept this egalitarian credo of the psychologists. Personal development is
encouraged but few norms for it are made explicit. The frequent
comment is that: "People are not the same, although we try
to give equal conditions and opportunities." Certainly,
kibbutz child-rearing and education occurs in this light,
just as the same reason is used to justify kibbutz society:

175

"We try to eliminate the worst aspects of the child's life,"
and "We try to eliminate the worst human problems."

Members were asked their attitudes towards personal
development [Question 31], interpersonal understanding
[Question 49], interpersonal honesty [Question 47], personality change [Question 53], and handling personal problems
[Question 57].

TABLE 27

Attitudes Towards Self-Development

Question: What is important for a person who wants to
improve oneself and strive for personal development?

1.   It depends on every individual according to   60%
     one's own nature.

2.   Studies and improvement of one's pro-   28%
     fession.

3.   Reading and personal study.   16%

4.   More honest relationships.   5%

5.   Meditation and self-understanding.   4%

6.   Art.   1%

7.   Other.   3%

_____

Valid answers: 135   Missing answers: 23

Since some persons answered more than once, percentages
shown indicate percent of all persons answering who choose
that answer.

_____

Members overwhelmingly favor an "Each to their own" philosophy or studies. (A majority of the answers showed a relationship between the two, that is, "People should do whatever they
feel improves them, and one of the best opportunities is
studying---in the university, or self-study, or vocational
training.") Less than 10% of the members participated in
courses in yoga and transcendental meditation for which tuition
is now a member right. Although there is no large movement in
Vatik in this direction the road is considered open. This
is in strict contrast to the community's view of a younger
member's trip to a European conference on Guru Maharaj Ji.
His preoccupation with spiritual development was much criticized;

177

nevertheless, when he returned some months later, he was accepted back into the community despite some friction.

In response to a question about how much personality change is possible [Question 53],* 12.6% felt that you are born a certain way, 34.7% saw it possible to change many qualities and 52.7% saw it possible to change some qualities.

Avraham Yassour, a kibbutz member and expert on the history of the movement has said that "Even in the early days of the kibbutz, spiritual development and changing the personality was never a strong goal as it is in many 'utopian' communities today. There was a greater concern for improving social life in general. The kibbutz's concern for individual development was contained within the context of concern for the group and the community, which they hoped would provide a more natural environment for the development of the person than their past social settings."** (Personal communications)

---

* Valid answers 150 - Missing answers 8

** Achieving equitable social relations was a goal of the early movement, and interpersonal closeness was defined as part of this goal. The kibbutz cannot now be conceived as an interpersonal growth-oriented community. It is no coincidence that the point of view that "human nature is good and bad and the social arrangement is what has importance" is an opinion naturally open to dealing with a wide variety of people. On the other hand, it is the irony of the kibbutz that despite its radical communal beginnings, extreme interpersonal closeness and diversity this area is probably the place where diversity is not accepted. Group marriage, homosexuality, and serial monogamy are definitely not accepted in kibbutz life; in fact, homosexuality and group marriage would be actively repulsed. Visiting homosexuals have been repulsed in Vatik, although not asked to leave; this was certainly a factor in denying membership to one prospective candidate. While sexual diversity may be fine in general, one would be hard-pressed to find a stable, small community where a candyshop of sexual styles is accepted. The weight of anthropological evidence certainly seems heavy in this regard. (O'Neill, pp. 23-24) There may be a limit to the number of sexual styles human beings can tolerate if they live in community.

In addition, the communal village form probably does not provide enough fellowship for aged members. A recent study of the aged in the kibbutz uncovered that 25% of the men and 15% of the women presently have no close friends, while 19% of the men and 34% of the women spend tea time alone. (Wershow, 1973) This level of loneliness in an organic community such as the kibbutz is unexpected, and it merits further attention.

Nevertheless, when asked about personal problems,* only 6.7% felt it best for the person not to worry but turn to other matters vs. 93.3% who agreed it was best to confront the problem directly even if it diverts him or her from other matters. In a question [Question 49]** on the amount of self-understanding possible only 8.1% thought that most people's lives were determined by forces they cannot understand. 77.9% felt that most people understand themselves and the reason for their behavior and have a lot of control over their lives, while only 14% said, you try to live your life and not worry about such things.

Strong matters of personal concern are brought out into the open and discussed. Observation of the involvement of committee members, kibbutz administrators, and members of the confidential counseling committee in members' personal difficulties, supports Erikson's statement that the inner life and social planning are one. Members usually have "seen" each other's development through the years, and gossip aside, know people not their friends quite well.*** Nina's comment on a middle-aged kibbutz man illustrates the point:

---

* Valid answers 136 - Missing answers 22

**Valid answers 149 - Missing answers 8

*** Members at Vatik clearly have a problem with gossip, which they solve by sharing intimate information with only a few friends, thus keeping the rest of the community guessing. Often, members can "figure out" someone's life just through observation. Several members advised that the best solution is to develop a "thick skin" to preserve a sense of privacy when you know they can see something even your shell cannot hide. On the whole, little vicious gossip was found, although everybody seems to be known for some unfortunate incident in the "collective mind"; the author never failed to find a few pieces of information about almost anyone when the right atmosphere and the properly flexible informer could be found.

He was always quiet as he is now,
you know kind of hiding in corners.
I remember when I worked in the children's
house he was looking at something
I took away and he was very hurt. I
always sensed him as so fragile and
sensitive, and even today I think his
mate takes care of him and makes a lot
of decisions for him and is certainly the
stronger of the two.

Diversity is encouraged by favoring variable approaches
to self-development, by not defining a specific quality of
inner life as a goal of the kibbutz personality and by not
favoring an ethic of overwhelming personal change. No observable community dynamics (as in earlier religious utopian
communities) are manipulated to "form the personality." There
is no "kibbutz character." The kibbutz as an institution is
oriented towards an active awareness of personality issues;
and the small community character of the village lends itself
to a public awareness of each other's developmental stages.

Re-Defining Social Roles In The Personal Lifecycle

Kibbutz Vatik must re-define social roles to deal with
life-cycle changes and their effect on personality. The time
it took to perceive this necessity is related to the increasing
acceptance of human diversity in kibbutz life. The young
members of Vatik in the thirties came from a movement calling
themselves the "Young Guard." As one member said, "We thought
we would never grow old." Yonina Talmon develops this notion:

The movement's founders had dis-
sociated themselves from traditional
Jewish life and had rebelled against the
authority of their elders. Most members
were trained in radical nonconformist
youth movements whose values and patterns
of behavior had a decisive and indelible
influence on the emerging patterns of
communal life. The original revolutionary
ideology was reinforced by the personal
experience of rebellion. All this
glorified youth as full of potentialities,

180

> free and creative, and emphasized
> discontinuity. (1972, p. 167)

Now the old are old. Perhaps this explains the difficulty
of older members of Vatik in correctly perceiving the motivation and attitudes of the younger generations.

Talmon has described the unique kibbutz approach to
aging. (1972) It solves many problems by ensuring members
economic security, communal services in case of ill health or
infirmity, and the possibility of social participation. The
emphasis on youth-centered values of work, productivity,
and radical ideology, however, is a source of strain, along
with the older generation's loss of its position and authority
to the second generation. She analyzes and suggests the
changes aging brings in each of the areas of kibbutz life we
have studied. Wereshow (1973, p. 218) found the aging population in the kibbutz mostly still working full-time despite
the fact they had passed retirement age, enjoying their work,
in good health, well-educated but somewhat lonely because of
a reduction in family and group interaction. He found that
the senior population was not suffering as much as Talmon
suggested, mainly because his work was completed after the
critical years (during which Talmon's investigations were
carried out) in which the generational succession occurred
and the tension and difficulty of "handing over responsibility"
had passed. Rosner (1975) found both generations satisfied
with the pace of advancement of younger members, although
in some areas of kibbutz life (work and the economy) younger
members are more willing to take over than older members
willing to give up positions, while exactly the opposite is
true in other areas (social life, culture, and politics).
Nevertheless, the majority of the respondents for both generations felt there was no discrimination between generations,
although older members perceived that higher education is
still considered more suitable and necessary for younger members and is in a sense a special privilege.

"While the second generation does not deviate from the
basic values of the kibbutz,...differences between the generations are to be found in the interpretation of these values
and in the attitude towards different concrete mechanisms and
organizational patterns intended to implement them." (Rosner,
1975, p. 5) The study found few interest conflicts between
generations in the kibbutz attributing this to the large number
of rewarding positions, the high degree of mobility in jobs
and absence of material rewards for advancement, the gradual

181

withdrawl of veteran members from their positions, and the
fact that while members are to an extent in competition they
have a common concern in seeing the future of the community
assured. However, the issue of generational conflict will
require greater attention in the next few years, when
thousands of members will reach retirement age simultaneously.

In Kibbutz Vatik aged members spoke proudly of the
security they felt. They seem not to be threatened by the
"giving over" of responsibility and control. Perhaps
equality takes the sting out of this change. No members
are in outside nursing homes, or in convalescent conditions
in the kibbutz. (Some parents of members who came to the
kibbutz in their old age have their own apartments and receive
home care.) All members are encouraged to do some kind of
work despite their infirmities or difficulties.

Although age is not thrown away as in our society the
seeds of problems exist in Vatik. Aged members are often
stuck with menial jobs (laundry, kitchen, plastics factory)
and many are so happy to have a job that a low level of
concern is shown for the quality of that job. For example,
one senior member trained in one of the professions does
monotonous assembly line work in the plastics factory. Work
change is often a crisis for members over 60, especially so
when the member does not have skills which can be used in work
outside the kibbutz (most of the outside workers are senior
members). One member studied gerontology and set up a committee; a small hospital is also under construction in preparation for members who may need supervision by a community
medical staff. But loneliness of members whose children have
left the kibbutz or whose mates have died is often searing to
behold. For those who cannot achieve a vibrant life, the inner
quality of their life strikes no one especially.* The senior

---

* Many members think, "They have a hobby program and a reading
room, and the gerontological committee looks after them; if
caring for these people is settled, why should I add my
energy?"

182

member who is not sick or in special need gets few visitors
This problem is not being confronted creatively in Vatik,
despite the laudatory degree of basic social support that
exists.

A society's management of the aged stage is a good indication of its attitude toward the self. In the next ten years
almost half of Vatik's fairly stable adult population of
approximately 400 will be over 65. That is an aging problem
of staggering proportions which does indeed point up the attitude
of Vatik towards the self. The kibbutz does not try to control
the inner life as do other utopian communities. The social
hazard here is that Vatik does not have sufficient awareness
of or interest in the inner experience of members to work
actively against the problems of loneliness and depression
in old age. While Vatik will prevent the major and minor
inconveniences of old age, and insure a productive life, little
is done to provide creative social roles; this can only be
interpreted as a blindness to the issue of self-development
in general.

The Meaning System of The Member

It might now be helpful to look at some of the underlying motivational structures responsible for the meaning
system in Vatik. While members were asked about their attitudes
towards specific areas of kibbutz life and specific ideological
issues, it was decided to seek out "enduring or central clusters
of beliefs, thoughts, feelings which influence or determine
important evaluations or choices." (Shaver, 1969, p. 94)
Asking for opinions on cooperation or the standard of living
sought such beliefs only in the context of relevant kibbutz
issues. We were interested, however, to determine the phil-
osophical-ideological system of members in the context of the
range of values of humanity as a whole. Thus, the Charles
Morris Philosophy of Life Measure was used. (Morris, 1951,
1956) Morris, a Harvard philosophy professor, did an exhaustive
amount of cross-cultural research and theory-building to construct
a set of 13 paths of life representing the cardinal ideas
of the world's main philosophical-religious systems.

The text of the paths of life is contained in Appendix I.
Each member was asked to evaluate each path according to
whether he or she: 1) liked it a lot; 2) liked it; 3) was neutral

regarding it; 4) disliked it; and 5) disliked it a lot.
Then, she or he was asked to rank the four most significant
philosophies important to her or his life at the end of the
evaluation. Table 28 summarizes the results. The percentages
show the number of members who liked the path a lot or just
liked it.

TABLE 28

Philosophy Of Life Of Kibbutz Members: A Descriptive Summary

(7)	Unselfish Concern And Helping Others	92.2%	
(13)	Combination of Privacy And Social Involvement	91.4%	Very central
(4)	Self-Control	80.6%	Chosen by 75%
(9)	Cooperation In the Social Group	80.6%	or more of
(10)	Emphasis on Scientific Advancement and Active Progressive Solution of Problems	75.2%	members
(3)	Concern With Bodily Energy And Physical Work	74 %	Moderately central
(5)	Active Community Participation To Preserve Tradition	65.3%	Chosen by 50%
(2)	Enjoyment Of Life's Moderate Pleasures	55.2%	or more of members
(12)	Being An Instrument For A Social Or National Cause	44 %	Not central/ Not unimportant
(1)	Emphasis On A Quiet Inner Meditative Life	40 %	As many members preferred as did not prefer or were neutral
(8)	Seek Variety of Sensuous Enjoyments	36.4%	Insignificant Twice as many or
(6)	Individualism And Self-Concern	18.8%	more members re-
(11)	Passive Receptivity In Spiritual Peace	7 %	jected or were neutral as accepted it

Average Valid Answers Per Question (Av. of All Valid Answers):   122

Average Missing Answers: 36

N.B. To check for sloppiness in answering the question and to cross-
validate respondents' answers, Morris designed the measure so that
the final results for each individual question (shown by percentages
above) could be compared with the order of respondents' ranking of
all paths at the end of the measure. When both methods of evaluation
were used here the order of correspondence was almost the same.
Dividing the order of the paths into several groupings above expresses
two facts that must not be misinterpreted: first, at times there
were subtle differences in how members as a whole evaluated a path of
life vs. how they ranked it (e.g. the Unselfish Concern Path was
ranked second but evaluated first, while the opposite was true of the
Combination of Privacy And Social Control Path) so the ordering here
according to percentages should not be seen as absolute rankings but
more like groupings into very important to less important paths of life;
second, given the limitations of statistical validity, in this case we
cannot say that a path seen as important by 75% of the population is
less important in the overall ideology than one rated for example 80%.
The data here are descriptive and do not express an absolute picture
of a motivational dynamic; this should not be misconstrued.

The paths of life considered unimportant or very central make logical sense in terms of the other findings. on the attitudes and practices of members in Vatik. The importance of unselfish concern for helping others and mutuality (7) in the kibbutz social structure is clear. Despite increased wealth, the preservation of a communal economy and equality remains a central concern. Contrasted with this is the strong rejection of extreme individualism which, with self-concern, is rated as insignificant.

The tension between the individual and the community has been featured as the most explanatory concept of the dynamic change of, the social development in, and economic distribution in the kibbutz. Members rate a combination of privacy and social involvement (13) as very high in their overall philosophy. This emphasis, along with the obvious concern for mutuality and maintaining the cooperative structure in the kibbutz (which involves a certain amount of individual limitation) makes the highly central appearance of self-control (4) and social cooperation (9) not surprising.

So too, Work is the medium of community life in Vatik, and an ever-present emphasis on progress, upgrading production, social advancement, scientific innovation and higher education, is both indicated by the placement of bodily energy and physical work (3) and of scientific advancement and progress (10) as central philosophies.

Conversely, the concern for self-control and social cooperation as central values certainly predicts the insignificance of sensuous enjoyments (8), and individualism (6), just as the emphasis on activity and work (3) and active scientific and progressive advancement (10) predicts the rejection of passive receptivity and spiritual peace (11), and the not central but not insignificant (let's call it moderate) emphasis placed on a quiet inner meditative life (1).

While rejecting extreme individualism, and spiritual receptivity and deemphasizing the meditative life the members of Vatik do not exhibit the old pioneering concern for asceticism and sacrifice for the nation. Therefore, being an instrument for a social or national cause (12) is accepted by as many members as reject it. This is surprising in terms of the initial importance that Zionism and founding of the state of Israel held in the kibbutz movement. Today, the kibbutz exists as a part of the state of Israel, and is not in the vanguard; it takes its support of Zionism as a matter of fact commitment. The point is not that Israel or Zionism is not central but that it is not perceived as the first-order cause to sacrifice on a day-to-day basis.* On the other hand, while sensuous enjoyment is rejected by two-thirds of the population the reasonable enjoyment of life's pleasures ("a comfortable home, talking to friends, relaxation, good food") is a moderately central value in Vatik.

There is a strong tendency to preserve the community nature of the village; thus the moderately central importance of active community participation to preserve tradition (5) is no surprise. But, the preservation of the kibbutz tradition per se is not a central value. The stronger values of mutualistic concerns, individual-community tension concerns, which make the structure "kibbutz" worthwhile in the first place and preoccupation with self-control and cooperation, all rated as very central values.

Three issues need exploration before the substance of this analysis can be appreciated: first, how much can this meaning system be called a "kibbutz ideology" shared by all individuals; second, and related, what do Morris' comparative data on world cultures indicate about the uniqueness or banality of this system of values; and third, taking both issues into consideration, how central is a superordinate ideology to the kibbutz?

First, this loosely labeled meaning system is not "a kibbutz ideology" in the sense of being a psychological construct. It is an ideology in the sense of Mannheim and German sociologists of the twenties in that it "denotes any set of ideas that directly express the interests of the social group." (Berger, 1972, p. 345) There is a strong relationship between what the members of Vatik say and do in their community and the ladder of centrality which their evaluation of ultimate human philosophies expresses. But these are still only averages, and despite the large percentage of agreement on the central kibbutz philosophies, the lack of 100 percent agreement indicates

---

* Kibbutz members, when called, serve their country without comparison. Nevertheless, it can be said that the exciting dream of building the state and embarking on the Zionist voyage is not a day-to-day excitement as it was in those "first times."

that most members tend in the direction of various central philosophies but also have individual interests. There were many different combinations, some members made minor or major changes in the set of interests expressed by the collectivity which probably have some effect on their actions and decisions. This further buttresses a notion of Vatik as a community organizing diversity.

Second, and closely related to an assessment of whether a "kibbutz ideology" exists here, is a review of comparative philosophy of life data. Charles Morris has such data from the nineteen-fifties from India, Japan, Norway and the United States. Because of the time lapse these comparisons must be put into perspective. Nevertheless, some strong trends emerge. First, when the Very Central and Moderately Central philosophies of Kibbutz Vatik are compared with the American college student sample in the middle nineteen-fifties, while a difference in order is clear, the only philosophy from the kibbutz group that is not in the top philosophies of the American group is "seek variety of sensuous enjoyment" (8). Americans give this a high rating, not an insignificant rating as in the kibbutz. Also, "unselfish concern and helping others" (7) and "self-control" (4) are at the very bottom of the eight most preferred philosophies in the United States while they are at the top of the kibbutz group. This makes sense, given the difference in society. Most interesting, however, is that both the American and kibbutz samples reject the same group of philosophies as insignificant: "emphasis on quiet inner meditative life" (1), "passive receptivity in spiritual peace" (11), "individualism and self concern" (6), and to some extent "being an instrument for a social or national cause." (12). Only sensuous enjoyment is significant for the United States and insignificant for the population of Vatik.

Thus, while values of mutuality and self-control are more important to Vatik's members, (and the order is different) both the American and the Kibbutz ideologies share the same elements and concerns. In fact, the above philosophies (1), (8), (12), and (11) are at the bottom of the ratings in India, Japan, Norway, the United States and the kibbutz! Receptivity in spiritual peace (11), as expected from the influence of oriental religion, was far more important in Japan, and given the time in history (independence), being an instrument for a social or national cause is far more important in India, but neither is central in either country. In all cases, the

comparison is with college students in these countries who
were probably more steeped in the Western scientific and
intellectual traditions than villagers, monks and primitive
tribes.

Vatik has basically a Western ideology with an uncommon
de-emphasis on spiritual development (1), (11) that has until
recently seemed to typify development in the industrial West
and the aspiring East. This strengthens the focus on and
criticism of spiritual and creative personal development in
the kibbutz, but places that comment in the context of a
general Western trend away from spiritual values.* The
kibbutz looks more and more like a better social arrangement
to deal with the diversity of people and the elements of modern
society. In comparison to the lives some people live it may
be a utopia (no where) but it is a very human and normal
place.

Third, in conclusion: how central is a superordinate
ideology to the kibbutz? If this means, "Is there a central
set of interests in kibbutz society?" the answer is "Yes."
The members of Vatik have constructed a social fellowship
where local community interests and social, economic and

---

* When the "first times" of a small community pass and the religion
of "intentionality" (the pioneering effort) is worn down, only
a unified spiritual tradition can bring peace to the aged and
a sense of meaningful involvement to the members. The kibbutz
faces individual-community tensions which could become conflicts
that threaten its nature as a cooperative community. The
person-community harmony, to effect a community and resolve
conflicts, needs to take place in the context of a vibrant
cultural, symbolic, and religious system. Judaism is the
closest and most logical direction to find such succor and it
may represent, ironically, the salvation of the kibbutz's
problems. The reader is referred to two excellent works:
The World of Primitive Man by Paul Radin (1953) develops the
notion that primitive societies were fundamentally cooperative
communities with spiritual-ethical traditions that guarded
the individual-communal harmony and Kibbutz Judaism, a brilliant
book by Shalom Lilker which constructs with expert historical
and theological evidence the spiritual system the author
intuitively believes might rescue the kibbutz if ever insoluble
conflicts threaten. (1972)

189

political cooperation comprise an identity limiting less-sought-after possibilities and arrangements. Adam Smith's philosophy does not rule the day. But, if it means a tightly held ideology is strictly and rigidly defined, or that a striving for ideological purity which seeks to neutralize or liquidate human diversity neither is existent nor central in Kibbutz Vatik. The kind of group consciousness and certain belief that many extremist politicians and ideologues, left and right, identify as a pre-condition for a good society does not exist in Kibbutz Vatik. Here, it is the arrangements people enter into and their attitudes toward those arrangements that produce a good society. Since a good society is defined in terms of constant striving for an individual-community harmony, tension, differences, disagreements, and diversity are welcomed and valued as much as group consciousness or certainty or strict ideological control in other circles.

The risk here is obvious and represents the pivotal trade-off of kibbutz life: how can we be sure that these tensions, differences, disagreements, and diversity will not lead to a rejection of the elements that make a kibbutz a kibbutz? Maybe some people will say, "We do not need small-ness, or local community, or economic cooperation, or basic social or economic rights, or direct diffuse democracy, or collective child-care, or cooperative work, or collegial decision-making on values and new challenges, or to worry and try to confront the individual-community tension. Let's throw some of these away." That risk is the price Kibbutz Vatik pays its side of the trade to get one of the few village-oriented, small rural, cooperative, communitarian settlement systems in the world which attempts to achieve its aims without fanatical ideologies, political force, rigid religions, economic impoverishment, or limiting social diversity, individual choice and certain amenities of modern life. True, the kibbutz is not perfect in achieving all of these goals. The statement is relative and made in a carefully constructed factual context that has been carefully knitted for the reader. The risk that people will come along and use their personal freedom to destroy or radically alter the kibbutz as a kibbutz depends on whether the community delivers to individuals and to the member-ship the implicit promise of this social arrangement. If it does not deliver, talk of a superordinate ideology is just a mist. This is the crux of the issue of motivation structures or overt behavioral patterns (as Oliver defines personality). In the end is it all satisfying? The risk of commitment to the cooperative community is not experienced as a great sacrifice if the commitment pays off. Rosabeth Kanter's painstaking review of the nineteenth century cooperative community trend in the United States, helped to bring the discussion of these social innovations to this crucial question. (1972, pp. 62-74)

In conclusion, the lack of a superordinate ethical and religious meaning system complicates the achievement of personal integrity since despite common interests, uncommon philosophies are present. In addition, we cannot conceive of a "kibbutz personality" that organizes personal identity since the community's open approach to self-development and personal problems encourages diversity. Without a clear approach to personality and the self it is reasonable to assume that the community will not be able to deal smoothly with significant changes in the person's life cycle. Nevertheless, this difficulty in managing life-cycle changes may be a cost which the kibbutz pays in order to have a diverse approach to personality, personal development, and personal meaning systems. In other words, this may be a problem that deserves greater attention and some attempts at solution, but the problem itself may be insoluble. Throughout this section, we have been careful to discuss issues in personality, rather than try with our present data to provide an over-arching theory of personality in the kibbutz or alternative societies. Further research may prove that we are wrong in asserting that the "organization of diversity" orientation is the most reasonable way to describe the salient data we have. Alternative interpretations, will, however, have to contend with the overwhelming evidence of attitudinal diversity - presented in preceding chapters -, our ethnographic evidence, and the likelihood that a unique kibbutz personality is indeed possible in a community whose system of personal meaning is not very different from any other Western societies. In addition to these considerations, our general orientation also supports the "organization of diversity" viewpoint: We view the kibbutz as an attempt to put together some positive features of integrative small communities without the disadvantages of tradition-bound, religiously fanatical approaches which would conflict with a maximum of human rights and freedom of expression.

191

<u>Section 2.</u>   <u>Life Satisfaction, Mental Health, and Social</u>

   <u>Support</u>

     This section will summarize data on life satisfaction,
mental health, and social support in Kibbutz Vatik's population. Measures of self-report were used, so our central
goal is to present a summary of the members' own reports
in these areas. No baseline data from other populations or
societies will be used. The goal here is not to compare
Vatik with another society. We want to know if specific
groups in Vatik's population are at an advantage or a
disadvantage in terms of life satisfaction, mental health
or social support. Should we find that Vatik disenfranchises
a specific group of members, this would emerge as a major
qualification of quality of life judgements on the community.

Life Satisfaction

     The measure of life satisfaction, taken from Shaver and
Robinson (1969) is a straightforward question about happiness
that is used extensively in social psychological research.
Members were asked: Taking all things into consideration
how happy would you say your life in the kibbutz is [Question
50]?

TABLE 29

Life Satisfaction of Community Members

1.	Very happy.	9.9%
2.	Somewhat happy.	70.4%
3.	Not so happy.	19.7%
4.	Very unhappy.	0%

Valid cases: 142   Mean   2.099

Missing cases: 16

N.B. These data are from Sample 1 and thus cross-tabulations with social, economic, historical, political, and personal attitudes are presented.

More than 80% of the community report that they are fairly happy, and without comparative data it is reasonable to assume that this represents a fairly positive situation.

It has been shown, however, that the usual measures of happiness do not consider the person's situation and environment sufficiently. Some researchers have criticized such an approach as simplistic and tried to extend the measure. (Bradburn, Caplovitz, 1965) A further question was added regarding the achievement of life's goals and the source of responsibility for such achievement or non-achievement. Members were asked: How do you view the planning of your life [Question 59]? Of paramount importance in the responses was the distinction between whether goals were achieved and who interfered with goal achievement: the person or the kibbutz.

TABLE 30

Degree And Cause of Goal Achievement

What happens to me is my own doing
and I reach my goals   39.3%

What happens to me is my own doing
but I do not reach most of my goals.   25.9%

I do not feel that I have enough control over my life but it is not the
kibbutz that interferes.   31.9%

I do not feel that I have enough control over my life and it is often the
fault of the kibbutz.   3%

Valid cases: 135

Missing cases: 23

N.B. These data are from Sample 1 and thus cross-tabulations
with social, economic, historical, political and personal
attitudes are presented.

Happiness does not necessarily predict goal achievement in
Vatik. While about 80% say they are somewhat or very happy,
only 40% report that they are reaching their goals in life
and have control over their lives. A Satisfaction Index was
created from both questions, since it was found that both
responses were highly related.* According to this index the
population can be divided into three groups. The High Satisfaction Group (34.8%) report they are very happy or somewhat
happy and that they have control over their lives and reach
their goals without exception. The Middle Satisfaction Group
(33.6%) reported that they were somewhat happy, but that they

---

* The relation was very highly significant and extremely
strong (.93).

did not reach their goals while it was of their own doing.*
The Low Satisfaction Group (31.6%) report that they are not so
happy and that they do not reach their goals, either because
of their own fault or that of the kibbutz. A cross-tabulation
was done between these three groups and all the other variables
in this study (see appendix I) to determine what the exemplary
qualities, if any, of the three groups were.

While workers in industry and service branches in Kibbutz
Vatik show no significant differences among themselves
regarding work satisfaction, the results show that agricultural
workers differ significantly from workers in industrial and
service branches.

TABLE 31

Differences In Satisfaction Index By Workplace (in %)

Coordinator=C   I=Industry   S=Service   SR=Special
Worker=W   A=Agriculture   E=Education   roles (outside
                                                kibbutz)

Satis-faction	CI	WI	CA	WA	CE	WE	CS	WS	SR
Low	0	26.3	0	0	0	0	10.5	57.9	5.3
Middle	2.1	22.9	4.2	16.7	0	4.2	6.3	37.5	6.3
High	4.9	7.3	7.3	31.7	0	19.5	12.2	7.3	9.8

Valid cases: 108   Missing cases: 50

N.B. This table is read in the following way: a percentage
indicates the percent of that Satisfaction Group who were
in a specific work classification, e.g. 26.3% of all members
in the low satisfaction group were workers in industry.

* A small number of this group (6.8%) did report that they
were somewhat happy and they achieved their goals.

195

Workers in agriculture and education are more satisfied than
workers in industrial or service branches. This supports
the conclusions of Chapter III, Section 2 that the structure
of new work tasks in the kibbutz and their effect on the
members merits much more discussion. Satisfaction, nevertheless, bears no strong relationship to being a branch coordinator. In fact, the most satisfied members of the
community had a moderately significant tendency* to have less
influence in the kibbutz administration regarding personal
matters [Question 35] or kibbutz matters [Question 36].
Satisfied members do not hold more political roles or have a
greater overall sense of political participation than less
satisfied members. Satisfaction is not related to the
increased ideological strength of a member's initial motivation
to join. The opposite is true; the more satisfied the
member the less ideological were his or her reasons for
joining. This is a highly significant moderate tendency.

Except for the association with low ideological
strength at the time of joining the community, satisfied
and dissatisfied members show no significant differences in
terms of their social, economic, educational, political,
or historical attitudes.

---

* All evaluations of significance and the strength of association
or correlation in all cross-tabulated tables have been
standardized according to accepted statistical practice; for
example, the use of the evaluation "very significant" or
"moderate relation" refers to the same numerical value in
all parts of the text. See Appendix I on Statistical Methodology for a listing of the standard usages.

* The attitudinal variables used in this and the other cross-
tabulations for which results are reported in this section can
be examined in Appendix I, Outline of Quality of Life Data For
Kibbutz Research Project.

The significant differences between the three groups
are in the area of personality; there is a very significant
moderate tendency for the Low and Middle Satisfaction
Groups to describe themselves as more unconfident and unsuccessful, according to the Unsuccessful Unconfident -
Successful Confident factor. This is in contrast to the
High Satisfaction Group. The Low and Middle Satisfaction
groups have a moderate tendency to evaluate themselves poorly,
to be followers, to report unhappiness as a trait of personality, to report an inability to achieve goals as a trait
of personality, to be more pessimistic. Also, the more
satisfied the group the more social support they have. The
correlation between the satisfaction and social support
indices is very strong with regard to social support from
fellow workers, moderately strong with regard to social support
from friends, and moderately strong with regard to social
support from relatives. In each case the differences are
significant. Thus, elements of work place, personality
and social support are most associated with satisfaction
and dissatisfaction.*

Mental Health

It seems to make sense that happiness and mental health
would be related; some researchers have maintained that
happiness can be used to mean mental health and that self-
reports on happiness are as valid as the ratings of experts
based on psychological tests (Bradburn and Caplovitz, 1965).

> But the equation happiness = mental
> health is not perfect because it
> fails to consider the person's sit-
> uation and environment. An individual
> who has just lost a loved one in an automo-
> bile accident may be deeply unhappy but not
> necessarily mentally ill. In fact, in
> this situation, not to be unhappy would
> more likely indicate mental instability.
> Unhappiness then fails, too, as an effec-
> tive measure of mental illness.
>
> (Perry and Perry, 1976, p. 408)

---

* A complete summary of cross-tabulations of all variables in
this study by over 20 demogrpahic groupings, in short, a fine-
toothed comb check for stratification of all types, is available
from the author.

Psychologists criticize the variety of methods used to classify the mentally healthy and the mentally ill (Perry and Perry, 1976, pp. 404-426). Because almost no research exists in the kibbutz dealing with mental health, it was decided until further work in this area is done that it would be best not to use interpretive techniques either never before used in Hebrew or never before used in a kibbutz population. In addition the author is not willing to be in the position of evaluating the mental health of persons for them. Therefore, two additional measures based on self-report were used: the Anxiety-Depression Index, the Locus of Control Index. A third index, the Composite Mental Health Index, was a combination of scores on these two.

The Anxiety Depression Index which we used has been used before in Hebrew. (Tannenbaum, Rosner, 1974) It has been in frequent use and was developed concurrently by several American mental health researchers. (Cobb, 1970) (Caplan et al., 1975) (Gurin et al., 1960), (Spielberger et al., 1970) and (Zung, 1965) Anxiety and depression are commonly classified with the neuroses and are basic components of mental health evaluation. Common symptoms are sadness, anxiety, insomnia, withdrawal from everyday life and relationships with others, reduced ability to function, and generally agitated and unrelaxed behavior. (Perry and Perry, p. 409)

TABLE 32

Kibbutz Vatik: Members' Self-Reports On Anxiety

And Depression Index

1.	All the time.	0%
2.	Most of the time.	14.1%
3.	Sometimes.	84.9%
4.	Never	1%

Valid cases: 66   Missing cases: 90   Mean: 2.907

N.B. The index was not figured if <u>any</u> answers were missing. This accounts for large numbers of missing cases.

The most important piece of information here is that <u>no</u> persons say they feel the symptoms of anxiety and depression "All of the time." It is noteworthy, however, that 84.9% report that they have the symptoms of anxiety or depression "sometimes," and that only 1% report having such symptoms "never." Kibbutz members are not insulated from the symptoms of personal difficulty, nor are large numbers in Vatik persistently beset by anxiety and depression except 14.1% "most of the time."

Do certain groups in the community report anxiety or depression more than other groups? The answer is no. Anxiety and depression as defined are distributed without significant differences among the dimensions of sex, age, kibbutz group, political participation, white collar <u>vs</u>. blue collar work or work in a service <u>vs</u>. a production branch. Several studies (Hollingshead and Redlich, 1965), (Miller and Mischler, 1959), (Rushing, 1969), (Kohn, 1968) have found that in the United States mental illness and neurotic symptoms are highly correlated with the lower socioeconomic classes. But in Vatik, when differences between persons which might be related to classes - if indeed classes can be said to exist in the village - are checked against anxiety and depression, no such differences are found. The only qualification to the data of other researchers in this sphere is that there is also a tendency for higher classes to get better care, to be more successful in avoiding hospitalization, and to be diagnosed by a middle-class therapist; this may account for their lower incidence of mental illness. But since our data is drawn from self-report and not hospital admissions and since it is not based on the evaluation of a person other than the member, these matters need not concern us.* There are members in Vatik who report

---

* The other studies cited were based on hospital admissions and not self-report tests. They are presented to illustrate the point that social class has been traditionally related to mental illness, and not to initiate a comparison of mental health in the community and the outside. Obviously, such work must be done. We need, for example, to know if the small number of persons reporting anxiety or depression is really small when compared to other societies!

symptoms commonly associated with mental illness; the group
is small, and not identifiable as a specific disenfranchised
class. It would seem then that the social arrangements of
Vatik have eliminated specific disenfranchisement of groups
in the community, but that egalitarianism, cooperation and
community do not eliminate the occurrence of personal problems.

The second measure of mental health used was the Locus
of Control Index.

> It refers to the extent to which
> persons perceive contingency re-
> lationships between their actions
> and their outcomes. People who
> believe that they have some con-
> trol over their destiny are called
> "Internals"; that is they believe
> that at least some control resides
> within themselves. "Externals," on the
> other hand, believe that their outcomes
> are determined by agents or factors
> extrinsic to themselves. For example,
> by fate, luck, chance, powerful others,
> or the unpredictable.

Shaver and Robinson, 1969, p. 169

This method of self-report was used because it allows a
person to report on possible environmental and situational
factors affecting mental health and well-being (i.e. control
relations in the environment.) It was noted earlier that
common measures of happiness and well-being often tend to
avoid this issue.* The Internal-External Locus of Control
measure used in this work was adapted for Hebrew and the kibbutz
by Menachem Rosner and Uri Levliatan at the Center for Social
Research on the Kibbutz at Givat Chaviva from several scales
presently in use (Rotter, 1966), (Gurin et al., 1969) and
(Levinson, 1972). (See Appendix I, Question 66 for Locus of
Control Scale). Because of its sensitivity to social situation-
specific issues it has been related to psychopathology* (Smith
et al., 1971); minority group status (Battle and Rotter, 1963)

---

* For both reasons this index is included in Composite
Mental Health Index.

200

(Lefcourt, 1966), success and achievement (Bartel, 1969),
(Coleman, 1966) (Epstein et al., 1971). The basic question
asked in the twenty measures used is: Do you perceive a
connection between effort and payoff in your environment over
which you have some degree of control?

TABLE 33

Internal External Locus Of Control In Kibbutz Vatik

Externals
Little Control Over Outcomes   5.5%

Middle Group   51.5%

Internals
Great Control Over Outcomes   43 %

Valid cases: 128   Missing cases: 28

The results indicate a small minority of members who
consistently responded that they had little control over
their lives. The approach used in understanding life satisfaction and anxiety and depression was also applied here,
by asking if any particular group in Vatik could be singled
out as having less control over their lives. Locus of Control
has no significant relation to age, kibbutz group, political
participation, or work in a white collar or a blue collar job.

TABLE 34

Sex and Locus of Control

	Low	Middle	High
Male	14 %	30 %	56 %
Female	51.4%	16.2%	32.4%

Valid cases:	87	Significance:	.008
Missing cases:	69	Measure of Association:	.40

There is a moderately strong correlation between sex and low locus of control, and men and women differ very significantly. We commented in Chapter III, Section 2 that women, concentrated in the service branches of the kibbutz, have been complaining loudly about the lack of opportunity in the work place. Not surprisingly, low locus of control is also related to lower education and to working in the service branches of the kibbutz, with the same significant differences and the same strength of association.

A central conclusion of previous research has been that people are handicapped by an external locus of control response and that they become more oriented to emotional non-goal oriented responses to their situation. (Shaver and Robinson, 1974, p. 197) Possibly, this explains why women in Kibbutz Vatik do not claim to enjoy their work significantly less than men, although we know that they criticize the work options available to them. Our conclusions about women in Vatik differ markedly from those of Shepher and Tiger (1976) who report that women in the kibbutz movement not only choose less professional types of education, and choose to work in service-related areas, but also, that they are not dissatisfied with this situation. We propose that women in Vatik (and possibly the whole movement) are not reporting their level of dissatisfaction in their work and lives because they have consistently had to fit their expectations to a situation they perceive as beyond their control. This is in fact the central conclusion of Rosabeth Moss Kanter's research on women in work organizations.* (1976, pp. 427-428), (1977)

The significantly higher amount of external control perceived by women does not, however, correlate with lower satisfaction or more anxiety and depression in women. The women of Vatik do not seem driven to depression by this situation. The general equality of the sexes in the kibbutz may explain this crucial variation.

The third index of mental health is the Composite Mental Health Index which we created from the previous two indices. Theoretically, it was based on a measure of neurotic symptoms (Anxiety Depression Index) and a measure of environmental factors (Locus of Control Index) in order to accommodate the increasing criticism of standard measurements of mental health. (Perry and Perry, 1976, pp. 405, 407, 419) Table 35 shows the number of persons who consistently report feelings of mental health or emotional problems on both indices together.

---

* What remains unexplained as far as the kibbutz is concerned is the fact that women do indeed have equal social, economic, educational and political rights. They were far more equal in the pioneering days of the community and have moved from that position. The argument here is how that change occurred. Shepher and Tiger ascribe the change to a basic orientation in females which is bio-socially conditioned (1976) whereas Kanter, with whom we concur, says that more subtle organizational strains which women begin to perceive as inherent in the male-dominated situation begin to shape the behavior and expectations of kibbutz women (1976). Unfortunately, there is no research in the kibbutz dealing with such subtle strains, or the inferred fact that women do perceive - albeit very subtly - such strains.

TABLE 35

Composite Mental Health Index Frequencies

1.	0%		5.6%
		Low	
2.	5.6%		
3.	90.2%	Middle	90.2%
4.	4.2%		
		High	
5.	0%		4.2%

Mean: 3.491

Valid cases: 72   Missing cases: 174*

N.B. Increasing numbers indicate more mental health.

This is a good estimate of the number of persons who, by their own report, persistently experience problems in their mental health, 5.6% of the population of Vatik.   When both factors of mental health are taken into account, no specific group in Vatik is overrepresented. It is especially relevant that the founders and the hashlama do not differ, for the founders have consistently reported that the hashlama because of their experiences in Europe and World War II are more unstable mentally. Few members report no problems; the large majority have some degree of difficulty in achieving their goals in life or maintaining happiness. The main differences are that service workers are more unhappy and women have less control over their lives.

Social Support

Our description of life satisfaction and mental health is guided by a very strong desire to explain many sides of the issue. Persons can be happy and not achieve most of their goals. They can be unhappy but not report persistent anxiety and depression. They can be equal but feel they have little control over opportunity in their lives. They can be unhappy and not be mentally

---

* The large number of missing cases are because either question was left out of the index if any part was left out.

ill. A final element of satisfaction is social support. French (1976) and Caplan et al., (1975) explains that social support is a significant buffer for stress in the social environment. Their study of worker health showed that persons under stress could cope if they had social support without persistent symptoms of mental illness.

Table 36 illustrates patterns of social support in Vatik. The members were divided into three groups, High, Middle, and Low social support depending on how frequently they reported support from a series of persons in their environment. The criteria for dividing groups was a interval division of the six-part Likert answer to this question.

TABLE 36

Social Support In the Village

Low	13.6%	No one available for social support or no social support.
Middle	83.4%	A little or some social support.
High	3 %	Very much social support.

Valid answers: 66   Missing answers: 90

A sizeable number of members perceive that little or no social support is available to them. Are these members identifiable in any specific group? Cross-tabulations of sex, political participation, kibbutz group, education, workplace (service/production or white collar/blue collar) have no relation to social support, but we note that there are some significant differences in terms of age.

The young report significantly less social support than the middle-aged and the older members of Vatik.

TABLE 37

Age And Social Support

		Social Support		
Age		Low	Middle	High
Young	15-29	56.5%	21.7%	21.7%
Middle	30-45	8.3%	58.3%	33.3%
Old	45-70	16.1%	48.8%	35.5%

Valid answers: 66   Significance: .0007
Missing answers: 90   Measure of association .32
                           (Cramer's V)

Upon further checking (cross-tabulating ten-year age groups by social support), the age group with the lowest social support is between 15-19,* the high school students. The age group 20-29 reports almost as much social support as other groups but, having passed the early stages of adolescence and having passed the Israeli army experience and re-joined their community as members, their situation differs markedly from that of high school students. In high school 80% report low social support (52.9% in 20-29 bracket); 20% report middle social support (17.6% in 20-29 bracket); and 0% report high social support (29.4% in 20-29 bracket). The differences are significant but because the sample of very young members is small (only 27 in this instance) they bear further exploration. Differences in social support according to education show up, but can be traced to age. The problem with social support among high school students is of particular concern given the much touted advantages of the collective educational system. However, it must be kept in mind that, as pointed out in the chapter on education, adolescence and the kibbutz high school remain the weakest portions of that system in Vatik.

---

* There was no one under 15 in the study.

An overall correlation between the Social Support Index and the Composite Mental Health Index is very low and has no significance. While the presence of social support may buffer stress, social support in and of itself does not necessarily produce positive mental health. Social support was related to satisfaction strongly and significantly, and about 27% of those members who report satisfaction also report high social support.

Kibbutz Vatik has suffered in the quality and intimacy of social relations because of its historical development from the small commune to the village system. No specific group is disenfranchised from social support. This is evidently a mixed blessing. At a time when psychological counseling is becoming a greater concern in Vatik, when personal development is more accepted, and when clinics are more accessible to the village, methods of increasing social support for individual members may prove more workable forms of "therapy." (Srole, 1976)

Mental Illnesses And Mental Health Services

For several reasons it was difficult to garner the normal kind of mental health statistics used in Western society for a kibbutz. For one thing, the kibbutz in question and the movement as a whole do not report such statistics or keep track of them. When one homicide occurs in a population of 100,000 persons in 50 years the reasoning is obvious. Crimes are petty in nature and social events which occupy the realm of gossip and speculation for months or even years. There is no police force, no massive public to impress with increasing or decreasing figures.

Admission to mental hospitals is a commonly used criterion. According to the social secretary of the kibbutz only four admissions have occurred in 40 years. Three of these subsequently returned to normal life in the kibbutz; one remained in the hospital. This seems like a very small number and it is difficult to avoid the inference that this kibbutz has reduced serious mental illness in comparison with the outside society. Unfortunately, the research necessary to deal with that issue is still in process, and a brief description of the mental health services available to members inside the community would be more productive at this time. This description is based on interviews conducted with several kibbutz secretaries and members of the "counseling committee" in the village. These members all discussed examples in general terms and were specific only about the number of members involved and the type of problem.

An adult member can get counseling or more formal kind of help by going to the counseling committee made up of a nurse, a physiotherapist, a special educator, a psychologist, a gerontologist and the social secretary (ex officio). After noticing that a need exists (for example, a sudden change in behavior, the obvious onset of depression or known marital problems), members of this committee recommend to a member, his or her family, or the social secretary that a conference occur. This process grows organically out of the sustained contact between members and their knowledge of each other.

Counseling in most adult cases is arranged with someone not a member of the community. These conferences occur in strict confidentiality and the secretariat is not informed of the members obtaining assistance. Nevertheless, the social secretary has pointed out that counseling is far more accepted today than it was in the past when "members thought you were crazy if you wanted to talk to a counselor."

In situations involving children the possibility of family counseling is discussed in the education committee, sometimes along with the counseling committee; the child care worker or nurse often initiates the discussion and explains the situation to the child's parents. Several members noted that family counseling is being used more than individual counseling when children are involved, since the view of the problem as something objective that exists in the child is no longer accepted. Parents unwilling to participate in a formal helping situation are never forced to get involved in such help. Often, however, if the problem with the child repeats and is serious these parents slowly come around.

The community uses counselors, psychiatrists, psychologists, and social workers from the Kibbutz Education College at Oranim or several regional kibbutz-run mental health centers for child-related problems. If adult problems (like a death in a family, or a work-related depression) cannot be handled by community personnel, the kibbutz mental health centers, a private psychiatrist, or a national health program psychologist is used. Two years ago the kibbutz Federations began training kibbutz member social workers to provide advice and counseling to communities other than their own. Vatik does not participate in this program yet. The community does its own evaluation and referral; it finances the cost of mental health care from a general health budget or members' insurance, and usually uses kibbutz federation facilities staffed mostly by kibbutz members or carefully chosen staff who have worked with the movement over many years.

Except for the few critical mental health situations that required hospitalization, and child and family counseling, three independent informers stressed the following problems as repetitive: family problems relating to death and family crises where short-term support is needed, marital conflicts and young members' anxieties either before entering the army or after returning. One member who has knowledge of the committee's work over several years reports that formal counseling must be considered for one or two members a month. The number of members currently being counseled in all areas is less than 10, and in the year of the research another member associated with the committee reported that three persons were receiving long-term counseling that year.

Unlike bureaucracies that identify persons in need of help according to their "admission," the kibbutz identifies situations especially those involving children, before they become critical and makes immediate recommendations to arrange helpful support and proper arrangements. This would have to be taken into account if a statistical comparison of mental health services were made between the kibbutz and the outside society.

Conclusion

Kibbutz Vatik emerges from our examination of personality issues and life satisfaction and mental health as a community which has a diverse population and deals with personality, self-development, and meaning systems to encourage that diversity. It has a sizeable but small number of members who persistently experience unhappiness, symptoms of depression and anxiety, loss of control over their lives or mental illness, lack of appropriate social support and occasional counseling problems. While it organizes diversity to eliminate the grossest human problems and sufferings, it is often at a loss to encourage smooth transitions at important junctures in the life-cycle among its members (especially the aged and the adolescent). The most important finding is that no particular group in the community - except for women in relation to their work options - are psychologically disenfranchised. Vatik seems then to be a "good society" in that it does not purposefully create conditions for social disintegration or willfully exploit specific groups. No claim is made that it is a better society than any other.

The identity of members is not uniform and not beyond question. The achievement of integrity is not automatic. People have common interests but various approaches to their meaning systems. While who they are and what they believe in does not predicate the exploitation of one group by another, neither is it the automatic guarantee of a life free of problems and psychological tension. As in other areas of life Vatik evolves a homemade arrangement to deal with issues of mental illness, even though the most serious forms of crime and mental illness have been surprisingly sparse. The inner life and social planning are not one in the kibbutz, and one senses that a far more rigid structure would be necessary to achieve that dubious goal.

Epilog

Before concluding, the judgment of the membership of Kibbutz Vatik on their community as a totality will be considered. For after all is considered the life is theirs and they know it intimately. So, instead of examining each area of life separately, we chose to ask the membership to evaluate the community by listing its most serious problems [Question 29], and its least problematic areas. Table 38 shows the results.

TABLE 38

Serious and Non-Serious Community Problems*

N.B. % indicates percentage of sample choosing that answer. Since members were asked for a maximum of four answers the distance between percentages has the meaning, not their size.

Serious	Problem	Non-Serious
39%	Low standard of work norm.	9%
37%	Loss of ideology.	5%
25%	Personal problems of members.	20%
18%	Unsuitability of members who have same rights as others.	18%
32%	Inequality.	13%
2%	Protexia (or favoritism).	28%
9%	Privileged use of cars.	24%
35%	Generational relations.	12%
15%	Relations between the members.	10%
14%	Collective education.	10%
9%	Standard of living.	28%
17%	Disagreement on norms.	3%
14%	Hired labor.	13%
4%	Richness of kibbutz among poverty of neighbors.	17%
7%	Excessive influence of one group.	17%
27%	Lack of normative discipline.	3%
2%	Oppression of women.	22%
15%	General lack of order.	13%
4%	Dissatisfaction with Secretariat.	5%
2%	Dissatisfaction with Committees.	4%

Serious problems:	Valid answers: 140	Missing cases: 18
Non-Serious problems:	Valid answers: 87	Missing cases: 71

211

TABLE 38

(Continued)

* The main way to check the accuracy of these evaluations was to compare the problems members considered most serious with the problems they considered most non-serious since a contradiction in both judgments would indicate that the question was not accurately answered. Also, since members were asked to rank their four choices, the rankings in each question were compared with the final results, i.e., the work norm, which in final analysis was considered the most serious problem, was also considered one of the least non-serious problems and was also ranked in the first place by a large number of members, who answered that question. The list of serious problems meets these criteria, and the results are intentional and accurate. Because of the closeness of the percentages for those issues indicated as problems they will not be ranked in the final results since they may mislead the reader into thinking that K is the central problem of the community when it is really a serious problem.

The most serious problems are: the low standard of the work norm, the loss of ideology, inequality, generational relations, personal problems of the members, and the lack of normative discipline. It is interesting to note about what members are mainly complaining here. Very few members or only a moderate number (2-9%) complain about the functioning of kibbutz institutions or its delivery of basic services and rights: protexia, privileged use of cars, the standard of living, dissatisfaction with the secretariat, dissatisfaction with the committees, the excessive influence of one group, the oppression of women. The orientation of this author has been that Vatik functions fairly successfully and the membership basically supports the way the community is put together. The standard of living is growing and tolerable; there is no sense that one group has control over the kibbutz or that central administrative institutions do not have the community's good at heart. Despite certain problems with the status of women regarding locus-of-control they are not viewed as oppressed, and despite the obvious and upsetting inequality in some areas of Vatik, the privileged use of cars is not a fundamental problem, probably because the community does have a fairly equitable car pool, outside workers who use personal cars must announce thier trips beforehand, and a free bus ticket policy throughout all of Israel is in force for all members. Even the richness of Vatik despite the stark poverty and the reeking incompetence of social welfare in a development town just a few miles away does not concern members much. They have little concern about the functioning of the kibbutz vis-a-vis this aspect of the outside.

About a series of other problems that concern a moderate number of members (15-20%) there is some contradiction. Almost an equal number of members view these as serious problems as do not: the personal problems of members, the unsuitability of members who have the same rights as others, the relations between the members, collective education. Since the check for accuracy in the evaluations for the most serious problems showed that their estimation was intentional, there is no reason to assume here that members are contradicting themselves. Rather, the assumption will be that some members view these as problems and others do not. What is relevant is that the difference is expressed in almost equivalent terms! About these moderate problems the following are tentative interpretations. Maybe those who have personal problems or come into contact with them often iew them as more important. Possibly the point behind a concern (and a lack of concern) that there are members unsuitable to be in the kibbutz and benefit from its life indicates that some members think the flexibility of recent years has led some

individuals to take advantage of collective institutions. Maybe
members (and here the percentage is quite small, 10%) who have
experienced bad personal relations themselves see this as a concern. As for collective education the dissatisfaction with the
functioning and planning of this area of Kibbutz Vatik was outlined in a detailed manner in the chapter on education. Now
let us return to the most serious problems.

If any common thread characterizes them most it is the individual-community tension. The weak work norm was consistently
criticized in the interviews as a serious difficulty and is
characteristic of the primal way we have defined the dilemma of
Vatik: Where are the limits, when you re-arrange individual and
communal obligations, beyond which you lose more than you gain in
a trade-off? How can you change and make trade-offs and yet
keep the limits in clear sight? The loss of an ideology that was
at one time ascetic, under emergency conditions (the founding of
the Zionist state and local military defense) and more closely
tied to a definite world view (socialism) is a problem because
that ideology once spelled out those limits.*

The central and very emotional concern with inequality is
the most heated daily expression of the confusion over limits
from both our point of view and that of the members themselves.
Generational tension is a sign that the confusion about limits
(and the passing of old limits - pioneering ideology) involves a
friction between old and young. Indeed, when a cross-tabulation
is done by age, older members perceive loss of ideology as a
problem significantly much more than younger members. This does
not mean that they are right and the younger members are the cause
of this lack of limits. While the concern here with the passing
of the old ideology is more dear to the senior members, they
participated and participate the same way in bringing about the
new circumstance. However, some of this tension is possibly
due to the separate problem of the social roles of the senior
members. The author conjectures that a good deal of this personal
difficulty may come from tension and struggle persons experience
related to the dilemmas the community is undergoing. The previous

----

* Please remember that when we speak about the loss of ideology
we mean the loss of the original pioneering ideology. As indicated earlier the loss of this pioneering ideology by the
middle-aged members and the younger generation is a myth perpetu-
ated by the older members and has little basis in fact.

section presented a format for this interpretation. The evaluation of Kibbutz Vatik's problems by its members then tends to give credence to what has been called the central dilemma of limits, and trade-offs, in the village.

To gain more insight into what members thought about the quality of life when they had to list criteria in general, they were asked: What are the criteria you use to evaluate the quality of life in a kibbutz? [Question 37] The reasoning behind this question was that attachment to particular problems of Vatik might cloud over some of the more fundamental judgments of the membership. The results are shown in Table 40.

TABLE 40

Quality of Life Criteria In Order Of Preference

Relationships between the members.	80%
Good cultural and social life.	65%
Social stability (in kibbutz terminology means number of members departing or staying).	55%
Equality.	50%
Extent to which many different and varied needs of members are met.	50%
Standard of living.	40%
Inner Democracy.	38%
Order - The rules of the Kibbutz are enforced and not ignored.	27%
The strength of the political ideology.	18%
No hired labor.	18%
Readiness to help other kibbutzim.	15%
Attachment to the Kibbutz Movement.	14%
Political involvement at large.	11%
Absorption of immigrants.	9%

Valid cases: 144   Missing cases: 14

Despite the passing of "first times" intimacy the social relations among the members, what has been called here the net of social agreements, is what most members see as characterizing the kibbutz. The importance of culture, to which our data point with great import, is heavily emphasized also. Members evaluate their quality of life according to some clear external criteria, how committed

people are to staying or leaving. It has been noted previously
that the kibbutz, as the author views it, is really built to
dynamically experience individual-community tensions, and that
few buffers (religion, strong purist ideology) exist to hide such
tension. Closely related are strong concerns by the members that
a good kibbutz has equality and the needs of individuals in balance
with the collectivity. Equality is another external and undoubted
way to know the cooperation is working and is not a farce. The
extent to which many different and varied needs of members are met
in the collectivity is one of the strongest and most recent criteria
applied throughout Vatik and the kibbutz movement as a whole.

The standard of living, inner democracy, and order of kibbutz
regulations are moderate concerns of less than half of the kibbutz
membership. Our interpretation of this is double-edged: first,
in and of themselves as central criteria they would not really
determine this phenomenon "kibbutz" that is being described; and
second, they can be seen as consequences of achieving what is most
important, as criteria to the membership. It must also be added
that political authoritarianism and poverty, and the breakdown of
all order (law-breaking, chaos, crime) are three phenomena with
which Vatik has never had problems.

Some cause for alarm, however, is found in the realization
of how little the membership is concerned in the larger political
scene. True, there are impressive numbers of kibbutz members in
the Israeli Congress and the Cabinet, but the criteria for evaluating the kibbutz as an institution place very little emphasis on
the strength of its political ideology, its political involvement
at large, the absorption of immigrants (considered a prime national
goal in Israel), and its use of hired labor. The seriousness of
the rejection of the basic socialist notion of self-labor by plac-
ing hired labor so low as a criterion cannot be overemphasized.
It is partially outweighed by the actual situation of hired labor
in Kibbutz Vatik, which is minimal and going further in that
direction (for complex economic and ideological reasons, and because the Kibbutz Artzi Federation looks down on this in its
member kibbutzim). Nevertheless, even the potential acceptance
that hired labor is not an important element in evaluating a kibbutz, rings a strong note of hypocrisy. Finally, the low emphasis
on the attachment to the kibbutz movement and the readiness to
help other kibbutzim indicates a fact that has been known for a
long time. The kibbutz movements started by drawing themselves
along political lines and because mutual aid between such communities was a necessary prerequisite to their survival. Since
the pioneering days have passed and the kibbutzim have really not
represented strongly extreme differences in Israeli politics, the

reasons for the federation and mutual aid between kibbutzim have to do with matters of survival more than substantive matters of ideology.

This then is Kibbutz Vatik. Its social arrangements and its budding tensions and dilemmas.

CONCLUSION

In Sociology As An Art Form, Robert Nisbet says:

> It occurred to me a number of years ago while I was engaged in exploration of some of the sources of modern sociology that none of the great themes which have provided continuing challenge and also theoretical foundation for sociologists during the last century were even reached through anything resembling what we are today fond of identifying as "scientific method."....Of course science is concerned with problems, with questions rooted in empirical observation as well as reflection.... The great harm of the present consecration of method, including theory construction, is that it persuades students that a small idea abundantly verified is worth more than a large idea still unsusceptible to textbook techniques of verification....The error is, as I have several times stressed, the belief that techniques peculiar to mere demonstration of something can be utilized also in the discovery of something. Deeply rooted in all such works is the delusion that the creative imagination works logically, or should work logically with everything neat and tidy....Finally, although the really vital unity of science and art lies in the ways of understanding reality, we should not overlook the important similarity of means of representing reality in the arts and sciences. We are familiar of course with the portrait as it is found in painting, sculpture and also literature. Portraiture is an ancient and universally recognized form in the arts. So is landscape which we see so widely in painting, but also in

> literature and music....A great deal of what
> is most important in sociology consists of,
> in effect, landscapes... (1976, p. 7, 8, 18, 21)

The aim of this work was to portray and evaluate the quality of
life in Kibbutz Vatik. Anthropological and social psychological
methods were used together.

The goal of Kibbutz Vatik has not been reached, because its
goal is a process, not utopia or the elimination of problems. The
community is experiencing many strains in the following six
areas of life.

Socially, the village has made the transition to normal life
without human diversity presenting an insurmountable problem.
Diversity has, in fact, helped to flavor the inevitable and
necessary attempt to constantly upgrade the job of balancing
individual and communal issues. The "outside" presents a stressful boundary problem. The social arrangement whereby some members work outside lends itself to inequality and jealousy, and
no clear approaches exist in this area. Vatik has diluted social
support for all members and runs the risk that in many situations
committees, extended families and intimate friend groups will
not reach all members. Members may tend to assume that a new hobby
program or a committee will alleviate the increasing loneliness
of the aged when they crave a selfless visit that cannot be
institutionalized!

Historically, the farm can no longer hope to reap the benefits of existing in a special historical period when "pioneerism"
and "self-sacrifice" and "dreams of a new society" dilute human
diversity and make the apportionment of resources much easier.
That time is long past. But change, especially under the guise
of technology, may be a recurrent sweat. Clear norms for its
introduction and influence on many hidden aspects of the social
milieu do not exist and are not being formulated with enough haste.
The kibbutz traded the power to freeze time when it decided to
opt for human rights and social flexibility.

Economically, inequality is the constant tug at Vatik's
existence. It is a small problem, with potentially large consequences if the concern about it reaches divisive proportions.
(The violations are not serious, and probably will not be for
the foreseeable future.) Since productivity and profit have become more resourceful the necessary connection between a simple
life and an equal community has been broken. However, their
original connection may not have been just a shotgun marriage.

Many members are very suspicious of the intimacy of affluence and egalitarian economic cooperation. A simpler approach to human needs and a simpler approach to productivity (by introducing ecology into production through self-sufficiency and profit through environmental impact) may make the long-term achievement of equality more possible.

As for work, too many members work for the sake of doing the job and are not evaluating their work task and role to insure the greatest amount of individual satisfaction. Awareness of the socio-technical aspects of work and broad-based attempts to help every member structure their work role will make this central area of life potentially less stressful. Possibly the absence of direct (vs. diffuse) and frequent democractic participation in some workbranches is related to this buckling. Women, concentrated in service branches and receiving less higher education, and the aged, willing to continue to sacrifice in their graceful transition, require immediate attention in the sphere of work.

Politically, the seizing of power is as little a threat as its maldistribution. The guaranteed vibrancy of culture was traded for the absence of a rigid religious spirit and structure. Diffuse participation is constantly being tugged at by the lack of a sufficiently involving non-goal-oriented celebration of community fellowship. Packaged culture plies the oar of democracy. The influence of a stable ethical system - like Judaism - is a close source of the "peace that surpasseth understanding." Ethical wholes are important in dilemma-laden situations.

Educationally, the kibbutz high school strains every nerve of the individual-communal dialectic. It is the potential breeding ground for polarization over the function of kibbutz society and the orientation the community should take about outside technical knowledge. If the technical inefficiency and the social efficiency of the high school are not tolerated together, the community may start socializing members for the wrong society, a Gesellschaft of some other name. The older generation must recognize the strain caused on the young by a condemnation of all their ideology when it is the pioneering ideology they mainly lack. Providing more cross-age support, more political participation of teenagers, more possibilities for new relationships to answer their slight problems of social support may relieve some of the tension of adolescence. We know too many cases of selfish kibbutz parents who are degree-hungry for their sons and daughters and through this express negatively their doubt about the educational efficiency of the community. In the childrens' houses, staffing problems abuse the unique method of education.

Personally, Vatik has much influence but little power. The conditions for personality are plentiful and their improvement can only enhance the changes people have to find happiness. The community is committed to not controlling or coercing the inner development life of members. Still, despite laudable achievements in the area of mental health and providing classless satisfaction, little is really understood about how members pose deeply personal questions in relation to the collective. The special strain of some women's sense of powerlessness and the clear tendency to dissatisfaction in old age must be fielded.

These stresses and strains are real. On the other hand, they cannot be seen out of perspective. Vatik has a unique set of clear, stable life arrangements based on volunteerism. The community's structural arrangements are unilaterally built for social fellowship, mutual aid, economic cooperation, diffuse power and informational networks, and visible non-exploitive labor. Education has an evident set of values and an enduring view of "the good life" in which they apply. The community has a school, but the community is a school. The social policy function of education, then, is effectively integrated with the population and the place which can benefit most from all the methods of learning and teaching employed. Thus, the setting of the landscape encourages a high quality of life by fairly efficiently organizing social functions. The channeling of human potentialities in Vatik's institutions is "consistent with basic needs of personal security and support," but also presents "breadth and looseness of cultural and social form." (Oliver, 1976, p. 104)

This is not enough. A consistent advantage of Vatik is the attempt to work for an urban-rural mix, a median social form that respects individual development and social fellowship. The functions of the kibbutz are not based on coercion or stressful socialization. They mix and attempt to balance both elements of Gemeinschaft and Gesellschaft. In this sense, a good quality of life avoids both extremes. The presence of stresses and problems is a sign of health, although health is not a sign of utopia. The dual culture dilemma of Vatik's members is widespread and systemic. As long as the members succeed in using this thing "kibbutz" as a common language, to integrate the opposites, a common landscape to blend the light and the dark aesthetically, the likelihood is high that people will continue to have a good quality of life. That means that the kibbutz will continue to deliver basic human needs without gross inequalities, without violating human rights, without crime, suicide, rampant mental illness, organized alienation, or massive dependence on some federal bureaucratic maze of programs. The contrasts of the

220

landscape involve trade-offs which exact good prices. A high
quality of life is not automatic, but the experience of a good
life is within reach given that the collective does not promise
absolute spiritual peace and interpersonal harmony. A society
with no problems can go in two directions: it can be privatized
so that persons are not aware of problems and thus do not have to
confront them in the fellowship. (Bureaucracies, budgets, and
paper-pushers do that.) Or, it can be a "herd," a community
where total identification is pushed, awareness strictly controlled, and confrontation over issues limited by the vested interests of power groups. Both possibilities of social problem resolution bastardize the function of education. The first make
it into a supermarket; the second make it into a church.

Vatik takes "the middle path." The word is 'takes,' not
'achieves.' "The central challenge for creating positive culture in modern society is inventing social institutions in which
the primal and the modern elements of human evolution are allowed
expression in non-destructive and non-competitive ways; or in
which modern and primal are integrated within a common setting."
(Oliver, 1976, p. 128)   Vatik is a good try.

Integration of functions does not eliminate the possibility
of exploitation. In Vatik diversity and equality of opportunity
and satisfaction are surprisingly compatible. A truly classless
society has been developed which avoids the invidious sufferings
of human difference. All pains are not avoided. The plight of
some women and the mounting aged population requires serious attention. In short, the kibbutz is not a bad society. The village is not structured to disenfranchise.*

Whether the kibbutz, according to Vatik's portrait, is a
better society than the cities, towns, neighborhoods, suburbs and
settlements of Western society is a question for comparison. This
has not been our goal. However, the kibbutz represents a median
form of cooperative community which may be timely at this point

---

* Possibly the reason why we emphasize human differences so much
in social and educational policy is that manageable social settings
really do not exist in most of Western society anymore. If social
action does not matter, then the narcissism of individual development and the creation of individualized pay-out government programs becomes the new common medium. (Lasch, 1976; Oliver, 1976,
pp. 165-166)

in history, given the mounting "rust of progress" (Nisbet, 1976, p. 115). Vatik gives us many good reasons to view microcommunity as a realistic alternative palatable to a large diversity of human beings.

Education is not simply a matter of schooling, but rather an atmosphere and an organization of skill and value transfer brought about by the environments we construct for human settlement. The more unintentional such environments, the more divorced from a balance of modern and primal human needs, the more the function of efficient schooling and child development is banalized.

National social policy need not be based solely on governmental programs which redistribute taxes into bureaucracies to pick up the pieces of "the rust of progress." Rather, the cooperative community form is evidence that broad, reasonable and efficient methods of organizing human settlements and communities exist which improve life by providing some basic elements of social form: smallness, fellowship, cooperation, work, participation, community-based learning, supportive personal atmosphere. Developing countries also need not copy the ways of western society. The cooperative community form has been applied in Tanzania and promises to become a viable alternative for the return to the native African form of "familyhood."*

The kibbutz also proves that the exigencies of human freedom and human dignity make the achievement of utopia a price too high for civilization to pay. Utopia is indeed nowhere, but viable alternatives do exist.

Only a poem is a fitting ending.

---

* The UJAMA experiment popularized by President Julius Nyere has met with mixed success. While a few voluntary model communities exist, there is evidence that the government has tried to force this alternative on other parts of the population.

Prospective Immigrants
Please Note

Either you will
go through this door
or you will not go through.

If you go through
there is always the risk
of remembering your name.

Things look at you doubly
and you must look back
and let them happen.

If you do not go through
it is possible
to live worthily

to maintain your attitudes
to hold your position
to die bravely

but much will blind you,
much will evade you,
at what cost who knows?

The door itself
makes no promises.
It is only a door.

Adrienne Rich
1962

APPENDIX I

RESEARCH BACKGROUND, MATERIALS AND METHODOLOGY

This Appendix consists of the following parts:

Schedule and Conduct of the Research

Statistical Methodology

Outline of Quality of Life Data for
Kibbutz Research Project

The Questionnaire

Schedule and Conduct of the Research

The settings of data collection for this study were two kib-butz communities in Israel. The first, a "pre-test community," was chosen at random. It was a smaller kibbutz, young, experi-encing some of the elements of the "intimate kibbutz" with which young communities are associated.

The community upon which the investigation is based was chosen in consultation with Dr. Menachem Rosner, Director of the Center for Social Research on the Kibbutz and Director of the Institute for Kibbutz Studies, University of Haifa, and Dr. Joseph Shepher, Chairman, Department of Sociology, University of Haifa, also of the Institute for Kibbutz Studies.

The parameters of the investigation were presented to a council made up of the social secretaries (the main executive officers) of the kibbutzim of one federation (the HaShomer HaTzair Federation, with 70 member communities) by Dr. Rosner, and sub-sequently we received invitations from several communities. Kib-butz Vatik (a pseudonym) was chosen over the others because it had all of the following qualities: a) it is relatively large (550 members) as opposed to very small communities; b) it included a mixture of agricultural and industrial plants (as opposed to communities leaning heavily in one direction); c) it was founded in 1936 and is considered "established" by the federation (as opposed to newer communities or very wealthy communities with inordinately successful industrial plants); d) it contains mem-bers with an ethnic mix and a broad distribution of age groups; and e) the community is not on a national border and has not seen military action in any war or skirmish since its inception. These qualities are considered those of a "normal kibbutz" and are rep-resentative of most kibbutzim. The preceding criteria were con-sidered significant in establishing the relevance of the study for the United States community.

The sample is a purposive sample of the membership. The fifty members interviewed were chosen in consultation with the previously mentioned sociologists and a sociologist of the Center for Social Research on the Kibbutz who resides in the community under study. Members were chosen to be representative of all age groups in proportion to population and representative of both sexes.

The sociological data of previous studies as well as the impressionistic data of previous descriptions of the kibbutz were used in constructing the research program, which was carried out during a fifteen-month period in Israel from July, 1973 to October, 1974 and again from December, 1975 to February, 1976. This work involved an ethnographic study of the community under consideration based on extended participant-observation while living in the community. This stage of the study was composed of the following components:

* residence of three months in Israeli city and suburbs for comparison with the kibbutz community.
* intensive study of Hebrew to allow a level of fluency for research and university study of kibbutz research.
* close work with the two senior Israeli kibbutznik (i.e., members) sociologists involving a review of existing research, planning the study, and reviewing problems of kibbutz investigation.
* living at a "pre-test" kibbutz community (not the community studied) in order to "pre-test" the interview schedule and examine relevant socio-economic and political issues along with personality issues (in a tentative manner) which would be dealt with in the questionnaires--this involved full work responsibilities in the community for a period of five months with research conducted after work hours.
* studying with kibbutz members (mostly social workers) at the Ruppin Institute for the Kibbutz, the kibbutz system's agricultural and vocational college, a course on kibbutz society given by Dr. Joseph Shepher.
* visiting various kibbutz communities and parts of the country to compare kibbutz and non-kibbutz life, and life in various villages and towns in the country.

As can be clearly seen, the author was engaged in an extensive preparatory program for the research. Following this period of approximately eight months, the main body of research was conducted at Kibbutz Vatik. This research involved the following components (on both field trips):

* participant-observation, living and working in the community as a full-time "member" for a period of six months, including complete access to meetings, archives, newsletters and related economic and social documents.
* interviewing members both for extensive non-structured data and for a purposive sample of fifty members using a directed questioning schedule regarding their commitment and attitude to the community and participation.
* administration of extensive questionnaires (in Hebrew).
* regular (bi-weekly) consultations with kibbutz member sociologists, especially Dr. Joseph Shepher and Dr. Menachem Rosner.

226

* preparation in consultation with kibbutz sociologists, community members and the results of a pre-test, of a comprehensive Hebrew questionnaire on attitude and commitment to the community, participation in the community, philosophy of life, philosophy of social structure, and personality.
* administration of the questionnaire to a representative sample of 108 members in addition to the fifty members participating in interviews.
* collection of historical material regarding developments in the social, economic and political structure from the community archives.
* initiation of a project to document the community photographically, beginning with slides.
* directed observation (note-taking, survey sampling, random checks) of various significant sectors of the community; for example, the political structure (through directed observation of general assembly meetings - their conduct, agenda, aftermath and continuation).
* collection of unpublished English material and published but significant Hebrew research on the kibbutz communities for reference in further stages of the research.

This phase of the research was completed in October, 1974. Since that time, the author has been involved in the following activities:

* translation of some of the interviews.
* review in more depth of previous research in order to summarize methods of analysis of social, economic, political and psychological material for use in the analysis phase.
* preparation of an extensive bibliography on the kibbutz and cooperative communities.
* teaching the experimental course Kibbutz Society and Community at the Harvard University Graduate School of Education in order to refine methods of presenting the community to people.
* extensive translation of materials (interviews, newsletters, meeting minutes, Kibbutz Federation documents) and reviews of pertinent recent developments on the kibbutz in the press and in the Congresses of the various kibbutz federations.
* computerization of all questionnaire data, construction of a computer program, generation and analysis of more than 10,000 pages of data according to the Statistical Package For The Social Sciences System (Nie, Bent and Hull, 1970).

During the most recent phase of the research Professor Avraham Yassour of the University of Haifa, a visiting associate at Harvard University, a kibbutz member and social historian for the kibbutz movement, acted as a devoted advisor to the author. Close and intense consultations continued with Dr. Joseph Shepher and Dr. Menachem Rosner, both of whom are, in addition to their positions (described earlier) at the University of Haifa, kibbutz members.

Statistical Methodology

Several technical matters must be dispensed with before examining the implications of members' diversities for quality of life. They are: aspects of quality of life under discussion, the method of analysis, the type of data under consideration and, finally, the statistical standards used to report the data.

"Quality of life" is taken to include attitudes, commitments and satisfactions. Attitudes of members toward each of the areas of life discussed in Part One were sought. One aspect of human diversity and the quality of life, then, will be whether different people view Kibbutz Vatik differently. Commitments here refer mainly to ideological motivation for joining or staying in the kibbutz and the commitment of oneself to participate in the community's activities (political participation). Satisfactions refer to the consequences specifically in terms of "good" or "bad" of a member's life in the community: standard measures of satisfaction, work satisfaction, happiness, mental health and anxiety-depression were used. The following section outlines all questions and indices (groups of questions) and factors (lumps of questions which statistical analysis proved measured one coherent factor) for which data were computed.

To avoid purporting to find something that is not actually there and to dispense with the possibility that slight tendencies in the data found now might mistakenly be used as the basis for sweeping conclusions later, very strict methods of statistical judgment were used and their use was standardized throughout this research.* Since the data in use will rely on cross-tabulations

---

* One of the most serious problems in the use of statistics in social research is that researchers often use different sets of words to refer to different relationships. For example, a "moderate tendency" is used by different researchers for different statistical meanings. Worse, however, is the possibility that once such usages are standardized they are still misunderstood. (continued on next page)

two kinds of statistics are of importance: measures of association and measures of significance. Measures of significance tell us whether there is an association between one variable and another (for example, sex and mental health) that has a high probability of not having occurred by chance and is probably related to an actual pattern in the population. The chi square statistic gives this information, and we have used conservative chi squares of .05 or greater (Hayes, 1973; Kerlinger, 1973; Marascuillio, 1971). All references to significance will be standardized as in Figure 8. Measures of association tell us how strong the relationship is and, to avoid an overemphasis on numbers to the detriment of the ideas under discussion, all references to the strength of the relationship between two variables will be standardized according to the method shown in Figure 8.

(* continued from preceding page)
For example, let us consider the cross-tabulation between sex and ideology. If men and women are associated with ideology without significant difference the measure of association would be very low. That would mean that both groups do not differ in how they are associated with the variable, ideology. If, however, they do differ significantly, and the strength of the association is .30, then one examines the table to find that a comparable number of men and women have low, middle and high ideology. The data show that far more men than women have high ideology. .30 tells us the strength of this association. In this case (and others under discussion) an association of .30 only accounts for a difference of 9%. (The approximate rule is to square the measure of association if it is comparable to r.) This means that only approximately 9% more men have higher ideology than women. It does not mean that men are more ideological than women, or that maleness causes ideological attachment. It simply states a relationship between two facts. The important fact is that while realizing the tendency exists (some more men are more ideological) one must continue to take into account that it is only 9% more for men than for women. Some researchers try to build global theories on mediocre correlations, and this is a disservice.

Figure 8

Measures of Association and Words Used to Describe the Association
and Measures of Significance to Describe Significance of Difference

Association*

.00 to .19	inconsequential
.20 to .29	very weak
.30 to .39	moderate
.40 to .49	moderately strong
.50 to .69	strong
.70 to .99	very strong
1.00	a direct relationship

Significance**

.05 to .01	significant
.009 to .001	very significant
.0009 to .0001	highly significant
.0000	very highly significant

* Since cross-tabulation data and not correlations are in use here the specific
statistic in use is Cramer's V, which is however comparable to Pearson correlation coefficient. Eleven other statistics were figured for each table and used
in the analysis to buttress this one.

** The meaning of significance measures is simple: .05 means that there were 5
chances in 100 that the differences in the data in the sample occurred by chance,
.009 means nine chances in 1000, .0001 means one chance in 10,000, obviously a
very good bet that the data reported show significant differences in the sample
which have a high probability of indicating differences in the population itself.

Outline of Quality of Life Data for the
Kibbutz Research Project*

I. Attitudes

History and Change - referring to issues discussed in Part One,
     Chapter I

     Question 27 - Attitude to Technical Innovation+
     Question 28 - Criteria for Technological Innovations+

Social - referring to issues discussed in Part One, Chapter II

     Question 27 - Types of Unacceptable Behavior+
     Question 24 - Attitudes to Studies Options
     Question 25 - Evaluation of Attitudes to Studies Options
          in Community (Flexible...)
     (Question 26 - Attitudes to Work Options)
     Question 42 - Social Relations With Neighbors
     Question 44 - Attitude to Source of Social Control+
     Question 45 - Attitude to Group Involvement+
     Question 46 - Attitude to Group Criticism+
     Question 55 - Attitude to Social Problem Resolution+
     Question 56 - Attitude to Social Cooperation+
     Question 29 - Evaluation of Main Problems of Kibbutz+
     Question 37 - Criteria for Evaluating Quality of Life in
          Kibbutz+

Economic - referring to issues discussed in Part One, Chapter III

     Question 16 - Attitude Toward Personal Cars+
     Question 17 - Reasons for Favoring Personal Cars+
     Question 18 - Reasons for Not Favoring Personal Cars+
     Question 19 - Attitude Toward Limiting the Living Standard+
     Question 20 - Reasons for Limiting the Living Standard+
     Question 21 - Attitude to Preferred Sources of Kibbutz
          Investment+
     Question 22 - Attitude Toward Simplicity+
     Question 34 - Attitude Toward Inequality+
     Question 38 - Attitude Toward Comprehensive Budget+
     Question 39 - Reasons for Favoring Comprehensive Budget+
     Question 40 - Reasons for Opposing Comprehensive Budget+
     Question 41 - Attitude Toward Economic Affluence+
     Question 43 - Attitude to Hired Labor+
     Question 56 - Attitude to Social and Economic Cooperation+
     Index**   Individualist-Communitarian Economic

<u>Work</u> - referring to issues discussed in Part One, Chapter II
and Part Two

Demographic - Previous Workplace+
Demographic - Classification of Previous Work According to
    Area and Role+
Demographic - Present Workplace+
Demographic - Classification of Present Workplace According
    to Area and Role+
Question A - Whether Person Works in His or Her Profession+
Question B - Whether Person is Satisfied With Above
    Circumstance+
Question 11 - Work Enjoyment
Question 12 - Evaluation of Aspects of Work+
Question 13 - Use of Talents in Work
Question 14 - Responsibility in the Workplace (Degree and
    Attitude To)+
Question 15 - Evaluation of Work Relations
Question 15B- Number of Persons in Work Group+
Question 26 - Attitude Toward Work Options
Index   Work Satisfaction Index**

<u>Political Participation</u> - referring to issues discussed in Part
    One, Chapter IV

Question 2 - Frequency of General Assembly Attendance+
Question 3 - Reasons for General Assembly Attendance+
Question 4 - Reasons for No General Assembly Attendance
Question 35 - Influence in Personal Matters
Question 36 - Influence in Kibbutz Matters
Question 54 - Degree of Overall Participation in Kibbutz+
Question 29 - Place of Political Considerations in Evaluation
    of Kibbutz Problems
Question 37 - Place of Political Considerations in Criteria
    for Quality of Life in Kibbutz
Index   Actual Index of Present Sense of Political
    Participation**
Index   Historical Index of Political Participation
    Through the Years**

<u>Educational and Cultural</u> - referring to issues discussed in Part
    One, Chapter V

(Question 24 - Attitude to Studies Options)
Question 32 - Advantages of Collective Education+
Question 33 - Disadvantages of Collective Education+
Question 58 - Attitude Toward Education in the Kibbutz
    High School+

Question 29 - Place of Educational Considerations in
    Evaluating Kibbutz Problems+
Question 37 - Place of Educational and Cultural Considera-
    tions in Criteria for Quality of Life in the Kibbutz+

Personality - referring to issues discussed in Part One, Chapter VI

Question 31 - Attitude Toward Personal Development+
(Question 35 - Amount of Influence in Personal Matters)+
Question 47 - Attitude Toward Interpersonal Honesty+
Question 48 - Attitude Toward Human Nature+
Question 49 - Attitude Toward Personal Understanding of Self+
Question 61 - Attitude to Source of Human Diversity in
    Success+
Question 62 Parts 1-25
            Self-Description According to 25 Descriptive
    Pairs of Adjectives
Question 63 Parts 1-13
            Attitude Toward 13 Philosophies of Life
Question 64 - Ranking of Four Most Important Philosophies
    of Life+
Question 29 - Place of Personal Problems in Evaluating
    Problems of the Kibbutz+
Question 37 - Place of Personal Problems and Fulfillments in
    Evaluating Criteria for the Quality of Life in the *
    Kibbutz+
Question 53 - Possibilities of Personal Change+
Question 57 - Attitude Toward Personal Problems+

II. Commitments

Question 8 - Reasons for Joining Kibbutz Originally
Question 9 - Reasons for Staying in the Kibbutz
Index**   Ideological Strength Index for Joining
Index**   Ideological Strength Index for Staying

Commitments to Political Participation (see above, Political
    Participation)

III. Satisfactions - referring to issues discussed in Part One,
                      Chapter VI

        Question 50 - Degree of Happiness of Life in General
        Question 59 - Degree and Cause of Achievement of Goals or
              Non-Achievement
        Question 51 - Degree of Tiredness
        Question 52 - Degree of Sickness
        Question 60 - Degree of Normlessness
        Index**   General Satisfaction Index
        Index**   Work Satisfaction Index
        Index**   Social Support Index
        Index**   Locus of Control (Over One's Life) Index
        Index**   Composite Mental Health Index
        Index**   Anxiety-Depression Index

IV. Demographic Variables

        Demographic   Age
        Demographic   Sex
        Demographic   Years in Kibbutz
        Demographic   Membership Status
        Demographic   Amount of Education

* Categorical variables of a non-continuous nature and dichotomous are marked with a +. When referred to in the text the statistic Cramer's V from the Statistical Package for the Social Sciences System is used as a measure of association between these and other variables. Where the relationship between diversity (e.g., being male or female and giving a particular reason or category more or less than another group, the accepted statistical procedure is used, i.e., the dichotomous variable is quantified by associating a +1 if it was observed and a 0 if it was not observed. Then it is possible to divide all persons using that category into two groups (those that chose the category or group scored as 1 and those that did not choose the category or group scored as 0) and do a statistical cross-tabulation between another variable and having chosen this particular category. Observations in the text on such associations often refer to the fact that "There is an association between being male and a moderate tendency to choose such and such." This language does not indicate causality, only an association between the frequency with which a member fell into the group male (for example) and the frequency with which a particular category was chosen. (Marascuilo, 1971, pp. 394-415) The evaluation of the tables is based on the method suggested by Kerlinger (1973, p. 172) for evaluating categorical data. The statistic Cramer's V, which is an adjusted statistic for Phi for N X N tables, is comparable in meaning to the Pearson product-moment coefficient. (Nie, 1972, p. 276)

** Indexes were explained in the text.

*** Following are components of indices not given in the text. The General Satisfaction Index is made up of questions 50 and 59. The Work Satisfaction Index is made up of questions 11, 12, 13, 14, 15. The Political Participation Index Historical is based on the number of committees, special public roles, number of times in special public roles (secretary, farm manager, branch coordinator, treasurer, executive committee) and question 5. The Economic Index is made up of questions 16 and 19. The Ideological Strength Indices were computed from questions 8 and 9.

Research On Communities

The purpose of this research is to understand the ideas and feelings of many different kinds of people who live in kibbutzim. In the past most work in English on the kibbutz has stressed a general description of the kibbutz, instead of a very specific personal description painting a realistic picture of all the complicated problems, the advantages of life on kibbutz. Also, it is hoped that from this work persons who are living on and trying to build communities around the world will find some inspiration, some learning, some realism that will help them build their communities and made more sense out of their lives. This questionnaire will be used to supplement a large number of personal interviews conducted on a small and a large kibbutz.

Age_____ Male_____ Female_____ Number of years in kibbutz_____
Work branch_____ Work outside the kibbutz (if any)_____
Committees or management positions_____
Previous work branch_____ Which profession did you want to study?
_____

Directions: Most of the issues or questions here offer multiple choice answers. Place the number(s) in the space to the left of each question, and write in your ideas if they are in the other category under that space. Give one answer to each question un-less otherwise indicated.

1.   From what group are you in the Kibbutz?
      1.   The founders
      2.   The Hashlama (1940's)
      3.   Another garin or hashlama
      4.   Son or daughter of the kibbutz
      5.   Came without a group and joined alone
      6.   Came from another kibbutz through marriage
      7.   Came from the outside through marriage
      8.   Other

2.   How often do you go to the general meeting?
      1.   Almost every general meeting
      2.   Frequently
      3.   Seldom
      4.   Never

<u>If you answered 1 or 2 to question 2 consider the following</u>
<u>question</u>:
3. Why do you go to the general meeting? Mark all answers
    relevant to you.
    1. Because as a member I must participate in kibbutz
        democracy.
    2. Because I want to have influence on decisions.
    3. It is interesting.
    4. It efficiently solves the problems of the kibbutz.
    5. I personally enjoy speaking and participating.
    6. Other.

<u>If you answered 3 or 4 to question 2 consider the following</u>
<u>question</u>:
4. Why don't you go to the general meeting? Mark all answers
    relevant to you.
    1. Every member need not participate in the democracy.
    2. I do not have enough influence.
    3. It is boring.
    4. It does not efficiently solve kibbutz problems.
    5. There is personal tension which I do not like.
    6. Other.

5. Please list the date of the last time you filled the
    following position in the kibbutz:
    Member of mazkirut_____ (indicate if mazkir, gizbar, or
    Head of a branch _____ farm manager, or chairman of
    Member of a com-   a committee)*
      mitee
    Head of a com-   _____
      mittee
    Other (e.g.madrich)_____

6. Do you work in your profession? _____yes _____no
    Are you satisfied with this situation? _____yes _____no
    Describe your education by listing the appropriate answer:
    1. Grammar school.
    2. High school (finished).
    3. High school (unfinished).
    4. Technical school or course.
    5. University (finished).
    6. University (unfinished).
    7. Other.

* Mazkir is the kibbutz social secretary; mazkirut is the
executive committee of the kibbutz; gizbar is the treasurer
and madrich is the guidance counselor in the school or youth
movement.

7. Are you a full member of the kibbutz?
    1. I am a member.
    2. I am a candidate from outside Israel.
    3. I am a guest.
    4. I am in the army.
    5. I am in the mosad.
    6. Other.

8. At the time in the past when you decided to join the kib-
   bitz, what attracted you to join then? List your reasons
   from the first most important reason, in order, to the
   reason of lesser importance for you.
    1. I liked the place, natural surroundings.
    2. Education of the children, which I like.
    3. Zionism and the building of the State of Israel.
    4. Personal reasons.
    5. Socialism - building a just society.
    6. Lack of pressure and absence of race after money and
       material comforts.
    7. I was attracted by agriculture and the kind of work.
    8. I was educated to this in the youth movement.
    9. I grew up here and have ties to the place.
   10. People I wanted to be with, friends and groups were here.
   11. I decided to come because of my marriage (partner wanted
       it).
   12. I am mixed in and invested here and simply can't go.
   13. It would have been too hard for me outside the kibbutz.
   14. I am mixed in and invested here and don't think of leaving.
   15. Other.

9. We recognize that sometimes over the years peoples' reasons
   change. Today, what are the most important reasons you live
   in the kibbutz. List your reasons from the most important
   to those of lesser importance.
    1. I like the place (surrounding environment).
    2. I have ties to the kibbutz (family, emotional..).
    3. Socialism - building an alternative and just society.
    4. Personal reasons.
    5. Education of the children.
    6. People I want to be with, groups and friends are here.
    7. Zionism and the building of the State of Israel.
    8. There is a lack of pressure and absence of race after
       money and material comforts.
    9. I am attracted to the kind of work (agriculture or other
       work), that I can do here.
   10. The influence of my education in the youth movement is
       still strong.

238

    11.   It would be too hard for me outside the kibbutz.
    12.   My partner wants to live here.
    13.   I am established and really cannot consider leaving.
    14.   I grew up here and this my home.
    15.   I am established and do not think of leaving.
    16.   Other.

10.   This question was especially constructed for young second-generation members and not used in our results.

11.   How do you feel about your work?
    1.   I enjoy it very much.
    2.   I enjoy it much.
    3.   I enjoy it very little.
    4.   I almost never enjoy it.
    5.   I hate my work.

12.   Following are reasons why people do or do not enjoy their work. List the different reasons that are relevant to you in the spaces.
    1.   The work is enjoyable in itself.
    2.   The work is not enjoyable in itself.
    3.   I feel I accomplish something.
    4.   I don't feel I accomplish anything.
    5.   A sense of professionalism.
    6.   My work lacks a sense of professionalism.
    7.   I like the relationships with the people.
    8.   I do not like relationships with the people.
    9.   Other

13.   Can you use your talents and potential in your work in a way you like?
    1.   Yes, a lot.
    2.   Sometimes.
    3.   Very little.
    4.   Never

14.   Do you have responsibility and enjoy having it in your work?
    1.   I have responsibility but do not enjoy having it.
    2.   I have responsibility and enjoy having it.
    3.   I do not have responsibility but would enjoy having some.
    4.   I do not have responsibility and do not want any.
    5.   I would like responsibility but would not enjoy it.

15A. How would you describe the relationships between you and the people that work in your branch?
   1. Very amicable relations but they are not my friends after work (do not drink tea with them).
   2. Very friendly and some are my friends after work.
   3. Correct relations, not friendly, not unfriendly.
   4. The relationships at work are not friendly.

15B. Do you work alone or with others?
   1. Alone (only person in branch)
   2. With others in a team.
   3. Around others but basically alone.

16. If the kibbutz had enough money to buy a car for each family would you vote for it?
   1. Yes
   2. No
   3. I don't know

17. If you answered yes to question 16, why? List all relevant answers.
   1. If we have the money the kibbutz can do everything.
   2. I myself would like a car.
   3. People need the opportunity to travel more outside the kibbutz.
   4. The kibbutz as a socialist society must prove it is as good as others.
   5. A car is an essential need today and must be satisfied.
   6. Other

18. If you answered no to question 16, why not? List all relevant answers.
   1. The kibbutz needs a certain distance as a society and the car would insure that distance from the outside.
   2. It would be a waste of money to maintain all these cars.
   3. I cannot even imagine this as a possibility.
   4. A car violates the simplicity of our lives.
   5. Other

19. Should the standard of living of the kibbutz be limited?
   1. Yes
   2. No
   3. I don't know.

20. If you think the standard of living of your kibbutz should be limited, why? Mark all relevant answers.
   1. Only the amount of money available is the limit.
   2. First, our social responsibility to help others who have less, is the limit.
   3. It should be limited so we do not become too materialistic and bourgeois.
   4. More possessions make members more competitive.
   5. The more material things the less you can devote to ideas.
   6. Other

21. What should be the criterion for distributing the kibbutz's wealth?
   1. More private property for members, but according to equality.
   2. More common projects for the whole kibbutz to enjoy (culture, building.. pool, moadon).
   3. It should go mainly into investment in the farm, for further production.
   4. Other.

22. Should simplicity be the basic value of the kibbutz way of life?
   1. Yes, definitely.
   2. No, it is not important now.
   3. No, but extravagance should not be allowed while recognizing everyone is different.

23. When you look at your kibbutz which cases of deviant behavior do you see as a violation of kibbutz values? List all relevant answers.
   1. Lack of mutual help.
   2. Persons who do not work well or skip hours.
   3. People who refuse to do "toranut," or "misloach."
   4. People who abuse outside sources of money.
   5. People with personal habits I find disagreeable.
   6. Dishonesty.
   7. I do not consider these important things.
   8. Other

24. In your opinion what should be the limit of your kibbutz's consideration of individual inclinations and desires of the members regarding higher education?
   1. All studies are ok, all requests should be positively accepted.
   2. All studies are ok, and people should go according to a tor (line).

3. All studies are ok, but the kibbutz should try to persuade people to study what it needs.
4. All studies are ok, but those who study what the kibbutz needs should get preference.
5. All studies are NOT ok, unless the kibbutz needs them.
6. All studies are NOT ok, since I am not sure a lot of higher education is a good idea.
7. Other.

25. Do you think that your kibbutz is too flexible or hard regarding members' inclinations about their education?
1. Too flexible.
2. Flexible.
3. Hard.
4. Too hard.

26. In your opinion what should be the limit of your kibbutz's consideration of individual inclinations and desires regarding work?
1. All work preferences should be accepted.
2. All work preferences are ok but the kibbutz must try to persuade people to do what it needs.
3. All work preferences are ok but often a member will have to compromise for a year or two before he gets what he wants.
4. The needs of the kibbutz are the main criterion of work possibilities.
5. Other

27. Assume that there are two alternatives for your kibbutz: one to relieve most of the members of physical work, and introduce machines (technology) which the member must supervise
OR
two, to continue to do most of the work physically given the kibbutz would lose no money with this present system. Which of these two alternatives would you vote for?
1. To introduce the technology, the first.
2. To continue the present system, the second.
3. Other

28. When the kibbutz has the opportunity to introduce technology what should be the main criterion? List all relevant answers.
1. Economic advantage and increased production.
2. The possible positive effect on the members.
3. The possible negative effect on the members.

29. Below are many problems of the kibbutz people talk about.
    Choose the four you consider the biggest problems of your
    kibbutz and place them in order from the most serious to
    the less serious problem.
    1. Low standard of work ethic.
    2. Personal problems of members.
    3. Loss of ideology.
    4. Large number of members not suitable for kibbutz life.
    5. Inequality, regarding standard of living.
    6. Protexia, persons who effect decisions through
       favoritism.
    7. Privileged use of cars.
    8. Conflict between the generations.
    9. Lack of good relationships between the members.
    10. Problems with communal education.
    11. Low standard of living and comfort.
    12. Difficult for member to get satisfaction from mazkirut.
    13. Lack of agreement on norms of behavior: what is allowed
        and good, what is not allowed and not good for the kibbutz.
    14. Hired labor.
    15. The richness of the kibbutz and the poverty of its
        neighbors.
    16. Excessive influence of one group of members on decisions.
    17. Work problems of women, and discrimination against women.
    18. Work problems of men.
    19. Difficult for a member to get satisfaction from the
        committees.
    20. Other

30. Which of the problems listed above are NOT serious problems
    in your kibbutz; in fact, you feel your kibbutz has done a
    lot successfully to solve them? List the four choices below.
    _____
    _____
    _____
    _____

31. What is important for a person who wants to improve himself
    and strive for personal growth and development?   From your
    perspective?
    1. Studies and improvement of profession.
    2. Reading and personal study.
    3. More honest relationships.
    4. Meditation and self-understanding.
    5. Art.
    6. Other

32. Below are different dimensions of communal education. In
     which areas do you see strong advantages of communal educa-
     tion in your kibbutz? List all relevant answers.
     1.   The children's society - education in peer groups.
     2.   The training of the staff in the children's houses.
     3.   The training of the mosad staff.
     4.   Relationships of metaplot with parents.
     5.   Early education of children.
     6.   Childhood without worries.
     7.   Type of studies in the mosad.
     8.   Seriousness of mosadniks (high school students).
     9.   Separation of parents from children.
     10. Relationships of metaplot with children.
     11. Other

33. Concerning communal education which of the above do you con-
     sider problems? List all relevant answers.

     _____
     _____
     _____
     _____

34. What do you think of equality in your kibbutz?
     1.   It is no problem.
     2.   It is a problem, but nothing can be done.
     3.   It is a problem, but there is no atmosphere here for
          more rules and order in this regard.
     4.   It is a problem which can be solved by more money.
     5.   It is a problem but greater order and rules AND more
          money is the solution.
     6.   Other

35. What kind of influence do you have in making decisions that
     relate to you personally in the kibbutz?
     1.   Very much.
     2.   A lot.
     3.   Some.
     4.   Little.
     5.   None at all.

36. What kind of influence do you have in making decisions that
     relate to the public life of the kibbutz?
     1.   Very much.
     2.   A lot.
     3.   Some.
     4.   A little.
     5.   None at all.

37. What are the criteria you use to evaluate the quality of life
    in a kibbutz? Below are some criteria. List in order from
    most important to least important the criteria you use to
    evaluate life in a kibbutz.
    1. Relations between the members
    2. Numbers of departures
    3. Standard of living
    4. Order - the rules of the kibbutz are enforced and
       not ignored.
    5. Strength of political ideology
    6. No hired labor
    7. Equality
    8. Good cultural and social life.
    9. Extent to which many different and varied needs of
       members are met
    10. Attachment to the movement
    11. Inner democracy
    12. Absorption of immigrants
    13. Political involvement
    14. Readiness to help other kibbutzim
    15. Other

38. Do you favor the inclusive budget (taksiv collel)?
    1. Yes
    2. No
    3. Unsure

39. If in question 38 you said you favored the comprehensive
    budget (taksiv collel) answer this question. Why? Mark
    all relevant answers.
    1. It is the best way to implement socialism - people will
       have what they need.
    2. People know better what their needs are.
    3. In the kibbutz the basics (food, education...) are given
       and how the rest is taken care of is not important.
    4. I generally favor the trend towards privacy.

40. If in question 38 you said you did not favor the compre-
    hensive budget, please answer this question. Why not?
    Mark all relevant answers.
    1. More private property would significantly change the
       kibbutz as a society.
    2. It opens the gate wider for outside sources of money.
    3. It gives rise to too many differences between people.
    4. People will not be able to manage their money.

41. The kibbutz is now entering a time of affluence and growth in the standard of living. Which of the following ways will it affect the kibbutz?
    1. Like the Roman Empire and the USA affluence and comfort cause less unity and consideration between people, until they have no agreement on values.
    2. A higher standard of living will bring a lesser need for cooperation. People will seek more privacy and property and maybe the kibbutz will (and it is not bad) substantially change as a form of life.
    3. There is no contradiction between a very high standard of living and a socialist society like the kibbutz. Cooperation and mutual help will grow.

42. How would you describe your relationships with your neighbors?
    1. Very friendly - we visit and drink tea together.
    2. Occasional help and visits.
    3. We just live next to each other. No real relationships.
    4. The relations are not good.

43. How do you feel about the hired labor in this kibbutz?
    1. It must be eliminated or we cannot call ourselves a kibbutz.
    2. In principle I'm against it, but because of labor power problems in cases we cannot oppose it.
    3. We have no other possibility and should not complain.
    4. We do not need hired labor. The problem is that the members will not do this work.
    5. Other

44. With which of the following opinions do you agree?
    1. It is better for the kibbutz to agree on specific rules to regulate the behavior of the members than to leave this up to individuals. This will insure order.
    2. It is better for a kibbutz to be flexible and more and more trust individuals to decide what is responsible behavior.

45. Which describes your attitude:
    1. People who identify themselves strongly with some group usually do so at the expense of their development and freedom as individuals, so social life must be limited.
    2. Individuals cannot really find happiness unless they involve themselves deeply in working with a group of people.
    3. It is possible to combine both attitudes. That is better.

46. How do you feel about criticism in the kibbutz?
    1. It usually does not help to criticize others. Nothing ever changes.
    2. Everyone is obligated to criticize the members of his community when they behave not well, or violate rules.
    3. Even if it would help the kibbutz it is wrong and not nice to point out others' mistakes.

47. Despite what we would like, everyone has a practical approach to other people. Which agrees with your approach? List all relevant to you.
    1. The best way to handle people is to tell them what they want to hear.
    2. One must tell people exactly what one feels no matter what the consequences.
    3. One should speak as little as possible to those not your friends.
    4. Although it is better to be open most people cannot be trusted with your real feelings.

48. What is your opinion about human nature?
    1. Human nature is not basically good but a strong society can organize people and at least eliminate many bad things.
    2. Human nature is bad. A person must be egoistic, since the society cannot improve the situation.
    3. Human nature is basically good and the society is not important.
    4. People are both good and bad and, the important thing is the society.

49. How much do you think people really understand their lives?
    1. You try to live your life and do not worry about such things.
    2. Most people understand themselves and the reasons for their behavior and have a lot of control over their lives.
    3. Most peoples' lives are determined by chance and forces they cannot understand. Life is a dark night.

50. Taking all things into consideration would you say that your life in the kibbutz is:
    1. Very happy
    2. Somewhat happy
    3. Not so happy
    4. Very unhappy

51. Are you:
    1. Tired a lot of the time.
    2. Tired some of the time.
    3. Tired occasionally.
    4. Tired never.

52. Are you:
    1. Sick a lot of the time.
    2. Sick some of the time.
    3. Sick occasionally.
    4. Sick never.

53. According to your experience in life have you found you and others can change their personalities?
    1. No, you are born a certain way and that is it.
    2. It is possible to change some qualities.
    3. It is possible to change many qualities but not radically.

54. Which most describes your life in the kibbutz?
    1. I am bothered about kibbutz problems and involved a lot in the public life.
    2. I am concerned about kibbutz problems and involved in public life but not a lot.
    3. I am more involved with my family and comforts than with kibbutz problems.

55. We always hear talk about social problems in the kibbutz. How would you describe your attitude toward them?
    1. Most social problems here can be solved by more money.
    2. Most social problems in the kibbutz are not paradoxes and can be solved by planning, decisions in the mazkirut, committees, and the sicha (general assembly).
    3. The attempts to solve social problems here are games. That life is better for some and not better for others cannot be changed.
    4. Most social problems stem from problems between people and groups in the kibbutz. Only by honesty and discussion, not just plans will they be solved.

56. What is your attitude towards cooperation between people? Mark all relevant answers.
    1. If we do not cooperate and work together we could not attain this standard of living.
    2. It is difficult for people to work together in the kibbutz or outside the kibbutz.
    3. Cooperation is the main value in life.
    4. Other

57. With which idea do you agree most:
    1. When a person has a problem or worry it is best for him not to think about it but to turn to other matters.
    2. When a person has a problem or worry it is best to confront it even though it is very upsetting and diverts him from other matters.

58. Following are some ideas about the education of the young. Mark all those with which you agree. This refers only to the MOSAD.
    1. What a youth needs to be free is to make up his own mind, to work for what he considers right personally.
    2. I really believe that education in the kibbutz shows the young the best society, in which many different people can find a place.
    3. I am not yet convinced that kibbutz education can both encourage our children to think freely as they want and at the same time educate them so that they will want to live in this kibbutz.
    4. Young people need direction and concern or they will get confused. Parents and teachers in the kibbutz must explain and show them and let them try our life.
    5. Kibbutz education must become more strict and academic. If we have good students who can go to the University they will stay in the kibbutz.
    6. Kibbutz education must become more like it was in the past: more freedom for the children to learn through doing, to decide on their own what to study. We must resist "packaged" education.

59. How do you view planning of your life?
    1. What happens to me is my own doing and I reach my goals.
    2. What happens to me is my own doing but I do not reach most of my goals.
    3. I don't feel that I have enough control over my life but it is not the kibbutz that interferes.
    4. I don't feel that I have enough control over my life and it is often the fault of the kibbutz.

60. People were better off in the times when everyone knew just how he was expected to act. Today there is so much change, and we are unsure about what is right or wrong.
    1. Very right.
    2. Right.
    3. Right to a certain degree.
    4. Not right at all.

61. How would you explain to yourself the diversity of success
    of people in the kibbutz?
    1. Some people have better qualities than others.
    2. Some people are more lucky and get more possibilities.
    3. Everyone has the same potential but it is effort that
       counts.
    4. Some people just know better how to get what they want.

62. The goal of this following part of the questionnaire is to
    describe in a general way your life in order to help under-
    stand your ideas on the kibbutz and your philosophy of life.
    Many people use the following qualities in self-description.
    Between each two qualities is a scale. Place yourself on
    this scale. For example:

Not Artistic _____ Artistic
             Very Little Both Little Very

Thus, if you see yourself as "a little" artistic mark "x"
in the place as shown:
_____/____/____/ X /_____

If you see yourself as "very unartistic" mark as shown:
     X /   /   /   /_____

Please mark the place closer to how you see yourself NOT how
you would like to see yourself. Use the scale to express
toward which you lean.

1.	Self-confident _____	Unconfident
2.	Flexible _____	Conservative
3.	Friendly _____	Unfriendly
4.	Independent _____	Dependent
5.	Do not care what others think of me _____	Check my ideas according to others
6.	Enjoys a rou- tined life _____	Prefers to try new and differ- ent experiences
7.	Express anger openly _____	Do not express anger openly
8.	I have some basic beliefs in life _____	I have no basic beliefs in life
9.	At times not fully honest when to my advantage _____	Always speak honestly even when not to my advantage
10.	Relaxed _____	Tense

11.	Active in social re-lations	Not active in social relations
12.	Have self-insight and understanding	Lack self-in sight and un-derstanding
13.	Skillful with others	Awkward with others
14.	Intellectual regarding books	More oriented to using my hands
15.	Affectionate	Hostile and moody
16.	Authoritarian - try to domin-ate decisions	Democratic - try to involve others in de-cisions
17.	Follower	Leader
18.	Fair	Unfair
19.	Cooperative	Competitive
20.	Value myself highly	Value myself lowly
21.	Closed about inner feel-ings	Open and free to express feelings
22.	A happy life	A life with much pain
23.	Responsible	Cannot take responsibility
24.	Unable to achieve goals	Decide on goals and achieve them
25.	Pessimistic	Optimistic

63. Each person has a philosophy of life which explains the life he chooses to live. Following are thirteen philosophies of life. In each question indicate how you feel about that way of life, NOT if you think that is the way life should be but if it expresses your philosophy of your life today. Use the following scale to indicate your feeling towards each, in the space below.
    1. I like this very much.
    2. I like this a little.
    3. I really do not care about this, am indifferent.
    4. I dislike this a little.
    5. I dislike this a lot.

      I   A quiet life is better where a person seeks meditation,
          inner feelings and ideas and an understanding of the
          universe. The external world is too big and cold for
          this.
     II   Enjoyment is the center of life, simple and easy
          pleasures and comforts: a comfortable home, talking
          to friends, relaxation, good food, moderate not intense
          pleasures.
    III   The use of your body's energy to build is the secret
          of a rewarding life. The hands need to make things.
          Life finds its zest in action, overcoming some obstacle
          by physical work and sport, not in relaxed ease.
     IV   Self-control in the keynote of life. To direct one's
          life by reason and know the limit of human power, con-
          trol your impulses, and by ideals determine your life.
      V   The individual should participate actively in the social
          life of the community not to change it but to reserve
          what we have attained, but this should not be in a
          radical way.
     VI   The individual should worry about himself, privacy in
          his home. You really can't achieve much by living on
          the outside all the time. Except for work it is better
          to avoid social groups. A more worthwhile life avoids
          dependence on these things.
    VII   This way of life means a concern for others. Affection,
          love, and lack of aggressiveness, and helpfulness to
          others is most meaningful, not overconcern for oneself
          or thoughts which hinder good relations.

   VIII   Life is to be enjoyed most of the time - sensuously
          enjoyed. One should be open to enjoying many kinds of
          people and things with few limitations, rather than
          sacrificing yourself to direct the course of society.
     IX   A man finds meaning in seeking the social group, compan-
          ionship and cooperation in realization of goals. One
          must not be too involved with one's self and ideas but
          try to work with others to build a good life.
      X   Life tends to stagnation so a person must stress con-
          stant activity, to solve problems as they appear, to
          make improvements all the time in the way of doing
          things by relying on scientific advances.
     XI   Receptivity should be the keynote of life. Good things
          come on their own. They cannot be found by constant ac-
          tion or enjoyment. When you are at peace with yourself
          you are nourished by the powers not of helpfulness or
          achievement but of nature or God.

XII   A person should let himself be an instrument to achieve great purposes of his society or state, with a commitment to perform for the social cause. For a person those goals and causes are more dependable, and from devotion he gets joy.

XIII One's way of life should be a combination. Life needs enjoyment of action and involvement in the social group AND quietness, privacy, peace, in equal amounts. When either is carried to the extreme we lose something important in life. At different times it is appropriate to be a different kind of person.

64.   Now that you have indicated how you feel about each approach to life please list here in order of preference the four ways of life that most fit your way of life today, from the first to the fourth in importance.

    _____
    _____
    _____
    _____

65.   How would you evaluate yourself according to the following:
1. Very very high evaluation.
2. Very high evaluation.
3. High evaluation.
4. Somewhat low evaluation.
5. Low evaluation.
6. Very low evaluation.

66.   After each question mark the appropriate number according to your feeling today as illustrated in the answer model below.

very right	right	not right not wrong	wrong	very wrong

1. I feel depressed.
2. Other people always have more than me.
3. I often feel bored.
4. It seems that I get what I deserve.
5. It seems to me that all I try to do fails.
6. I feel sometimes that my life is not working.
7. It is impossible to rely on others.
8. Today it is impossible to find real friends since everyone thinks about himself.
9. I never have the kind of influence on things I want.

10. Public affairs are so complicated that it is impossible to influence them.
11. Despite all its advantages it is science that has complicated our lives.
12. I can never get involved with what I really want to because conditions oblige me to other things.
13. Life is so complicated so there is no chance to express myself.
14. People like me cannot influence things, only the leadership has influence.
15. It is hard to discriminate between good and bad.

67. How much do people from each of the following groups go out of their way to help you?

1	2	3	4	5
very much	somewhat	a little	not at all	do not have any such person

1. Branch coordinator
2. Fellow workers in branch
3. Your partner
4. Friends
5. Your relatives

68. How easy is it to talk with each of the following people? Indicate your choice according to the answer model in question 67.
1. Branch coordinator
2. Fellow workers in branch
3. Your partner
4. Friends
5. Your relatives

69. How much can each of the following people be relied upon when things get tough? Indicate your choice according to the answer model in question 67.
1. Branch coordinator
2. Fellow workers in branch
3. Your partner
4. Friends
5. Your relatives

70. How much is each of the following people willing to listen to your personal problems? Indicate your choice according to the answer model in question 67.
1. Branch coordinator
2. Fellow workers in branch
3. Your partner
4. Friends
5. Your relatives

71. Here are some items about how people may feel. When you think about yourself and your life nowadays, how much of the time do you feel this way?

1	2	3	4
Never or a little of the time	Some of the time	A good part of the time	Most of the time

1. I feel sad
2. I feel unhappy
3. I feel good
4. I feel depressed
5. I feel blue
6. I feel cheerful
7. I feel uncomfortable
8. I feel nervous
9. I feel relaxed

Married _____ Single _____ Divorced _____   Number of children ___
Their Ages _____.

NOTE: Shaver and Robinson (1959) served as a helpful source book for many questions and constructions used herein.

Bibliography

Abel, Theodore M. and Diaz-Guerero, Regelio. "Discussion of
A. I. Rabin's 'Kibbutz Adolescents.'" American Journal of
Orthopsychiatry 31, July, 1961.

Altman, A. "The Japan Kibbutz Association." Asian and African
Studies 6, 1970.

Amir, Yehuda. "Effectiveness of the Kibbutz-born soldier in the
Israeli Defense Forces." Human Relations 22:333-344.

Antonovsky, Helen. "Commitment in an Israeli Kibbutz."
Human Relations 27 (March 1974): 303-319.

Arian, A. Ideological Change in Israel. Cleveland: The Press of
Case Western Reserve University, 1968.

_____. "Utopia and Politics: The Case of the Israeli Kibbutz."
Journal of Human Relations 14 (1966): 391-403.

Arian, A. ed. The Election in Israel - 1969. Jerusalem:
Jerusalem Academic Press, 1972.

Auerbach, H. A. "Social Stratification in Israel's Collective."
Rural Sociology 18, 1953.

Bakan, David. The Duality of Human Existence: Isolation and
Communion in Western Man. Boston: Beacon Press, 1966.

Baldwin, Elaine. Social and Economic Relations in an Old-
Established Cooperative Farming Community in Israel.
Manchester, England: University of Manchester, 1968.

Banfield, Edward C. Government Project. Glencoe, Ill.: The
Free Press, 1951.

Baratz, J. Dagania: The Story of Palestine's First Collective
Settlement. Tel Aviv: Zionist Organization, Youth
Department, 1945.

_____. A Village by the Jordan, The Story of Degania.
London: Harvill Press, 1954.

Barkai, H. "The Kibbutz--An Experiment in Microsocialism."
     In Israel and Arabs: View from the Left. Edited by I. Howe,
     New York: Bantam Books, 1972.

Barker, Roger. The Midwest and Its Children: Psychological
     Ecology of a Town. Evanston, Illinois: Harper and Row,
     Publishers, 1954.

Barkin, D. and Bennett, J. W. "Kibbutz and Colony: Collective
     Economies and the Outside World." Comparative Studies in
     Sociology and History. 14 (September 1972): 456-483.

Barnett, L. D. "Kibbutz as a Child-rearing System: Review of the
     Literature." Journal of Marriage and Family. 27 (August
     1965): 353-359.

Barriga, Claudio. Management in Cooperative Farming: Its
     Importance for Agricultural Development, with a Comparative
     Study. Madison, Wisconsin: The University of Wisconsin
     Press, 1972.

Bartol, N. R. "Locus of Control for Middle and Lower Class
     Children." Abstraction International 29 (1969): 2991.

Bar-Yoseph, R. "The Pattern of Early Socialization in the
     Collective Settlements in Israel." Human Relations 12 (1959):
     345-360.

Battle, E. S. and Rotter, J. B. "Children's feelings of personal
     control as related to social class and ethnic group."
     Journal of Personality 31 (1963): 482-490.

Bauer, Raymond, ed. Social Indicators. Cambridge: M.I.T. Press,
     1976.

Becker, Howard. German Youth: Bond or Free. New York: Oxford
     University Press, 1946.

Ben-Gurion, D. "Three New Friends for Zionism, Bolshevik Diplomat
     Hails the Kibbutz." Jewish Observer and Middle East Review
     13 (March 13, 1964) 18.

Bentwich, N. "Religious Stirrings in Israel." Contemporary Review
     212 (May 1968): 241-246.

Berdichevsky, M. J. The Collected Writings of M. J. Berdichevsky.
     Harvard University, Hebraica Collection, Widener Library.

Berger, Peter and Berger, Brigitte. Sociology: A Biographical Approach. New York: Basic Books, Inc., 1972.

Bergman, Samuel Hugo. "A. D. Gordon: The Recovery of Cosmic Unity." In Faith and Reason: Modern Jewish Thought. New York: Schocken Press, 1961.

Bernan, Yitzhak. "Some Problems of the Aged in the Rural Milieu in Israel." International Journal of Aging and Human Development 5 (Summer 1974): 257-263.

Bernstein, S. and Weintraub, D. "Social Structure and Modernization: A Comparison of Two Villages." American Journal of Sociology 71 (March 1938): 509-521.

Bettelheim, Bruno. The Children of the Dream. Communal Childrearing and American Education. New York: The Macmillan Company, 1969.

Bien, Yehudah. "Culture of Leisure in the Kibbutz." In Kibbutz Changes: Collection of Articles, pp. 31-43. Givat Haviva, Israel: Center for Social Research on the Kibbutz, 1973.

Billis, David. The Process of Planning in the Kibbutz: A Case Study. London: University of London, 1971.

Bishop, Claire Huchet. All Things in Common. New York: Harper and Brothers, 1950.

Bitton, Livia E. A Decade of Zionism in Hungary, the Formative Years--The Post-World War I Period: 1918-1928. New York: New York University Press, 1968.

Blasi, Joseph R. "The Kibbutz: Integrated Learning Environment and Social Alternative." The Journal of Educational Research, forthcoming, 1977.

_____. "The Kibbutz as a Learning Environment." In Education and Community, pp. 201-204. By Donald W. Oliver. Berkeley, California: McCutchen Press, 1976.

_____. The Kibbutz as a Social Alternative. Cambridge, Massachusetts: Institute for Cooperative Community, 1975.

Blasi, Joseph R. and Murrell, Diana L. "Adolescence In The Kibbutz." Adolescence, forthcoming, 1977.

Blitsten, Dorothy R. The World of the Family: A Comparative Study of Family Organizations in their Social and Cultural Settings. New York: Random House, 1963.

Blumberg, Paul M. Workers' Management in Comparative Analysis. Berkeley, California: University of California Press, 1966.

Blumberg, R. L. "Women of the Kibbutz." Center Magazine 7 (May 1974): 70-72.

Borman, Stuart A. The Prague Student Zionist Movement: 1896-1914. Chicago: University of Chicago Press, 1972.

Bowlby, J. Maternal Care and Mental Health. Geneva: World Health Organization, 1951.

Bradburn, Norman and Caplovitz, David. Reports on Happiness. Chicago: Aldine Publishing Company, 1965.

Braham, Randolph. Israel: A Modern Education System. Washington, D.C.: U.S. Government Printing Office, 1966.

Bronowski, Jacob. The Ascent of Man. Boston: Little, Brown and Company, 1974.

Buber, Martin. Paths in Utopia. Translated by R. F. C. Hull. London: Routledge and K. Paul, 1949.

_____. "What is Common to All." Review of Metaphysics: A Philosophical Quarterly. 11: 359-79.

Byles, Marie B. Paths to Inner Calm. London: Allen and Unwin, 1965.

Cantril, Hadley. The Pattern of Human Concerns. New Brunswick, N. J.: Rutgers University Press, 1965.

Cohen, Eric. "Changes in the Social Structure of Work in the Kibbutz." Economic Quarterly [Riv' on Lekalkala] 10 (1963): 378-388 in Hebrew.

_____. A Comparative Study of the Political Institutions of Collective Settlements in Israel. Jerusalem: Hebrew University, 1968.

_____. "Progress and Communality: Value Dilemmas in the Collective Movement." International Review Of Community Development 15-16 (1966): 3-18.

Cohen, E., and Leshem, Elazar.   "Public Participation in Collec-
    tive Settlements in Israel." International Review of
    Community Development 19-20 (1968): 251-270.

_____. "Survey of Regional Cooperation in Three Regions of
    Collective Settlements."   In Publications on Problems of
    Regional Development Translated by Yaacov Gazit.
    London: (2) Keter Publishing House, Ltd. 1969.

Cohen, Erik, and Rosner, Menachem. "Relations Between Genera-
    tions in the Israeli Kibbutz." Journal of Contemporary
    History 5, January 1970.

Coleman, J. S. et al. Equality of Educational Opportunity.
    Washington, D.C.: Government Printing Office, 1966.

Communities: Journal of Cooperative Living. Louisa, Virginia:
    Community Publications Cooperative, 1975.

Constitution of the Kibbutz. Government of Israel, Ministry of
    Labor, Registrar of Cooperative Societies, 1976.

Caplan, Robert; Cobb, Sidney; French, Jr., John R. P.; Harrison,
    RiVan; and Pinneau, Jr., S. R. Job Demands and Worker
    Health. Washington, D.C.: Government Printing Office, 1975.

Criden, Yosef, and Gelb, Saadia. The Kibbutz Experience:
    Dialogue in Kfar Blum. New York: Herzl Press, 1974.

Cronn, A. D. "Changing World of the Kibbutz." Middle East
    Journal 19 (Autumn 1965): 422-34.

Cobb, S. "Class A Variables from the Card Sort Test CA Study
    of People Changing Jobs." Project Analysis Memo No. 120.
    Ann Arbor: University of Michigan, Institute for Social
    Research, 1970.

Curtis, Michael. Israel: Social Structure and Change. New
    Brunswick, N.J.: Transaction Press, 1973.

Davis, Anne. "Communal Work and Living." Sociology and Social
    Research 55 (1971): 191-202.

Davis, Anne and Olesen, Virginia. "Communal Work and Living:
    Notes on the Dynamics of Social Distance and Social Space."
    Sociology and Social Research 55 (1971): 191-202.

Deveraux, E. "Socialization practices of parents, teachers, and peers in Israel." _Child Development_ 45 (June 1974): 269-281.

Diamond, S. "The Kibbutz; Utopia in Crisis." _Dissent_ 4 (1957): 132-140.

_____. "Kibbutz and Shtetl; the History of an Idea." _Social Problems_ 5 (1957): 71-79.

Durant, Will. _The Reformation_. New York: Simon and Schuster, 1957.

Durkheim, Emile. _Suicide_. Glencoe, Illinois: The Free Press, 1947.

Eden, D. and Levitan, U. "Farm and Factory in the Kibbutz; A Study in Agro-industrial Psychology." _Journal of Applied Psychology_, forthcoming.

Edenberg, L. and Newbauer, P. "Mental Health Issues in Israeli Collectives." _Journal of American Academy of Child Psychiatry_ 4 (1965): 426-442.

Eisenstadt, S. N. _Israeli Society_. New York: Basic Books, Inc., 1967.

_____. "Studies in Social Structure: Age Groups and Social Structure: Comparison of Some Aspects of Socialization in Cooperative and Communal Settlements of Israel." Hebrew University, Jerusalem, 1950. (Mimeographed)

Eisenstadt, S.N., Bar Yoseph, R., and Adler, B., eds. _Integration and Development in Israel_. New York: Praeger, 1970.

Ellul, Jacques. _The Technological Society_. New York: Random House, Inc., 1964.

Ember, Carol and Ember, Melvin. _Anthropology_. Englewood Cliffs, N.J.: Prentice Hall, 1973.

Epstein, R. and Komorita, S. S. "Self-Esteem, Success-Failure, and Locus-of-Control in Negro Children." _Development Psychology_ 4 (1971): 2-8.

Erikson, Erik. _Childhood and Society_. New York: W. W. Norton & Company, Inc., 1950.

_____. _Insight and Responsibility_. New York: W. W. Norton & Company, Inc.

261

Etzioni, Amitai. "Agrarianism in Israel's Party System."
Canadian Journal of Economics and Political Science
23 (1957): 365-375.

_____. "The Organizational Structure of the Kibbutz."
Ph.D. dissertation University of California, Berkeley,
1958. Also in Human Relations 12 (1959): 549-555.

_____. "Solidaric Work-Groups in Collective Settlements
(Kibbutzim)." Human Organization 16 (1957): 2-6.

Faigin, H. "Social Behavior of Young Children in the Kibbutz."
Journal of Abnormal and Social Psychology 56 (1958): 117-129.

Faris, Robert and Dunham, Warren. Mental Disorders in Urban
Areas Chicago: University of Chicago Press, 1939.

Fellows, Lawrence. "Spirit of Kibbutz Fading in Israel."
New York Times June 18, 1961.

Fishman, Aryeh. "The Religious Kibbutz." Sociology Department,
Hebrew University, Jerusalem, 1967.

Fishman, A. ed. The Religious Kibbutz Movement. Jerusalem:
Religious Section of the Youth and Hehalutz Department of
Zionist Organization, 1957.

Freeman, Erika Padan. Psychological Study of a Family in a
Kibbutz in Israel. Ph.D. dissertation. Columbia
University (Teachers College), 1964.

Freud, Anna and Dann, Sophie. "An Experiment in Group Upbringing."
The Psychoanalytic Study of the Child, Vol. VI., pp. 127-169.

Fromm, Erich. The Sane Society. Greenwich, Connecticut:
Fawcett Publications, 1955.

Gans, Herbert. The Urban Villagers. New York: The Free Press,
1962.

Gerson, Menachem. "The Child and his Family in the Kibbutz: The
Family." In Children and Families, pp. 251-262. Edited
by A. Jarus, et al. New York: Gordon and Breach, 1970.

_____. "Women in the Kibbutz." American Journal of Ortho-
psychiatry 4 (1971): 566-573.

Gitlin-Betensky, Mala. "The Role of The Adolescent In The Israeli Collective." Ph.D. dissertation. New School of Social Research, 1957.

Golan, Sh. Collective Education in the Kibbutz. Merchavia, Israel: Education Department of the Kibbutz Artzi Hashomer Hazair, 1961.

Golan, Sh., and Lavi, Z. "Communal Education." In Collective Education in the Kibbutz. By Sh. Golan. Merchavia, Israel: Education Department of the Kibbutz Artzi Hashomer Hazair, 1961.

Goldberg, H. E. "Egalitarianism in an Autocratic Village in Israel." Ethnology 8 (January 1969): 54-75.

Golomb, Naphtali. "The Kibbutz in the Seventies." Unpublished manuscript. Kibbutz Management Center, Ruppin Agricultural School and Institute, Netanya, Israel, 1972.

Golomb, N., and Katz, D. The Kibbutzim as Open Social Systems. Netanya, Israel: Ruppin Institute, 1970.

Golubchick, L. "A Comparison of Attitudes Toward Family, Friends, Nationalism and Education of Kibbutz Reared High School Students." Ph.D. dissertation. New York University, 1972.

Gouldner, Alvin. The Coming Crisis of Western Sociology. New York: Basic Books Inc., 1970.

Greenspan, S. "Leaving the Kibbutz." Psychiatry 35 (August 1972): 291-304.

A Group of Young Kibbutzniks. The Seventh Day. Baltimore, Maryland: Penguin Books, 1971.

Gurevitch, Michael and Loevy, Zipora. "The Diffusion of Television as an Innovation: The Case of the Kibbutz." Human Relations 25 (1972): 181-197.

Gurin, G., Verloff, J., and Feld, S. Americans View Their Mental Health. New York: Basic Books Inc., 1960.

Halevi, N., and Klinov, R. The Economic Development of Israel. New York: Praeger Press, 1968.

Halperin, Haim. Agrindus: Integration of Agriculture and Industries. New York: Praeger Press, 1963.

Havens, Joseph. "A month in the Itto-En religious community." Inward Light 24, Fall-Winter 1961.

Hawkes, Jacquetta. The World of the Past. New York: Alfred A. Knopf, Inc., 1963.

Heschel, Abraham Joshua. The Earth is the Lord's. Cleveland: Meridian Books and the Jewish Publication Society of America, 1963.

Heymont, I. "Israeli Nahal Program." Middle East Journal 21 (Summer 1967): 314-324.

Hill, Warren. "Yin and Yang." Unpublished paper. University of Pittsburgh, 1972.

Hillery Jr., G. A. "Definitions of Community: Areas of Agreement." Rural Sociology 20 (1955): 111-123.

Hollingshead, A. C. and Redlich, Fredrick C. Social Class and Mental Illness: A Community Study. New York: John Wiley & Sons, Inc., 1958.

Hostetler, John. Amish Society. Baltimore, Maryland: Johns Hopkins University Press, 1968.

_____. Hutterite Society. Baltimore, Maryland: Johns Hopkins University Press, 1974.

Infield, H. F. "Boimondau: A French Community of Work." In Communes: Creating and Managing the Collective Life, By Rosabeth Kanter. New York: Harper & Row, Publishers, 1973.

_____. Cooperative Communities at Work. London: Kegan Paul, Trench, Trubner and Company, 1947.

Irvine, E. E. "Children in Kibbutzim: Thirteen Years After." Journal of Child Psychology and Psychiatry 7 (1966): 167-168.

Jaffe, E. "Child Welfare in Israel." In Children and Families In Israel, pp. 331-350. Edited by A. Jarus, et al. New York: Gordon and Breach, 1970.

Jarus, A., Marcus, J., Oren, J., Rapaport, Ch., eds. Children and Families in Israel: Some Mental Health Perspectives. New York: Gordon and Breach, 1970.

Jay, Jeffrey, and Bimey, Robert. "Research Findings on the Kibbutz Adolescent: A Response to Bettelheim." _American Journal of Orthopsychiatry_ 43 (April 1973): 347-354.

Jerome, Judson. _Families of Eden: Communes and the New Anarchism_ New York: Seabury Publications, 1974.

Kaffman, Mordeci. "Characteristics of the Emotional Pathology of the Kibbutz Child." _American Journal of Orthopsychiatry_ 42 (July): 692-709.

_____. "Children in the Kibbutz: Clinical Observation." In _Current Psychiatric Therapies_ Vol. 3. Edited by Jules H. Masserman. pp. 171-179. New York: Grune and Stratton, 1963.

_____. "A Comparison of Psychopathology: Israeli Children from Kibbutz and From Urban Surroundings." _American Journal of Orthopsychiatry_ 35 (1965): 509-520.

_____. "Evaluation of Emotional Disturbance in 403 Israeli Kibbutz Children." _American Journal of Psychiatry_ 117 (1961): 732-738.

_____. "Survey of Opinions and Attitudes of Kibbutz Members toward Mental Illness: Preliminary Report." _The Israel Annals of Psychiatry and Related Disciplines_ 5 (1967): 17-31.

Kagawa, Toyohiko. _Brotherhood Economics_. New York: Harper & Row Publishers, 1936.

Kanovsky, Eliyahu. _The Economy of the Israeli Kibbutz: A Study of Kibbutz Productivity and Profitability and the Position of the Kibbutzim in the Economy of Israel_. Cambridge, Harvard Center for Middle Eastern Affairs, 1967.

Kanter, Rosabeth M. _Communes: Creating and Managing the Collective Life_. New York: Harper & Row Publishers, 1973.

_____. _Commitment and Community_. Cambridge: Harvard University Press, 1974.

_____. "The Impact of Hierarchical Structures on the Work Behavior of Women and Men." _Social Problems_ 23 (1976): 415-430.

_____. Men and Women of the Corporation. New York:
Basic Books, Inc., 1977.

_____. "Structure, Function, and Impact of Urban Communes."
Grant, 23030. 1972-1974.

Kardiner, A. "The Roads to Suspicion, Rage, Apathy, and Social
Disintegration." In Beyond the Germ Theory. Edited by
I. Galdson. New York: Health Education Council, 1954.

Kehiliatevau. Kibbutz Aleph, Haifa-Jida Road, 1922. Reprinted.
Jerusalem: S. Monson, 1964.

Kerem, Moshe. "The Kibbutz: State of the Dream." Judaism
22 (1973): 182-193.

_____. "The Child and his Family in the Kibbutz: The Environ-
ment." In Children and Families in Israel, pp. 237-250.
Edited by A. Jarus, et al. New York: Gordon and Breach,
1970.

Kibbutz Artzi. Kibbutz Gan Schmoel, Israel: Congress on Kibbutz
Industry, 1976. (In Hebrew)

Kincade, Kat. A Walden Two Experiment. New York: William Morrow
and Company, Inc., 1974.

Kinloch, Robert F. Agricultural Settlement in Southern Israel.
Cambridge: Cambridge University Press, 1963.

Klayman, Maxwell I. The Moshav in Israel: A Case Study of
Institution Building for Agricultural Development.
Cambridge: Harvard University Press, 1968.

Kluckhohn, Florence and Strodtbeck, Fred. Variations in Value
Orientations. New York: Greenwood Publishers, 1973.

Kohen-Raz, Reuven. From Chaos to Reality: Experiences in the
Re-education of Emotionally Disturbed Immigrant Youth in
Kibbutzim. New York: Gordon and Breach, 1972.

_____. "Mental and Motor Development of Kibbutz, Insti-
tutionalized and Home-Reared Infants in Israel." Child
Development 39 (1968): 489-504.

Kohlberg, Lawrence. Cognitive-Developmental Theory and the
    Practice of Collective Education in Group Care: An Israeli
    Approach, pp. 342-379. Edited by Martin Wolins and M.
    Gottesman.

Kugel, Yerechmiel. Communalism, Individualism, and Psychological
    Modernity: A Comparison of Kibbutz and Moshav Members on
    the Overall Modernity and Dogmatism Scales. East Lansing,
    Michigan: Michigan State University, 1970.

Kurokawa, Colbert N., ed. What is Itto-en? Yamashina:
    Itto-En Publishing House, 1959.

Lasch, Christopher. "The Narcissist Society." The New York
    Review, September 30, 1976, pp. 5-13.

Lefcourt, H. M. "Internal vs. External Control of Reinforcement:
    A Review." Psychological Bulletin 65 (1966): 206-220.

Leon, Dan. The Kibbutz: Portrait from Within. London:
    Oxford Pergamon Press, 1969.

Leviatan, U. Process of Industrialization in the Israeli
    Kibbutzim. Paper presented at the Ninth International
    Congress of Anthropological and Ethnological Sciences,
    Chicago, 1973.

_____. "Status in Human Organization as a Determinant of
    Mental Health and Performance." Ph.D. dissertation.
    University of Michigan, 1970.

Lifschitz, Michalla. "Social Locus-of-Control Dominance as a
    Function of Age and Social Milieu." Child Development
    44 (1973): 538-546.

_____. "Encopresis Among Israeli Kibbutz Children."
    Israel Annals of Psychiatry and Related Disciplines
    10 (1972): 326-340.

_____. "Impact of Social Milieu on Nature of Adaptive
    Emotional Difficulties." Journal of Marriage and Family
    37 (February 1975): 221-228.

Long, B. "Self-other Orientations of Israeli Adolescents."
    8 (February 1973): 300-308.

Luria, Zella and Goldwasser, Miriam. "Response to Transgression in Stories of Israeli Children." Child Development 34 (June 1963): 271-280.

Lynd, Robert and Lynd, Helen. Middletown. New York: Harcourt, Brace and World, 1929.

McKinney, John C. Constructive Typology and Social Theory. New York: Appleton-Century-Crofts, 1966.

McKinney, John C. and Loomis, Charles P. "The Application of Gemeinshaft-Gesellshaft as Related to Other Typologies." Community and Society, pp. 12-29. By F. Tonnies. New York: Harper Torchbook, 1957.

Macarov, P. "A Test of the Two Factor Theory of Work Motivation in an Isreali Kibbutz." Proceeding of Industrial Relations Research Association, 1971.

Marbert, J. "Development of Kibbutz Girl who Lost her Father." Acta Paedopsychiatrica 89 (1972): 59-66.

Marcus, Joseph, Thomas, Alexander, and Chess, Stella. "Behavioral Individuality in Kibbutz Children." Israel Annals of Psychiatry and Related Disciplines 7 (1969): 43-54.

Marcuse, Herbert. One Dimensional Man. Boston: Beacon Press, 1964.

Meadows, D. H. and Meadows, D. L. The Limits To Growth. New York: New American Library, 1973.

Mednick, Martha. "Social Change and Sex Role Inertia: The Case of the Kibbutz." Washington, D.C.: Howard University, 1975.

Melman, Seymour. "Managerial vs. Cooperative Decisionmaking in Israel." Studies in Comparative International Development, Vol. 6. Beverly Hills, California: Sage Publications, 1970.

Miller, D. R. "Identity, Situation, and Social Interaction: The Impact of Social Structure on Motivation." In Psychology: A Study of A Science, pp. 639-787. Edited by S. Koch. New York: McGraw Hill, 1963.

_____. "Self-Identity as an Integrating Concept." Unpublished manuscript. University of Michigan, 1959.

Miller, Daniel. *The Religious Kibbutz*. Oxford: University of Oxford Press, 1962.

Miller, S. M. and Mischler, Elliot G. "Social Class Mental Illness and American Psychiatry: An Expository View." *Milbank Memorial Fund Quarterly* 27, April 1959.

Minkovitz, Moshe. *A Study of the Settlement of a Community of Moroccan Jews in an Israeli Cooperative Village*. Manchester, England: University of Manchester, 1968.

Morris, Charles. "Comparative Strength of Life Ideals in Eastern and Western Cultures." *Essays in East-West Philosophy*, pp. 353-370. Edited by C. Morris. Hinikuku, Hawaii: University of Hawaii Press, 1951.

_____. *Paths of Life*. 2nd ed. New York: Braziller, 1956.

_____. *Varieties of Human Value*. Chicago: University of Chicago Press, 1956.

Morris, G. and Jones, L. "Relations Of Temperament To The Choice of Values." *Journal of Abnormal and Social Psychology* 53 (1956): 346-349.

_____. "Values, Scales and Dimensions." *Journal of Abnormal and Social Psychology* 51 (1955): 523-535.

Mowrer, Ernest. *Family Disorganization*. New York: Arno Publishers, 1972.

Mushakoji, Saneatsu. *Kono Michi o aruku* [Walking This Way]. Tokyo: Kadokswa shoten, 1958.

Nagler, S. "The Child and his Family in the Kibbutz: Mental Health." In *Children and Families in Israel*, pp. 300-328. Edited by Jarus, et al. New York: Gordon and Breach, 1970.

Newmann, Fred M. and Oliver, Donald W. "Education and Community." *Harvard Educational Review* 37 (1967): 63.

Neubauer, P. B., ed. *Children in Collectives: Child Rearing Aims and Practices in the Kibbutz*. Springfield, Illinois: Charles C. Thomas, Publishing, 1965.

Nie, Norman H; Dent, Dale H.; and Hull, Nadlai C. *SPSS: Statistical Package for the Social Sciences*. New York: McGraw Hill, Inc. 1970.

Nisbet, Robert A. Community and Power: A Study in the Ethics of Order and Freedom. New York: Oxford University Press, 1962.

_____. Quest for Community. Oxford: Oxford University Press, 1960.

_____. Sociology as an Art Form. New York: Oxford University Press, 1976.

Nordhoff, Charles. Communistic Societies of the United States: From Personal Visit and Observation. New York: Schocken Press, 1965.

Oliver, Donald. Education and Community. Berkeley, California: McCutchen, Publishers, 1976.

Ortar, Gina A. "Educational Achievement of Primary School Graduates in Israel as Related to their Socio-cultural Background." Comparative Education 4 (1967): 23-24.

Orsi, Uri. "Progress and Cooperation." Niv HaKvutza, September-December 1968. (In Hebrew)

Oz, Amos. Elsewhere, Perhaps. New York: Harcourt, Brace and Jovanovich, 1973.

Park, Robert E. Human Communities. Glencoe, Illinois: The Free Press, 1952.

Parsons, Talcott and Shils, E. Toward A General Theory of Social Action. New York: Harper Torchbook, 1952.

Passamanick, B. and Rettig, S. "Some Observations in the Moral Ideology of First and Second Generation Collective and Non-Collective Settlers in Israel." Social Problems 11 (1963): 165-178.

Pelto, P. Anthropological Research: Structure of Inquiry. New York: Harper & Row, Publishers, 1970.

Peres, Yohanan. "The General Assembly in 'the Kibbutz.'" Oranim 3 (1962): 105-197. (In Hebrew)

Perry, John and Perry, Erna. Face to Face: The Individual and Social Problems. Boston: Little, Brown and Company, 1976.

Peskin, H. "Birth Order in Child Psychiatric Referrals and Kibbutz Family Structure." Journal of Marriage and Family 36 (August 1974): 615-618.

Piaget, Jean. Six Psychological Studies. New York: Random House, 1967.

Pironjnikoff, Leo and Hadar, Illana, and Hadar, Avner. "Dogmatism and Social Distance: A Cross Cultural Study." Journal of Social Psychology 85 (December 1971): 187-193.

Plath, David. "The Fate of Utopia: Adaptive Tactics in Four Japanese Groups." American Anthropologist 68 (October 1966): 1152-1162.

Plath, David and Sugihara, Yoshie. "A Case of Ostracism--and Its Unusual Aftermath." Transaction 5 (January-February 1968): 31-36.

_____. "Ostracism and Beginning of the Shinkyo in Japan." In Communes: Creating and Managing the Collective Life, pp. 55-64. By Rosabeth Kanter. New York: Harper & Row, Publishers, 1973.

Poplin, Denis. Communities: A Survey of Theories and Methods of Research. New York: Macmillan, 1972.

Poppel, Stephen M. Nationalism and Identity: German Zionism, 1897-1933. Cambridge: Harvard University Press, 1973.

Posnik, Gerilyn. "The Kibbutz School: A Proposal to Israeli Educators." Unpublished manuscript. Harvard University, 1973.

"Principles, Types and Problems of Direct Democracy in the Kibbutz. In The Kibbutz As A Way Of Life In Modern Society, pp. 31-43. Edited by Menachem Rosner, Givat Haviva, Israel: Center for Social Research on the Kibbutz, 1972.

Rabin, Albert I. "Attitudes of Kibbutz Children to Family and Parents." American Journal of Orthopsychiatry 29 (1959): 172-9.

_____. "Culture Components as a Significant Factor in Child Development: II, Kibbutz Adolescents." American Journal of Orthopsychiatry 31 (1961): 493-504.

_____. Growing Up in the Kibbutz. New York: Springer Publishing Company, 1965.

_____. "Infants and Children under Conditions of 'Intermittent' Mothering in the Kibbutz." American Journal of Orthopsychiatry 28 (1958): 577-584.

_____. "The Israeli Kibbutz (collective settlement) as a 'Laboratory' for Testing Psychodynamic Hypotheses." Psychological Records 7 (1957): 111-115.

_____. "Personality Maturity of Kibbutz (Israeli Collective Settlement) and Non-Kibbutz Children as Reflected in Rorschach Findings." Journal of Projective Techniques 21 (1957): 148-153.

Rabkin, Leslie Y. "Some Notes on the Kibbutz Voices." Art and Science of Psychotherapy 6 (1970): 20-24.

_____. "A Very Special Education: The Israeli Kibbutz." Journal of Special Education 2 (1968): 251-261.

Radin, Paul. The World of Primitive Man. New York: Henry Schuman, 1953.

Rapaport, D. "The Study of Kibbutz Education and Its Bearing on the Theory of Development." American Journal of Orthopsychiatry 28 (1957): 587-597.

ben Raphael, Eliezer. "Processes of Change in the Israeli Kibbutz." Unpublished manuscript. Hebrew University, 1975.

Rawls, John. A Theory of Justice. Cambridge: Harvard Belknap Press, 1971.

Redfield, Robert. The Little Community. Chicago: University of Chicago Press, 1955.

Reifen, David. "Children in Communal Settlements." New Era 30 (1949): 195-198.

Reimer, Joseph B. "The Development of Moral Character in the Kibbutzim with a Special Focus on Adolescents." Special Qualifying Paper. Harvard University, 1972.

Rettig, Solomon. "Anomie in the Kibbutz." International Journal of Group Tensions 2 (1972): 37-52.

_____. "Relation of Social Systems to Intergenerational Changes in Moral Attitudes." Journal of Personality and Social Psychology 4 (1966): 409-441.

Rich, Adrienne. *Adrienne Rich's Poetry*. Edited by Albert Gelpi and Barbara Charlesworth Gelpi. New York: W. W. Norton and Company, 1975.

Riesman, David. *The Lonely Crowd*. New Haven, Connecticut: Yale University Press, 1961.

Rose, Herbert H. *The Life and Thought of A. D. Gordon*. Jerusalem. Hebrew Union College-Jewish Institute of Religion, 1962.

Rosenfeld, Eva. "Institutional Change in Israeli Collectives." Ph.D. dissertation. Columbia University, 1952.

_____. "Social Stratification in a Classless Society." *American Sociological Review* 16 (1951): 770-774.

Rosner, Menachem. "Communitarian Experiment, Self-management Experience and Kibbutz." In *The Kibbutz as a Way of Life in Modern Society*. Givat Haviva, Israel: Center for Social Research on the Kibbutz, 1972.

_____. "Difficulties and Rewards in the Role of Branch Manager." *Hedim* 46, 1963. (In Hebrew)

_____. "Perception of Intergenerational Relations in the Kibbutz." Paper delivered at 10th International Congress on Gerontology, Jerusalem, 1974.

_____. *Research on the Second Generation*. Givat Haviva, Israel: Center for Social Research on the Kibbutz, 1967-1976.

Rosner, Menachem, ed. *The Kibbutz as a Way of Life in Modern Society*. Givat Haviva, Israel: Center for Social Research on the Kibbutz, 1972.

Rotter, J. B. "Generalized Expectancies for Internal vs. External Control of Reinforcement." *Psychological Monographs* 80 (1966): 1-28.

Rudolf, Allan E. *A Theoretical Analysis of the Kibbutz as a Producer's Cooperative*. New York: Columbia University Press, 1970.

Ruppin, Arthur. *The Agricultural Colonisation of the Zionist Organization in Palestine*. London: Martin Hopkinson and Company, Ltd., 1926.

Rushing, William. "Two Patterns in the Relationship between
     Social Class and Mental Hospitalization." American
     Sociological Review 34 (August 1969): 533-541.

Sadan, Ezra. Agricultural Settlements in Israel: A Study in
     Resource Allocation. Chicago: University of Chicago Press,
     1962.

_____. "Capital Formation and Growth in the Israeli Co-
     operative Form." American Journal of Agricultural Economy
     50 (November 1968): 975-990.

_____. "Co-operative Settlements in Israel: Problems of
     Resources Allocation." Journal of Farm Economy 45.
     (August 1963): 547-557.

Samuel, J. "Kibbutz as a Welfare State in Miniature."
     Contemporary Review 218 (January 1971): 1-6.

Sarel, Moshe. "Research Report on the Second Generation in
     the Kibbutz." Jerusalem: Hebrew University, 1959.
     (Mimeographed in Hebrew)

Sartre, J. P. "The Polyvalent L." New Outlook 10 (1967): 15-17.

Schmalenbach, H. "The Communion." In Theories of Society,
     pp. 331-347. Edited by T. Parsons: Glencoe, Illinois:
     Free Press, 1961.

Schwartz, Richard D. "Democracy and Collectivism in the Kibbutz."
     Social Problems 5 (Fall 1957): 137-147.

_____. "Functional Alternatives to Inequality." American
     Sociological Review 20 (1955): 424-430.

_____. "Social Factors in the Development of Legal
     Control: A Case Study of Two Israeli Settlements."
     Yale Law Journal 63 (1954): 471-491.

Seeley, John R., Sim, Alexander and Loosley, Elizabeth.
     Crestwood Heights. New York: Basic Books Inc., 1956.

Segal, M. "The Child and his Family in the Kibbutz: School Age."
     In Children and Families in Israel, pp. 271-283. Edited by
     A. Jarus, et. al. New York: Gordon and Breach, 1970.

Shapira, Ariella. "Cooperation, Competition, and Conformity among City and Kibbutz Children in Israel." Ph.D. dissertation. University of California. Los Angeles, 1970.

Sharp, Gene. The Politics of Non-Violent Action. 3 vols. Boston: Porter Sargent Publishers, 1973.

Shaver, Phillip and Robinson, John. Measures of Social Psychological Attitudes. Ann Arbor, Michigan: Institute of Social Research, University of Michigan, 1959.

Shaw, Clifford R. Delinquency Areas. Chicago: University of Chicago Press, 1929.

Shdemot: Literary Digest of The Kibbutz Movement. (English version) Tel Aviv, Israel: Youth Division Ichud HaKvutzot veHakibbutzim.

Shepher, Joseph. "Familism and Social Structure: The Case of the Kibbutz." Journal of Marriage and the Family 31 (1969): 567-573.

_____. "The Kibbutz." In Sociology in Israel. Edited by L. Weller. Westport, Connecticut: Greenwood Press, 1974. pp. 229-274.

_____. "Mate-Selection Among Second Generation Kibbutz Adolescents and Adults." Archives of Sexual Behavior 1, 1974.

_____. "Motivation Work and Social Activity in Kibbutz Society." Proceedings of the International Symposium of Cooperative Rural Communities 1 (1968): 205-207.

_____. "Public Activity Outside the Kibbutz." Niv HaKvutzah 15 (1966): 39-59. (In Hebrew). Available in English: Dr. Joseph Shepher, University of Haifa, Mt. Carmel, Israel.

_____. "Self-imposed Incest Avoidance and Exogamy in Second Generation Kibbutz Adults." Ph.D. dissertation. Rutgers University, 1971.

_____. The Sociology of the Kibbutz (in hebrew). Netanya, Israel: The Ruppin Institute, 1977.

Sherwood, J. "Self-Identity and Self-Actualization: A Theory of Research." Ph.D. dissertation. University of Michigan, 1962.

Shey, Thomas. "Study of Communes in Denmark." NIMH Grant. Center for the Studies of Social Problems, NIMH. 1975. Personal Communication.

Shalom, Saar. "A Study of the Educational Systems of the Urban School and the Kibbutz." Unpublished paper. Harvard University, 1975.

Spielberger, C. D., Gorsuch, R. L., and Lushene, R. E. Manual for the State-Trait Anxiety Inventory. Palo Alto, California: Consulting Psychologist Press, 1970.

Spiro, Melford. Kibbutz: Venture in Utopia. Cambridge: Harvard University Press, 1956.

_____. "The Sabras and Zionism: A Study in Personality and Ideology." Social Problems 5 (1957): 100-109.

_____. Children of the Kibbutz. Cambridge: Harvard University Press, 1958.

Srole, Leo. "The Natural Therapeutic Community: 1475-1975." New York: Kittay Scientific Foundation, Fourth International Symposium on "A Critical Appraisal of Community Psychiatry," 1976.

_____. "Social Integration and Certain Corollaries: An Exploratory Study." American Sociological Review 21 (1965): 709-716.

Srole, Leo, Langner, T. S., Michall, S. T., Oeler, M. K., and Rennie, T. A. C. Mental Health in the Metropolis: The Midtown Manhattan Study. New York: McGraw-Hill Inc., 1962.

Stein, Maurice. The Eclipse of Community: An Interpretation of American Studies. Princeton, N. J.: Princeton University Press, 1960.

Stern, B. "New Look Kibbutz." Jewish Spectator 31 (March 1966): 21-25.

_____. The Kibbutz that Was. Washington, D.C.: Washington Public Affairs Press, 1965.

Suttles, Gerald D. The Social Order of the Slum: Ethnicity and Territory in the Inner City. Chicago: University of Chicago Press, 1968.

Talmon-Garber, Y. _Family and Community in the Kibbutz_.
Cambridge: Harvard University Press, 1972.

_____. "Mate Selection In Collective Settlement."
American Sociological Review 29 (1964): 491-508.

Tannenbaum, Arnold. _Hierarchy In Organization: An International
Comparison_. San Francisco, California: Jossey Bass
Publishing Company, 1974.

Tauber, Esther. _Molding Society to Man: Israel's New Adventure
in Cooperation_. New York: Block Publishing Company, 1955.

Taylor, Gordon Rattray. _Rethink Radical Proposals to Save a
Disintegrating World_. Baltimore, Maryland: Penguin Books,
1972.

Thomsen, Harry. _The New Religions of Japan_. Rutland, Vermont:
Charles E. Tuttle, 1963.

Tiger, Lionel and Shepher, Joseph. _Women of The Kibbutz_.
New York: Harcourt, Brace, and Jovanovich, 1975.

Toffler, Alvin. _The Eco-Spasm Report: The Breakdown of Industrial
Civilization on the Planet_. New York: Bantam Books, Inc.,
1975.

Tonnies, Ferdinand. _Community and Society_. New York:
American Book Company, 1940.

Vallier, Ivan Archie. _Production Imperatives in Communal Systems:
A Comparative Study with Special Reference to the Kibbutz
Crisis_. Cambridge: Harvard University Press, 1959.

Veysey, Laurence. _The Communal Experience: Anarchist and Mystical
Counter-Cultures in America_. New York: Harper and Row,
Publishers, 1973.

Vidich, Arthur J. and Bensman, Joseph. _Small Town in Mass Society_.
Princeton, N. J.: Princeton University Press, 1958.

Viteles, Harry. "Cooperative Agricultural Settlements in Israel."
Sociology and Social Research 39 (1955): 71-76.

_____. _The Evolution of the Kibbutz Movement_. Vol. II: _A
History of the Co-Operative Movement in Israel_. _A Source-
book_, London: Valentine, Mitchell, 1966.

Wallace, Anthony. _Culture and Personality_. New York: Random
House Inc., 1970.

Wallfish, A. "Americans in Carmiel: An Experimental Urban
Kibbutz." _Hadassah Magazine_ 50 (1969): 12-13.

Weintraub, D. _Moshava, Kibbutz and Moshav: Patterns of Jewish
Rural Settlement and Development in Palestine_. Ithaca,
New York: Cornell University Press, 1969.

Weller, L. _Sociology in Israel_. Westport, Connecticut:
Greenwood Press, 1974.

Wenner, Kate. "Nation Builders in Tanzania." In _Communes:
Creating and Managing the Collective Life_, pp. 48-54.
By Rosabeth M. Kanter. New York: Harper and Row, Publishers,
1973.

_____. _Shamba Letu_. Boston: Houghton Mifflin Company, 1970.

Wershow, Harold J. "Aging In The Israeli Kibbutz: Some Further
Investigation." _International Journal of Aging and Human
Development_ 4 (1973): 211-227.

Wilhelm, Richard. _The I Ching or Book of Changes_. Translated
by Cary F. Baynes. Princeton, N. J.: Princeton University
Press, 1967.

White, Alan. _Kibbutz, A Novel_. London: Barrie and Jenkins, 1970.

Whyte, William. _The Organization Man_. Garden City, N. J.:
Doubleday Anchor Books, 1957.

_____. _Street Corner Society_. Chicago: University of Chicago
Press, 1955.

Winograd, Marilyn. "The Development of the Young Child in a
Collective Settlement." _American Journal of Ortho-
psychiatry_ 28 (1958): 557-562.

Wirth, Louis. _The Ghetto_. Chicago: University of Chicago
Press, 1928.

_____. "Urbanism As a Way of Life." _American Journal of
Sociology_ 44 (July 1938): 1-24.

Wolins, Martin. "Group Care: Friend or Foe?" Social Work 14 (1969): 35-53.

_____. "The Kibbutz as Foster Mother: Maimonides Applied." Paper presented at the 48th Annual Meeting of the American Orthopsychiatric Association, New York, 1959.

_____. "Political Orientation, Social Reality and Child Welfare." Social Service Review 38 (December 1964): 429-442.

Yarrow, L. J. "Maternal Deprivation: Toward an Empirical and Conceptual Re-Evaluation." Psychological Bulletin 58 (1961): 459-490.

Yuchtman, E. "Reward Distribution and Work Role Attractiveness: Reflections and Equity Theory." American Sociological Review 37 (October 1972): 581-595.

Zablocki, Benjamin. "Investment of Self in the Urban Group." NIMH Grant No. 1R01 MH 25525. 1974-1975.

_____. The Joyful Community. Baltimore: Penguin Books, 1971.

Zbrowski, Mark and Herzog, Elizabeth. Life is with People. New York: International Universities Press Inc.,1952.

Zung, W. W. K. "A Self-Rating Depression Scale." Archives of General Psychiatry 13 (1965): 63-70.

Zweig, Ferdynand. The Israeli Worker: Achievements, Attitudes and Aspirations. New York: Herzel Press and Sharon Books, 1959.